DEVELOPMENT, CHANGE, AND GENDER IN CAIRO

INDIANA SERIES IN
ARAB AND ISLAMIC STUDIES

SALIH J. ALTOMA, ILIYA HARIK, AND MARK TESSLER
GENERAL EDITORS

DEVELOPMENT, CHANGE, AND GENDER IN CAIRO

A VIEW FROM THE HOUSEHOLD

EDITED BY

DIANE SINGERMAN
AND
HOMA HOODFAR

INDIANA UNIVERSITY PRESS

BLOOMINGTON AND INDIANAPOLIS

Library of Congress Cataloging-in-Publication Data

Development, change, and gender in Cairo : a view from the household /
edited by Diane Singerman and Homa Hoodfar.
p.   cm. — (Indiana series in Arab and Islamic studies)
Includes index.
ISBN 0-253-33027-0 (cl : alk. paper). — ISBN 0-253-21049-6 (pa : alk. paper)
1. Households—Economic aspects—Egypt—Cairo Region.   2. Social
change—Egypt—Cairo Region.   3. Poor—Egypt—Cairo Region.
4. Women—Employment—Egypt—Cairo Region.   5. Sex role—Egypt—
Cairo Region.   6. Women—Egypt—Cairo Region—Social conditions.
I. Singerman, Diane.   II. Hoodfar, Homa.   III. Series.
HC830.D48   1996
339.2'2—dc20   95-34930
1   2   3   4   5   01   00   99   98   97   96

KATAYOON H
AND TO OU
WHO HA
WITH T

S,
SINGERMAN,
KIN TIES,
RS CAN,
PORT

CONTENTS

❖

ACKNOWLEDGMENTS

WE WOULD LIKE to thank, first of all, the hundreds of women, men, and children from Cairo who were so patient with our questions and so generous with their hospitality. Neither the editors nor the contributors could have learned much about the household if so many households and families had not shared their experiences and thoughts with us. To each and every one of them, we are extremely grateful. In particular, Diane Singerman would like to thank the family of Abla Biadha who invited her to live with them and taught her so much about Egypt and resourcefulness. The memory of Abla Biadha lives on in her family and friends and in the pages of this book. Homa Hoodfar would like to thank Leila Al-Kilani, who opened her house and her heart to her, treating her as a daughter, and the households in Bulaq al-Dakrur who for years patiently answered her questions and treated her as a sister.

We are both deeply appreciative of the constant support which Fred Shorter has demonstrated toward this project and our research in general. As Senior Representative of the Population Council in Cairo, he organized a research seminar in 1988 where most of the contributors to this book presented their work. We would like to thank Hoda Zurayk, Barbara Ibrahim, and Ann Lesch for their support and encouragement at that seminar and throughout the course of this project. In particular, we are grateful for Barbara Ibrahim's thorough reading of the manuscript. Karen Glasgow and Carolyn Makinson have helped our efforts in many tangible and intangible ways, including Karen's editing talents. We would like to thank our research assistants, Quintan Wiktorowicz, Ryan Rusek, and Candace Walsh, at the American University and Marlene Caplan and Heather Howard at Concordia University for their prodigious assistance. We would also like to thank our husbands, Tony Hilton and Paul Wapner, both of whom came on the scene at a point where their support and good humor was very appreciated. During the summer of 1988, we were lucky to have had the editorial and graphic arts assistance of two dear friends, Chuck Raht and Kevin Rimmington, who have since died. They are sorely and deeply missed.

❖

INTRODUCTION

The Household as Mediator: Political Economy, Development, and Gender in Contemporary Cairo

DIANE SINGERMAN AND HOMA HOODFAR

THIS BOOK PRESENTS a perspective largely missing from social science research on contemporary Cairo. Through this collaboration and presentation of our diverse research we hope to demonstrate the important role the household plays in the political economy, social structure, and political life of Egypt. This perspective has evolved from detailed and sustained field research and interviews among lower-income groups in Egyptian society within neighborhoods and communities of the Greater Cairo region, including those once at the threshold of the lower middle class who are rapidly losing economic ground.[1] The contributors to this volume represent the spectrum of the social sciences: political science, anthropology, economics, sociology, and communications. Each of us began to work on quite unrelated topics of research, such as food subsidies, housing, female participation in the labor force, migration, maternal health care, political community, literacy, and the political economy of households, yet we shared the gradual realization that the household was far more important to our research than we had originally realized. Singular issues that we concentrated upon could not be understood only in terms of individual actions, of policies of the state, the bureaucracy, and voluntary agencies, or of cultural norms of Egyptian society. In this collection we suggest that scholars, researchers, and policy makers must understand the structure and the underlying principals of the household to better grasp the complexity of economic and political development in Egypt. The household, we argue, is a very significant institution, mediating the relationships between individuals, local communities, markets, and the state. It is this institution which encourages the interdependence of formal and informal socioeconomic structures.[2]

The household is not transhistorical but rather shapes, and is in turn shaped by, larger socioeconomic and historical forces (Yanagisako 1979; Redclift 1985; Wilk 1984; Netting et al. 1984). Hence we have purposefully limited this collection to a specific period (1984–1994), economic stratum, and geographic area.[3] By focusing on households within the socioeconomic and political environment of Cairo, the authors in this volume have scrutinized the impact of social change and have tried to reflect and articulate the political and economic concerns of lower-income groups during this turbulent last decade or so.

Our emphasis on the household and the informal socioeconomic structures of lower-income communities is not meant to minimize or underestimate the influence of other forces and centers of power and authority in Egypt. Structural forces such as the ideology of the state, industrialization, changing labor market conditions, the state's distribution of public goods, and patterns of income distribution clearly influence individuals, gender roles, and the Egyptian economy and polity. As Emmanuel Wallerstein argues, the household unit is a part of an interrelated set of institutions that constitute the operational structure of the social system, which is in a continuous process of change (Wallerstein 1984, 17). Indeed, macroeconomic and political changes during the past decade in Egypt have shaken the foundations of the household, its norms, and its gendered division of labor. People must face the challenges of new pressures and opportunities at the level of the household. Most recently, radical Islamist activists have used the increasing economic, social, and moral predicaments of lower-income communities as fodder for their opposition to the Mubarak regime. One can better understand the strength of this Islamist challenge to the status quo if one takes into account the changes within the household and the ways in which these changes have affected the lives and hopes of many Egyptians.

The Economic and Political Context

Egypt became increasingly integrated into the international economy following two agreements which laid the groundwork for a new era during the tenure of President Anwar Sadat: the economic Open Door Policy in 1974 (*al-Infitah al-Iqtisadi*) and the Camp David agreements in 1978. These developments also marked an abrupt shift in Egypt's political alliances as the nation withdrew from the Soviet sphere of influence and crafted an economic and military alliance with Western nations, particularly the United States.[4]

Internally, this new economic and political alliance threatened Egypt's previous commitment to state capitalism and the social welfare policies developed under Gamal Abdel Nasser (1952–1970). The Open Door Policy, followed by the implementation of gradual but steady structural adjustment policies, retreated from the most important elements of Nasser's ambitious social agenda, which took on the responsibility of providing basic goods and services to the Egyptian people. The most significant of these were free public education, free health care, employment opportunities, old-age pensions, and affordable basic food commodities. While many of these provisions have been scaled back by the Mubarak regime, food subsidies in particular are politically sensitive and their direct or indirect reduction remains a source of popular discontent.

To a large extent the delivery of these provisions during the 1960s and 1970s induced considerable upward social mobility on the part of less-privileged social groups and raised the expectations of others. These policies, which were perceived as a "social contract" between the state and its citizens, radically influenced resource allocations within the household. In particular, they affected prospects for a new and more extended role for younger women, at least in urban areas. As a part of modernization and Egyptian-style socialism, the state encouraged women to become educated and seek employment in the then-expanding state and public sector, which also offered relatively high wages. Subsidies of food and basic health care made it possible for households to direct their scarce resources toward educating their children, including daughters. However, as the state, under Sadat and his successor, Hosni Mubarak, withdrew from its provisionary role, the economic burdens of the household radically increased,[5] particularly as the inflation rate rose in the mid-1980s and 1990s.[6] The food and beverage index, which measures the cost of basic food commodities, rose from 100 in 1966 to 1839.8 in 1990, demonstrating the escalating burdens on lower-income households to feed their families (CAPMAS and UNICEF 1993, 88).

Some new policies were introduced in the hope of attracting foreign investment. However, it was domestic and not foreign investors who largely responded. Private investment rose from £E 113 million in 1982 to £E 1.02 billion in 1983; and by 1990 the figure stood at £E 10.7 billion, of which 64 percent was Egyptian, 19 percent Arab, and the remaining 17 percent from other sources (Day 1991, 399). Such data indicate that the pressure for economic liberalization emanated from domestic as well as foreign constituencies (see Harik and Sullivan 1992 and Barkey 1992). Even with domestic and foreign support for economic liberalization, the Egyptian economy remains dominated by the public sector.[7] At the same time, these developments signal a restructuring of national capital from public to private, though the government's commitment to economic liberalization is, at times, still ambivalent. Increased private investment has induced a new wage structure in which private sector wages are often more attractive than public sector wages. This situation, on the one hand, has reduced the burden on the government to create jobs within the public and state sector and, on the other hand, has created considerable dissatisfaction on the part of government and public sector employees who once, as privileged workers, were the government's most solid supporters.[8]

Some of the economic growth of this period was fueled by increasing foreign debt, which Egyptians from various political perspectives (including government bureaucrats) argued eroded Egypt's economic and political autonomy.[9] Scarce government resources were absorbed to service the debt, and the nation's vulnerability to economic shocks from the international economy and foreign economic and political influence rose, causing much resentment and debate among opposition forces, as well as among some elites within the government.[10]

Egypt became far more integrated into the international economy since the 1980s, bearing the positive and negative consequences of such a trend. (See Chaudhry 1993 for a discussion of the relationship between the international political economy and structural adjustment pressures.) Foreign exchange income from petroleum, the Suez Canal, tourism, and workers' remittances rose from only 6 percent of gross domestic product (GDP) in 1974 to 40 percent of GDP in the mid-1980s (Day 1991). Tourism, previously untapped, became the primary hard-currency earner and the largest employer in the country by 1993 (Mattoon 1993, 10).[11] Ironically, tourism has also made the government vulnerable and open to attack by opposition forces. In the 1990s, Islamists, the most outspoken political opponents of the regime, began attacks on foreigners in order to weaken the government both nationally and internationally. The consequences of these attacks (though actually very few in number) have been disastrous. One source estimates that the economy lost at least U.S. $1 billion in revenues as vacancy rates in the plethora of luxury hotels that were built in the 1980s skyrocketed and thousands of employees in the tourist industry lost their source of livelihood ("Egypt: Staying Away" 1994, 45–46).

Despite the increasing vulnerability of the Egyptian economy, it experienced strong growth as well. Per capita income doubled, from $334 in 1974 to $700 by 1984 (Handoussa 1991, 3). Rising wage levels in Egypt (International Labor Office 1991, 497, 793) and the huge increases in labor remittances from abroad, which rose from $0.37 billion (Tesche and Tohamy 1994, 57) to $3.55 billion in 1985–1986 (Sullivan 1990, 129) and $5.2 billion in 1991–1992 (Tesche and Tohamy 1994, 57), spurred tremendous growth in the service sector and in the construction industry.[12] These socioeconomic changes have had a significant impact on the development of human resources and social welfare in Egypt: per capita nutritional level increased by 21 percent over a ten-year period; life expectancy increased to sixty-one years from fifty-five; and child mortality dropped from 116 to 85 per thousand (Handoussa 1991, 3). Despite increasing discontent with the quality and performance of the national education system, primary school enrollments increased between 1979 and 1985 by 23 percent among boys and 38 percent among girls, secondary school enrollments by 15 percent and 18 percent respectively, and university enrollments by 20 percent and 24 percent (CAPMAS 1986). Yet wages were increasingly inadequate to keep up with the rising cost of living, thereby fueling discontent among many Egyptians and opposition to the government.[13]

The economic boom Egypt experienced in the late 1970s and early 1980s could not be sustained, as the nation felt the effects of the international recession in the mid-1980s and increasingly burdensome government spending. The remittances from Egyptians working abroad leveled off as employment opportunities in the Gulf countries decreased; Egypt's own petroleum industry no longer produced the high revenues of earlier periods as the international price of oil declined; and the flow of net aid to Egypt declined as international lending agencies and foreign governments began slashing their foreign aid programs (Abdel-Rahman and Abu Ali 1989, 43). Domestically, unprofitable public sector industries, the subsidies bill, continued high military spending, and debt servicing added to the regime's economic woes and people's burdens, particularly among the poor and those who had just crossed the threshold to the lower middle class.

While Egypt's economic policies have changed significantly, political liberalization has lagged behind. Opposition parties, though more vocal owing to a generally freer press, remain hampered by a barrage of government regulations and electoral and legislative restrictions (Makram-Ebeid 1989; Lesch 1989; Post 1987; Hendriks 1987; Bianchi 1989; Abdalla 1991). The National Democratic party, through its use of government funds and its overwhelming majority in Parliament, remains the strongest political party, even though its power is fairly hollow, since it lacks real grassroots support. Sadat encouraged the organization of Islamic cultural, political, and religious groups as a strategy to outflank the Nasserists and leftists of the early 1970s and paradoxically Islamists have now become the government's most threatening opposition force (El-Guindi 1981; Ibrahim 1980; Kepel 1986; Ayubi 1991).

Though the movement incorporates a variety of ideological positions, Islamists generally condemn the government for its peace accord with Israel, its close alliance with the United States and the West, government corruption, income disparities and poverty, and the ill effects of Westernization on the culture, mores, and religious piety of Egyptians (see Ibrahim 1980; Kepel 1986; Sivan 1985; Ayubi 1991; Ramadan 1993; El-Sayed 1990; and Saeed 1994). Because Islamists remain the strongest threat to the government, it has never allowed any group within this general category to register or operate openly as a political party. Therefore, none of the Islamist groups has presented a specific social, political, or economic platform beyond the vague claim that it wants to build a just Islamic society. Hence, these groups can attract members from all segments of society, particularly low-income persons who have suffered in the rapid process of social and economic change. Secular opposition forces, interest groups, professional syndicates, and private voluntary organizations who still play by the regime's rules of political participation have also been critical of government policies and are severely hampered by government repression, legal restrictions, a lack of resources and organized popular support (Sullivan 1994; Abdalla 1991; El-Sayyid 1990; Middle East Watch February 1991, June 1992, October 1993). Hence, it is the Islamists, operating outside the system, who remain the more potent threat to the Mubarak regime, despite the crippling attacks against them by government security forces.[14]

Development policies have been, and continue to be, enacted in the name of the Egyptian people, and yet we know little about the ways in which Egyptians from the low-income group and lower middle class (i.e., the majority of the urban and rural population) cope with and react to fundamental economic or political change. Substantive, detailed studies of income distribution, economic stratification, and poverty in Egypt are still sporadic, and government sensibilities toward these issues obstruct comprehensive studies on these topics (Hussein 1973; Abdel-Fadil 1980; Hansen and Radwan 1982; Waterbury 1982; Alderman and Von Braun 1984; Amin 1989; Zaytoun 1991). "Progress" and development affect different economic strata differentially. Policy makers may be well-intentioned and specific programs may benefit Egypt in the long term, yet in the short term these same changes may produce major dislocations for individuals, households, and local communities—as they would in any society which underwent such changes. While people with fewer resources are the supposed beneficiaries of many of these programs, they are also more vulnerable to rapidly changing economic conditions. Their vulnerability may encourage them to react to new policies in ways which policy makers never imagined, even if the policies were designed to help them.

The questions which motivate our work differ from conventional scholarship, which largely focuses on the causes behind the recent economic and political changes in Egypt. We will not enter into that debate here. We begin with the fairly obvious statement that significant policy changes which emanate from elites have both intended and unintended consequences for those who are economically disadvantaged and politically marginalized in society. What we have tried to demonstrate so briefly above is the scope of changes which directly and indirectly affected all segments of Egyptian society, but particularly its most vulnerable members.

The Household in the Context of Social Change

In this book, we propose that the reactions of many Egyptians to the rapidly changing economic and social conditions we describe above can be better understood through the lens of the household. For most Egyptians, the family remains a central and valuable institution in their everyday lives (Rugh 1984). But people in low-income communities rely on their families to an even greater extent, since they have fewer ties to other structures of power in society, upon which middle and elite families can rely (Singerman 1995). Few individuals in Cairo live independently from their kin or in single-person households (Zurayk and Shorter 1988). We define the household as "a group that ensures its maintenance and reproduction by generating and disposing of collective income" (Wood 1981, 339). As a collective institution, the members of the household, men, women, and children, negotiate and renegotiate their roles and positions, according to the changing circumstances within and outside the household.[15]

Detailed anthropological studies have demonstrated that households are not egalitarian institutions but are often marked by many disparities and inequalities, and Cairene households are no exception (Beneria and Roldan 1987; Booth 1993; Folbre 1984; Papanek 1990; Sharma 1986). Households in Cairo are characterized by what Amartya Sen terms "cooperative conflict" (Sen 1990). Members of households cooperate to minimize threats from outside forces and to increase the collective interest of the household, but this does not exclude pursuit of individual self-interest within the structure of the household. Men and women are continually bargaining, negotiating and renegotiating their position within the household and community. The bargaining power of individuals reflects their actual and potential contribution of labor and of material and nonmaterial resources to the household as well as other currents of power, such as an unequal gender ideology within the larger society. Therefore, a prevailing atmosphere of cohesion and cooperation in the household may not only go hand in hand with many legitimized inequalities but may also contribute to the reproduction or even exacerbation of these inequalities (Sen 1990). A strategic choice which yields the highest return for all members of the household may be a clearly unfavorable option to a particular member, who may not have the power to prevail. Therefore, national development policies which attempt to benefit vulnerable groups should strive to reduce existing inequalities at all levels of society, particularly within the household.

As Egypt's economy has become more market-oriented, the rapid commercialization of daily life has emphasized the need for cash. In this transformation, women have lost many of their domestic functions to the market, as many of the services they used to perform became commodified. Noncash contributions to the household, traditionally made by women, once formed the basis of their power and status within the household and the community. While new economic developments have brought about cash-earning opportunities for women, their lack of marketable skills and specific gendered roles and responsibilities, such as mothering, has placed different constraints on them than on their male counterparts. Even if increasing numbers of women enter the labor force, traditional neoclassical notions of work and employment fail to understand that working women may actually lose the power and status they had in the household because when they work their noncash contributions to the household decline. Their position is doubly weakened because Egyptian women, like women in all other societies, typically earn far less than men. This lack of attention stems from underestimating as well as misunderstanding the political economy of the household and the changing role of women within the household.

As the rising demand for cash has increased women's dependence on their husbands and male folk, women have become critical, if not suspicious, of the trends of economic change, even if they hold a wage-earning job. Understandably, they become receptive to alternative economic and ideological anchors that offer them more acceptable prospects. As Arlene Elowe MacLeod's essay demonstrates (chapter 2), even those segments of the female population which benefited from the educational and nationalist policies of the earlier era and became lower-level clerks or bureaucrats in the public sector found themselves in contradictory binds. Their salaries, though offering minimal economic security, remained so low that they offered no noticeable degree of economic independence. Neither did they compensate for some of the material, nonmaterial, and emotional costs of venturing outside the household.

What our diverse research reveals is that collective behavior in Egypt is heavily influenced by the needs and demands of the household and that the household and intrahousehold relations are a crucial and central variable in development. An alert reading of economic and political realities suggests that the actual and perceived needs of the household are an underlying force behind many contemporary problems. For instance, given the new economic situation and wage structures that favor technical skills, sons are persuaded to leave school and begin apprenticeship programs to support the family while daughters, who have fewer labor market opportunities, may be allowed to attend school longer. Husbands may disagree with their wives' desire to work (it is believed that a husband has the religious right to restrict his wife's physical mobility) because they are supposed to take care of children. A teenage girl might be forced into an unwanted marriage by her family because of a groom's wealth or status. An educated young man might be persuaded to accept a five-year contract for a low-skilled job in Saudi Arabia in order to save enough money for his marriage and establish his own household. It is the needs and demands of the household and rarely the individual which represent the prime force behind these decisions.

While too much attention is paid to the actions of elites (particularly by political scientists and economists), it is the cumulative effect of individual and collective behavior which influences the most ambitious and well-funded policies of the government. The essays in this collection share a "bottom-up" approach, or what John Gray and David Mearns, in their study of households in South Asia, called the "inside-out" approach (1989). It is an approach which explores "the ways in which wider social structure is sustained, altered or generated by social actors operating through small groups such as the household" (Madan 1989, 11). This approach recognizes the cumulative importance of common practices, desires, and preferences of millions of households throughout Cairo. In order to understand the logic of people's choices and their reactions to government policies or changing economic, political, or cultural conditions, one must consider the household arena and its effect on macro social, political, and economic forces.

Our observations reveal that men and women in densely populated neighborhoods certainly have a good grasp of the consequences of new conditions or policies in the international or national arena on their daily lives. For example, workers in public sector factories and the civil service understand that pressures from international lending agencies and financial institutions to privatize the public sector and reduce the government workforce will probably mean a decrease in their benefits and even, perhaps, unemployment. Similarly, men and women, many of whom worked abroad in the Arab oil-rich countries in order to finance major expenses (particularly marriage), are aware that their jobs are affected by national and international politics. Many were quick to recall the deportation of thousands of Egyptian workers from Libya in the 1980s as a result of animosities between the governments of Egypt and Libya. The Gulf conflict of 1990–1991 forced Egyptian workers who had been working in Kuwait and Iraq to relocate. In fact, as Homa Hoodfar points out in chapter 1, many Egyptians believe that international migration acted as a buffer against rapid inflation and the rising cost of living after the introduction of the Open Door Policy, particularly for lower-income and unskilled workers. Migration has reduced income disparities within Egypt and facilitated rising economic mobility among peasants and disadvantaged urban groups, even though the capital for this indirect redistribution of wealth largely came from outside Egypt. Despite this commonsense knowledge freely available to listening ears, the early literature (largely produced by academics and development specialists) on the impact of migration on the Egyptian economy and society was primarily negative (Amin and Awny 1984). As decreased migration opportunities put more pressure on the economy and unemployment rose, the attitudes of intellectuals and social critics toward labor migration grew more positive (Said 1990).

Gender and Development

Perhaps the most significant consequence of ignoring the role of the household has been the construction of a gender-blind notion of development (Elson 1991; Brydon and Chant 1993; Tinker 1990).[16] The patriarchal conceptual framework, which saw the world populated with individuals (i.e., men) and viewed gender as a neutral and unimportant variable, rendered women invisible and powerless (Folbre 1986; Rogers 1980; Waring 1978; Elson 1991). As many feminist scholars have explained, a male-centric view of society led to a peculiar situation in which women, half the population, were transformed into the "other," an object of society (Moore 1988). Minimizing the role of the household has particularly distorted analyses of the role of women and the impact of socioeconomic change and policies on their position and status in society. Anthropological and ethnographic research, due to its historical interest in the household, kinship, and family, has been critically important in the push for rethinking the role of gender not only in small communities but also in relationship to economic production, national identity, culture, and policy making.

The realization that women had been overlooked in the study of societies led to a corrective move, by feminist scholars, to conduct research on women (Moore 1988; Rogers 1980). Though the early profusion of research on women expanded the breadth of our knowledge available on women and gender relations, it also made it clear that focusing on women and theoretically and methodologically isolating them as a meaningful social category is as partial as a male-centric point of view. It perpetuates an inaccurate and incomplete view of society. Moreover, this approach could marginalize women, hence defeat the very purpose it set out to achieve. The paramount goal must be to integrate the study of women into the study of society. The fact remains that the real world of women is the real world of men, although women may experience life differently because of gender and age hierarchies. Even in the most segregated societies, and certainly in our case study of Egypt, men and women are in constant interaction and therefore any research should take account of this context. Each chapter in this collection is an effort in this direction.

Looking at women in relation to men in their shared social context can also help to avoid what Edward Said refers to as positional superiority, a principle that ensures seeing others through a Western cultural grid. A rich debate among feminists from "Third World" nations and the Middle East questions the portrayal of women in "other" cultures as oppressed, passive victims (hooks 1984; Mohanty et al. 1991; Lazreg 1988, 1994; Hoodfar 1994; Nader 1986, 1989). Laura Nader suggests that "in the writings of American feminist scholars, there is a hint of the same viewpoint held by the general population that while it may be bad here, somehow it is really worse in the Middle East, or Africa, or Asia, or Latin America. And sometimes it is worse, but as anthropologists have pointed out, not always" (Nader 1986, 380). Chandra Mohanty warns against a homogeneous notion of the oppression of women because it produces the image of an "average third-world woman."

This average third-world woman leads an essentially truncated life based on her feminine gender (read: sexually constrained) and being "third world" (read: ignorant, poor, uneducated, tradition-bound, religious, domesticated, family-oriented, victimized, etc.). This . . . is in contrast to the (implicit) self-representation of western women as educated, modern, as having control over their own bodies and sexualities, and the "freedom" to make their own decisions. (Mohanty 1988, 65; see also Mohanty et al. 1991).

It is the recognition of the agency of women in their social context that is most widely shared by the authors in this collection, some of whom have different and, on occasion, conflicting conclusions about the nature of patriarchy and gender relations in Egypt. Egyptian women and men, as social agents, protect their interests and fight to promote them within a wide range of constraints. The opportunities a high school graduate from an upwardly mobile working-class family may have, for example, are very different than those open to a lower-middle-class, widowed, illiterate mother of five. In fact, many of the authors draw different conclusions about the larger questions of gender, power, and class, because even within the boundaries of low-income communities in Cairo, regional, educational, class, racial, and religious diversity makes generalizing difficult. Recent immigrants to Cairo living in the neighborhood which Hoodfar studied have different interests and problems than working-class and lower-middle-class long-time residents of one of Cairo's oldest neighborhoods, which Diane Singerman studied. The housing problems of families who had lived in "temporary" facilities for twenty years which Nawal Hassan investigated are very different from the problems which migrant laborers face after living abroad for years, problems that Hoodfar analyzes. While we hope to offer a sense of how several low-income communities have responded to tremendous changes, our research is largely based on qualitative studies of specific communities, using intensive methods of participant observation and informal interviewing. We have not drawn, nor would we draw, generalizable or predicative conclusions from our research.

What is common to all the contributions is evidence of the actions which men and women take to make the best of their individual circumstances, sometimes working in collective ways to reach shared goals (particularly with other members of their families and communities), sometimes competing with others for scarce resources. Many of these "coping strategies," as they are often referred to in the anthropological literature, can be seen as forms of resistance to structures of power and domination—whether expressed through gender norms, the state, the culture, or the economy. While the nature of this resistance has been more difficult to recognize and has not been carefully documented, it is nevertheless extremely important in people's struggles to support, shape, or transform relations of power in their society. As James Scott argues, "the basis of class struggle . . . is first and foremost, a struggle over the appropriation of work, production, property and taxes. 'Bread and butter' issues are the essence of lower-class politics and resistance" (Scott 1985, 295–296). Men and women in Cairo were preoccupied and in some circumstances almost obsessed by such "bread and butter" issues. It is this struggle to provide for individual and collective needs, within a specific social, economic, and political context of Cairo at a crucial juncture in its history, which is reflected so vividly in these contributions.

The Chapters

Before we can begin to understand the effect of macro changes on the material positions of households in low-income communities, Homa Hoodfar suggests, we must understand the nature of income and the intricate webs of household economies. In the first chapter of this volume, she offers a four-part explanation of the nature of household income in Cairo which incorporates cash and other sources of material benefits. She argues that conventional economic analysis has overemphasized the role of cash at the cost of devaluing other forms of material contributions to the household. Egyptian gender norms and Islamic law demand that the male/husband/father has the sole responsibility to support the household financially. The contributions of women, which are also the material basis of their power in their households, were primarily in the areas of subsistence activities such as housework, production of food stuffs, and child care. Since Nasser's era, when social welfare expenditures increased dramatically, it also became the time-consuming responsibility of women to channel public goods and services to their households.

Through a detailed analysis of the political economy of households in the neighborhoods of her study, Hoodfar argues that as a result of the process of commercialization and the reduction of public subsidies and government services, women have lost many of their domestic functions to the market, a loss which has increased the household's need for the cash. However, since neither the organization of domestic life nor market opportunities have been hospitable to increasing the ability of women to earn cash, the process of economic change has left them economically more dependent on their husbands. This situation has been exacerbated by the rapidly spreading market ideology, which places more emphasis on cash as the only source of income. Slowly and somewhat imperceptibly, the balance of power has shifted within the household in favor of men, who are able to command more cash. Yet the nonmonetary contributions of women remain essential to survival strategies of low-income households, and it is difficult for women to take up paid positions, which would make their contribution more visible. Hence many women feel ambivalent about the process of development and modernization and are more cautious about devaluing traditions and embracing "modernity."

Exacerbating this changing balance of power has been the declining and stagnating wages of many women in these communities who chose to work in the public sector because of the benefits, the shorter working hours, and the availability and public respectability of government employment. This financial predicament has been used by opponents of the right of women to "work" in Egypt to suggest that women should give up their jobs and remain at home, since employment for low-paid employees makes less and less economic sense, as salaries barely cover costs of travel, clothes, and food consumed during the workday. The voices of those who argue against the right of women to work outside the home have grown stronger recently as more and more Egyptians, particularly within these communities, have become supportive of a wide range of Islamist activists, politicians, and theologians, as their economic position deteriorates, and as their communities are rent by social crises.

The relationship between Islamic and traditional gender ideologies, women's roles and identities in the family, and economic change is examined by Arlene Elowe MacLeod. In chapter 2, she argues that the recent stagnation of government wages and the increasingly high cost of living have raised new problems for working women. Earlier assumptions about the relationship between female employment, "progress," and female liberation articulated by some feminists and modernization theorists suggested that employment outside the home would lead to greater earning power and autonomy for women. These scenarios, once again, are challenged by MacLeod's case study of lower-ranking female government employees in Cairo, or *muwazzifaat*, who work but are nevertheless losing power and influence. For many couples from traditional working-class or lower-middle-class backgrounds who struggle to attain and retain middle-class status, both husband and wife must engage in cash-earning activities. Owing to rising consumer expectations after the Open Door Policy and the commercialization of many services, contributions from the wife are no longer a luxury but a necessity. These couples, "tottering on the edge of the divide between the 'poor' and the 'lower middle' class," are not merely interested in surviving but are ambitious and believe government promises that they will prosper with education and hard work.

The paradox of female employment in Egypt is that women from lower-income communities largely fill the lower rungs of employment, their earning power has been on the decline, they resent the tedium and bureaucratic control of government offices where there is little substantive work, and by working outside the home, they lose the traditional sources of power and influence which women yield as *sitaat al-bayt*, or housewives (a translation which does not do justice to this female domain in Egypt). As MacLeod argues, the economic ideology of the lower middle class pushes women into the workplace, but the gender ideology of Islamic societies, which argues that men should be financially responsible for their households, strongly opposes this move. One of the ways in which Cairene women have managed to ameliorate these tensions, MacLeod suggests, is to adopt an Islamic mode of dress, which publicly identifies them as pious, serious women committed to Islamic moral codes, a "traditional" gender ideology, and an improved middle-class standard of living for their families.

In Hoodfar's second contribution to this volume (chapter 3), she examines the effects of an overwhelming surge in Egyptian labor migration to Arab countries, a surge which began shortly after the oil boom in 1973. As it is largely men who migrate, there is an increasing number of de facto female-headed households in Egypt, particularly in urban areas. This phenomenon has raised many questions about the effects of migration on the traditional sexual division of labor, the prevailing gender ideology, and family and parental relations.

Exploring the changes in the sexual division of labor, household expenditures, and prevailing gender roles among migrant households, Hoodfar suggests that the impact of male migration on low-income families and children is fairly positive, as migration is the only option for achieving a higher standard of living for the unskilled and less-educated men. However, Hoodfar's data suggest that the impact of migration on women is more diverse. She found that traditional and less-educated wives managed to improve their position within the household and vis-à-vis their husbands both during and after the migration. Whereas better-educated wives, particularly those who had been white-collar workers, lost much ground to their husbands, less-educated women became more self-confident as they were forced to deal with various arms of the bureaucracy, make financial investments, supervise schooling, and accomplish a variety of other tasks which their husbands had typically been responsible for before they migrated. However, educated women enjoyed such self-confidence prior to the migration of their husbands, and moreover they enjoyed a degree of financial independence, which they viewed as a means of claiming more equal partnership with their husbands. Successful migration increased the husband's cash contribution and strengthened the traditional gender ideology, which designated women as economically dependent on males despite some apparent changes in the sexual division of labor in the household. Thus, many educated women, though they enjoyed a higher standard of living as a result of migration, felt that their previous influence and role in the family had declined. What Hoodfar's study underscores is the importance of understanding the complex impact of economic and social changes on men and women within the household.

The consequences of Egypt's move to a more market-oriented economy and resultant changes in gender ideology are also examined by K. R. Kamphoefner in her study of low-income illiterate women in Cairo. She argues that Egypt, in its move to embrace Western-style industrialization, is departing from a system of traditional patriarchy and toward a social system of sexism. Women are no longer supported by the separate power domain of the household, which the traditional patriarchal structure of Egyptian society afforded them. Nor are they benefiting from the traditional status and respect associated with the role of housewife and mother—roles that within the old structure offered them the possibilities of building political alliances and social and economic connections to benefit themselves and their families. Changing the locus of women's activity toward the workplace means that they lose their power base in the household and their community.

Kamphoefner argues that the state actively supports education, not so much for the knowledge imparted as for the sense of organization schooling teaches, in that it trains people for participation in the labor force. Yet at the same time, the public educational system is extremely overextended and ill equipped both to educate an increasingly youthful population and to offer literacy programs to the still-significant percentage of the population that remains illiterate. Among women in Egypt, illiteracy is predominant (approximately 70 percent). To date, Kamphoefner argues, literacy programs and the Egyptian educational system have been irrelevant to women's roles in the household and their educational needs. Policy makers have not incorporated the everyday realities of low-income adult illiterate women into their design of all aspects of literacy programs. Kamphoefner argues that the Egyptian state, both for the sake of the position of women and for the sake of successful literacy programming, must reshape literacy programs and education to make them more relevant to the role of women in the household and the context of Egyptian culture and economy.

The symbolic and substantive commitment of the state to social welfare is explored as well in Nadia Khouri-Dagher's analysis of the place of food subsidies in the political economy of lower-income communities. Food is an obvious requirement for survival and a crucial component of the household budget in lower-income households. As such, the state's ability to fulfill its role as food provisioner is the basis of much of its popular credibility and legitimacy. Even with the subsidies still largely in place, Egyptians spent approximately 50 percent of their household budget on food in the mid-1980s, while poorer families spent proportionately even more. More specifically, Khouri-Dagher suggests that the price of bread has come to be regarded as a gold standard which indexes the performance of the economy and the government's commitment to social-welfare policies.

In the working- and lower-middle-class community which Khouri-Dagher studied, most people, whatever their educational level, had an intuitive understanding of the inflationary spiral of food prices. When the government tried directly or indirectly to increase the price of bread, people did not demonstrate out of hunger but because they understood Egypt's complex economy and knew that price increases for bread were pegged to other commodities. The riots and demonstrations that followed these price increases were not hunger riots (1977, 1981, 1984) but protests against the diminution of the state's role of food provisioner and its commitment to social welfare polices. What is at stake is the ideological basis of the modern Egyptian state, and the barometer of the government's commitment to the welfare of its citizens is its subsidy policy. Yet, at the same time, if people cannot purchase subsidized goods, or if they cannot stem government price increases, they engage in what Khouri-Dagher calls postrationalization, or the ability to turn imposed situations into what appear as choices. If they cannot find subsidized chickens, they insult the quality of subsidized chicken; if they cannot influence the government to maintain subsidies, they point out the corruption of the system and the burden it places on the national budget while devising illegal and extralegal methods to obtain subsidized food. These communities develop systems that are parallel to the market or to the state system of distribution because they are marginalized vis-à-vis both the market (by their low incomes) and the distribution system (because of defects in the system and allocation priorities). Although people identify themselves as victims of the system and complain about their marginalization, they also become actors and develop parallel networks of exchange, information, and assistance which bring together relatives, neighbors, colleagues from work, and people from one's village. Khouri-Dagher points out that the role of food in household economies and in the political economy of Egypt is not new; the food-provisioning role of the state has its historical precedent in Ottoman and Mamluk Egypt. Thus, over time, people have grown accustomed to government intervention in food distribution, and these popular expectations have an inscribed place in the consciousness of Cairenes.

A similar story of the consequences of macroeconomic changes on the urban poor can be seen in Nawal Mahmoud Hassan's study of the displacement of families from so-called temporary housing in the Gamaliyya district of Islamic Cairo (they had lived in these quarters since the Nasser era). Not only was housing abruptly withdrawn from the very poor owing to the demands of tourism and gentrification following the reinvigoration of Egyptian tourism after the Camp David accords, but working- and middle-class residents of these neighborhoods could no longer afford to live there and establish businesses because of real estate speculation during the Infitah era. Hassan's study complements the other chapters in the volume because it documents the efforts of an advocacy group and examines the housing crisis in Cairo at a slightly earlier point: in the late 1970s, when population pressures, a growing deterioration of the housing stock, a construction boom, and increased consumer demand for products and services sent the prices of housing and commercial property skyrocketing.

The Centre for Egyptian Civilization Studies, a private voluntary organization located in Gamaliyya and directed by Hassan, played an important advocacy role in assisting the residents of the "temporary" housing facilities and historic buildings which were being bulldozed by speculators. The Centre promoted the interests of residents of these neighborhoods whose lifestyles and sources of livelihood were being threatened by the "modern" and "rational" designs of areas on the outskirts of Cairo where they had been relocated. The Centre worked in league with local politicians, sympathetic provincial authorities, lawyers, bureaucrats, and international development agencies to demand that the government pay more attention to the needs and the lifestyle preferences of public housing residents. Hassan calls for policies which permit families to work in their own neighborhoods and which support many of the communal and traditional aspects of Old Cairo that make it such a vibrant area. She questions the attitude of government officials who want to replicate the housing and lifestyles of the West rather than support indigenous living and work patterns that have made these neighborhoods thrive for centuries.

Even when the authorities are sympathetic to the needs of neighborhood residents, Hassan argues, market forces supersede their power and real estate speculators from outside these neighborhoods are able to destroy housing and neighborhoods that should be preserved and restored. The government's fear of any popular mobilization, along with the various bureaucratic and political obstacles which advocacy groups must contend with in Egypt, weakens the ability of residents in Old Cairo to resist both government policies and market forces that threaten their households, workplaces, and lifestyles.

In the context of authoritarian rule in Egypt, where political organization and oppositional politics are strictly controlled despite the facade of pluralism, Diane Singerman argues in chapter 7 that men and women in lower-income communities are excluded from the formal, political arena. Yet, that does not mean they are only repressed victims, apathetic or powerless. Rather, they establish and maintain institutions such as the family and informal networks which serve their interests and which support their ideological preferences and social norms. Women and men use informal networks, based in the household yet extending through all aspects of the community and beyond it, to promote their economic interests and the collective interests of the family. Since networks bring together unrelated individuals, households, and families, they serve to aggregate interests even further.

The political institutions of lower-income communities are supported by what Singerman calls the "familial ethos," a set of norms and traditions which encourage family solidarities and the regeneration of the family itself. The family strives to fulfill the material and social needs of individual members of households, arbitrates conflict between individuals and among households, and promotes the ideological and communal norms of the community. She emphasizes the political nature of the family, which stems from its structural role. It maintains its place in the community, and within the larger political economy of Egypt, because it is the vehicle not only for reproduction but also for economic production. Familial enterprises (both formal and informal) and self-employment are still vital components of the local economy.

Noting the collective aspects of networks and families, however, Singerman also argues that households are characterized by competition for resources and contests of power which do not follow prevailing gender or age stereotypes. Women actively defend their interests, and the model of patriarchy distorts the analysis of male-female relations. Many women resist their position of structural subordination through the use of the familial ethos, informal networks, family enterprises, and informal institutions. However, familial demands and needs influence the lives of men as well as women, and both sexes are bound by family expectations and obligations. The informal politics of lower-income communities and the financial role of the family are most apparent in the lengthy and costly struggles to marry off the younger members of the family. Marriage, or the regeneration of the family itself, which is such a highly valued social institution in Islamic societies, absorbs the financial, political, and emotional resources of these communities for years on end. It is extremely difficult to understand the reactions of Egyptians to macroeconomic changes unless one considers the Herculean struggle, which almost every household confronts, to marry off their children in a climate of escalating costs and dwindling financial resources.

The Egyptian state, in a variety of explicit and implicit policies, understands the popular attachment to the familial ethos and the financial burdens on lower-income families. The state is pervasive in the everyday lives of women and men in these communities and it has tremendous power, if and when it is willing to exert it. Yet, because these communities articulate and organize their interests, even though this organization is largely informal and invisible, the government is persuaded to maintain vestiges of the Egyptian "social contract" referred to earlier, even if many of these programs are underfunded and oversubscribed. Typically, the government favors discreet and indirect methods of reducing public expenditures to avoid further opposition to the government, even though it understands that Egyptians closely follow market fluctuations. The organization and role of familial institutions and informal networks in lower-income communities, Singerman suggests, is a crucial but largely ignored aspect of politics in Egypt, and it is a politics in which both women and men are active participants.

These essays are rich in surprising examples of the consequences of significant change in Egypt during the era of Infitah. What we have attempted to do, in concentrating on the household and gender in lower-income communities, is to shift attention away from questions of elite politics, macroeconomic analysis, and ideological debates to look at some of the material consequences of a wide spectrum of change. It is not that we are uninterested in class formation, income distribution, or party politics, but we believe much more empirical research must be conducted among diverse communities in Egypt before we can understand who is winning, who is losing, and who is merely surviving these changes. But we must also be conscious of our assumptions of what constitutes winning and losing. For example, while Western social scientists have assumed that working outside the home will improve the autonomy and position of women, Hoodfar, MacLeod, and Kamphoefner suggest that the issue is far more complicated and that some of the consequences of increased Westernization and economic liberalization have worsened the economic position of some women and decreased their authority. This analysis, some might argue, is apologist and only supports those political and economic forces in Egypt that call for women to remain in the home. Rather than confuse our analysis with prescription, we suggest that we must be very sensitive to the costs of change for both men and women and try to anticipate difficulties so that mechanisms can be put in place to support vulnerable groups, as they work and live in different ways. This is an agenda which many people share in Egypt, and we believe this agenda will be enhanced by paying far more attention to the variable of the household.

NOTES

1. The Greater Cairo region includes the administrative units of Cairo, Giza, and Qalubiyya provinces. For a thorough study of the growth of this region, see Shorter 1989.

2. The term *informal* is used here to identify activities which are not recognized, enumerated, taxed, or licensed by the state. More commonly, the term *informal activities* refers to a range of economic activities which evade the reach of the state, but the term can also be used to describe political activities which elude the state's reach (see Abdel-Fadil 1980; Singerman 1995; Castells and Portes 1989; Hart 1973). For further elaboration, see Singerman, chap. 7 in this volume.

3. Most of the fieldwork for our research was conducted between 1983 and 1986, although we have also returned to Cairo repeatedly to conduct additional research. Nawal Hassan's contribution, however, is based on research conducted in the late 1970s. We have not included scholarship on the household in rural areas of Egypt to maintain the specificity of this collection, though one could argue that the role of the household in the Egyptian countryside and in other provincial cities is probably even stronger than it is in Cairo. For a discussion of the effects of recent socioeconomic changes on rural Egypt, see Toth 1991; Hopkins 1987; Adams 1985 and 1989; Khafagy 1984; Taylor 1984; Sadowski 1991; Kupferschmidt 1987; and Abaza 1987.

4. When the Open Door Policy was announced, the United States did not have a program of military assistance to Egypt. By 1979 U.S. military assistance to Egypt had risen exponentially to $1.5 billion, and by 1985 it had leveled off to $1.1 billion (Roy 1990, 165). The U.S. program of economic assistance began modestly after the Open Door Policy, reaching $346 million in 1975, and surging to $1.3 billion by 1985. The annual U.S. disbursement of economic aid averaged $721 million between 1975 and 1984 (Handoussa 1990, 112–114). In the early 1990s the aid continued at similar levels; Egypt ranked second to Israel as a recipient of U.S. foreign aid, and by 1995 the embassy in Egypt was the largest U.S. embassy in the world.

5. While describing the extent of changes in Egypt during this period, it is also important to note that many pre-Infitah policies and patterns were maintained, including subsidy policies, public employment policies, social welfare benefits, and extensive price controls. There was a careful effort on the part of the government to introduce policy changes slowly and indirectly to avoid popular dissatisfaction, economic hardship, and opposition to the government (for an example, see the analysis of the gradual removal of bread subsidies in the essay by Khouri-Dagher, chap. 5 in this volume).

6. While official inflation rates are politically sensitive and difficult to estimate, one source suggests an annual inflation rate between 1980 and 1988 of 18 percent (Sherif and Soos 1992, 61). Inflation rates rose slightly in the early 1990s to approximately 20 percent and declined again to 9 percent by 1993 (Tesche and Tohamy 1994, 58; see also Yang 1994; Timwell 1993; and Bromley and Bush 1994).

7. A decade after the launching of the Open Door Policy, public enterprises still accounted for 70 percent of total gross fixed investment and as much as 80 percent of manufactured exports (El-Naggar 1989, 8). For an analysis of the ways in which interest groups and trade unions have fought privatization strategies, see Posusney 1993.

8. Apart from changes in the wage structure, the Mubarak regime introduced competitive examinations for government positions to reduce its obligation to provide jobs for all high school and university graduates—a commitment made by Nasser's government. In the mid-1980s, the average wait for government appointment increased to five years for university graduates and six years for intermediate degree holders and technical school graduates (Assaad 1989, 5–8).

9. Egypt's debt to Eastern bloc countries in the late 1960s was just over U.S. $1 billion, while its debt to Western countries was only U.S. $35 million (World Bank 1984, 46). In the next two decades Egypt's debt soared. In 1975 it reached U.S. $76 billion and had risen to $21.6 billion by 1985 (World Bank 1987, 382).

10. The U.S. Congress, acting unilaterally, canceled $7 billion of Egypt's debt to the United States after Egypt supported the international alliance against Iraq after Iraq's invasion of Kuwait in 1990. At the same time, in gratitude for Egypt's position, the United States and its allies in the Paris Club of Western creditors canceled debts worth approximately $10 billion (Reed 1993, 95); this figure includes the $7-billion debt which the U.S. Congress canceled. Even those who supported Egypt's stand against Iraq were troubled by the obvious quid pro quo represented by the debt forgiveness.

11. By 1993, tourism alone provided 10 percent of Egypt's gross domestic product ("Egypt Exploits Its Gulf War Bonus" 1993, 139). The tourist industry is vulnerable not only to attacks on tourists by opposition groups but also to perceptions concerning the safety of traveling to the country and the region. After the Iraqi invasion of Kuwait, tourists stayed away from Egypt, and direct tourist revenues dropped by $1.2 billion, with indirect losses estimated at $1.8 billion (ibid.).

12. While labor remittances from abroad have been a critical source of foreign currency reserves in Egypt and have provided sources of employment for many Egyptians,

particularly young men, the economy is also that much more vulnerable to abrupt changes in migration opportunities abroad. For example, following the Iraqi invasion of Kuwait in 1990, one source estimated that Egypt lost $3.7 billion in remittances from 700,000 Egyptians employed in the Gulf ("Egypt Exploits Its Gulf War Bonus" 1993, 138). Since significant labor remittances from abroad enter Egypt through the informal economy, estimates of their value are, at best, crude. Nevertheless, one source in the Ministry of Migration estimated that actual remittances entering Egypt annually amounted to $10 billion: $2 billion through official channels and $8 billion through informal channels (Lesch 1985, 8). In 1985, the GDP of Egypt equaled approximately $33 billion (World Bank 1989, 235). Obviously, remittances are extremely important to the Egyptian economy when they comprise almost a third of its GDP.

13. The consumer price index in the mid-1980s and early 1990s often rose by approximately 20 percent per year. For example, in 1986 the increase reached a high of 23.9 percent; in 1989 it was 21.3 percent, while it was slightly lower in 1988 (17.6 percent) and 1992 (13.6 percent). This economic indicator is particularly useful to assess the impact of economic trends on lower-income groups, who spend far more of their incomes on direct consumption than do middle- or upper-income groups (Tesche and Tohamy 1994, 54).

14. In the past several years hundreds of people have been killed due to Islamic activist opposition to the government and the government-sanctioned violence against the Islamists. For example, 201 persons were killed in civil unrest in 1993 and 286 in 1994. Thousands remain in prison, held without charge, and torture is used systematically by the Egyptian security forces. Eleven persons "disappeared" in 1994 after unrest, three in 1991, and three in 1993 (U.S. Department of State January 1994 and February 1995. See also Middle East Watch February 1991, June 1992, October 1993).

15. We use *household* to refer to the primary unit that pools its resources together. We use *family* when we refer to kin relationships; relatives may or may not be members of a particular household.

16. Here *gender* refers to a cultural set of rules that are defined as appropriate to the sexes in a given society at a given time. As Lerner argues, "it is a costume, a mask, a straitjacket in which men and women dance their unequal dance" (Lerner 1986, 238).

WORKS CITED

Abaza, Mona. 1987. "Feminist Debates and 'Traditional Feminism' of the Fellaha in Rural Egypt." Working Paper, no. 93. Sociology of Development Research Center, University of Bielefeld.

Abdalla, Ahmed. 1991. "Structure of Political Participation in Egypt." Paper presented at the annual meeting of the Middle East Studies Association, November, Washington, D.C.

Abdel-Fadil, Mahmoud. 1980a. "Informal Sector Employment in Egypt." Series on Employment Opportunities and Equity in Egypt, no. 1. International Labor Office, Geneva.

———. 1980b. *The Political Economy of Nasserism: A Study in Employment and Income Distribution Politics in Urban Egypt, 1952–1972.* Cambridge: Cambridge University Press.

Abdel-Rahman, Ibrahim Helmy, and Mohammed Sultan Abu Ali. 1989. "Role of the Public and Private Sectors with Special Reference to Privatization." In *Privatization and Structural Adjustment in the Arab Countries*, ed. Said El-Naggar, 141–181. Washington, D.C.: International Monetary Fund.

Abu-Lughod, Leila. 1986. *Veiled Sentiments: Honor and Poetry in a Bedouin Society.* Berkeley: University of California Press.

Adams, Richard H., Jr. 1985. "Development and Structural Change in Rural Egypt, 1952 to 1982." *World Development* 13: 705–723.

———. 1989. "Worker Remittances and Inequality in Rural Egypt." *Economic Development and Cultural Change* 38: 45–71.

Alderman, Harold, and Joachim Von Braun. 1984. "The Effects of the Egyptian Food Ration and Subsidy System on Income Distribution and Consumption." Research Report, no. 45. International Food Policy Research Institute, Washington, D.C.

Amin, Galal A. 1989. "Migration, Inflation, and Social Mobility: A Sociological Interpretation of Egypt's Current Economic and Political Crisis." In *Egypt under Mubarak*, ed. Charles Tripp and Roger Owen, 103–121. London: Routledge.

———, and Elizabeth Awny. 1984. "International Migration of Egyptian Labor: A Review of the State of the Art." International Development Research Center, Ottawa and Cairo. Manuscript report.

Assaad, Ragui. 1989. "The Employment Crisis in Egypt: Trends and Issues." American University in Cairo, January. Mimeographed.

Ayubi, Nazih N. M. 1991. *Political Islam: Religion and Politics in the Arab World.* London: Routledge.

Barkey, Henri, ed. 1992. *The Politics of Economic Reform in the Middle East.* New York: St. Martin's Press.

Beneria, Lourdes, and Martha Roldan. 1987. *The Crossroads of Class and Gender: Industrial Homework, Subcontracting, and Household Dynamics in Mexico City.* Chicago: University of Chicago Press.

Bianchi, Robert. 1989. *Unruly Corporatism: Associational Life in Twentieth-Century Egypt.* New York: Oxford University Press.

Booth, William James. 1993. *Households: On the Moral Architecture of the Economy.* Ithaca: Cornell University Press.

Boxer, Marilyn J. 1982. "For and about Women: The Theory and the Practice of Women's Studies in the United States." In *Feminist Theory: A Critique of Ideology*, ed. N. Keohane, M. Rosaldo, and B. Gelti. Brighton: Harvester Press.

Bromley, Simon, and Ray Bush. 1994. "Adjustment in Egypt? The Political Economy of Reform." *Review of African Political Economy* 60: 201–213.

Brydon, Lynne, and Sylvia Chant. 1993. *Women in the Third World: Gender Issues in Rural and Urban Areas*. New Brunswick: Rutgers University Press.

CAPMAS (Central Agency for Public Mobilization and Statistics). 1986. *Statistical Year Book: Arab Republic of Egypt, 1952–1985*. Cairo: CAPMAS.

CAPMAS and UNICEF. 1993. *The State of Egyptian Children and Women*. Cairo: CAPMAS and UNICEF.

Castells, Manuel, and Alejandro Portes. 1989. "World Underneath: The Origins, Dynamics, and Effects of the Informal Economy." In *The Informal Economy: Studies in Advanced and Less Developed Countries*, ed. Alejandro Portes, Manuel Castells, and Lauren A. Benton, 11–40. Baltimore: Johns Hopkins University Press.

Chaudhry, Kiren Aziz. 1993. "The Myths of the Market and the Common History of Late Developers." *Politics and Society* 21 (September): 245–274.

Day, Alan J. 1991. *The Middle East and North Africa, 1992*. London: Europa, 399–411.

Dwyer, Daisy, and Judith Bruce, eds. 1988. *A Home Divided: Women and Income in the Third World*. Stanford: Stanford University Press.

"Egypt: Staying Away." 1994. *Economist*, February 19, 45–46.

"Egypt Exploits Its Gulf War Bonus." 1993. *Euromoney*, April, 138–141.

Elson, Diane, ed. 1991. *Male Bias in the Development Process*. New York: Manchester University Press.

Folbre, Nancy. 1984. "Household Production in the Philippines: A Non-Neoclassical Approach." *Economic Development and Cultural Changes* 321: 303–330.

———. 1986. "Cleaning House." *Journal of Development Economics* 22: 3–40.

———. 1990. "The Demographic Logic of Patriarchal Capitalism." Washington, D.C.: Population Council and International Center for Research on Women. Mimeographed.

Gray, John N., and David J. Mearns. 1989. *Society from the Inside Out: Anthropological Perspectives on the South Asian Households*. London and New Delhi Park: Sage.

Guindi, Fadwa El-. 1981. "Veiling Infitah with Muslim Ethic: Egypt's Contemporary Islamic Movement." *Social Problems* 28: 465–485.

Handoussa, Heba. 1990. "Fifteen Years of U.S. Aid to Egypt—a Critical Review." In *The Political Economy of Contemporary Egypt*, ed. Ibrahim M. Oweiss, 109–124. Washington, D.C.: Center for Contemporary Arab Studies.

————. 1991. "Crisis and Challenge: Prospects for the 1990s." In *Employment and Structural Adjustment: Egypt in the 1990s*, ed. Heba Handoussa and Gillian Potter, 3–24. Cairo: American University in Cairo Press.

Hansen, Bent, and Samir Radwan. 1982. *Employment Opportunities and Equity in a Changing Economy: Egypt in the 1980s*. Geneva: International Labor Office.

Harik, Iliya F., and Denis J. Sullivan, eds. 1992. *Privatization and Liberalization in the Middle East*. Bloomington: Indiana University Press.

Hart, Keith. 1973. "Informal Income Opportunities and Urban Employment in Ghana." *Journal of Modern African Studies* 11: 61–89.

Hendriks, Bertus. 1987. "Egypt's New Political Map: A Report from the Election Campaign." *MERIP Middle East Reports*, July–August, 23–30.

Hoodfar, Homa. 1994. "Situating the Anthropologist; A Personal Account of Ethnographic Fieldwork in Three Urban Settings: Tehran, Cairo, and Montreal." In *Urban Lives: Fragmentation and Resistance*, ed. Vered Amit-Talai and Henri Lustiger-Thaler, 206–226. Toronto: McClelland and Stewart.

hooks, bell. 1984. *Feminist Theory: From Margin to Center*. Boston: South End Press.

Hopkins, Nicholas S. 1987. *Agrarian Transformation in Egypt*. Cairo: American University in Cairo Press.

Hussein, Mahmoud. 1973. *Class Conflict in Egypt, 1945–1970*. Trans. Michel and Susanne Chirman et al. New York: Monthly Review Press.

Ibrahim, Saad Eddin. 1980. "Anatomy of Egypt's Militant Islamic Groups: Methodological Note and Preliminary Findings." *International Journal of Middle East Studies* 12: 423–453.

International Labor Office. 1991. *ILO Yearbook of Labor Statistics*. Geneva: ILO.

Kabeer, Naila. 1991. "Gender, Production, and Well-Being: Rethinking the Household Economy." Institute of Development Studies, no. 28. Brighton: Sussex University.

Kepel, Gilles. 1986. *Muslim Extremism in Egypt*. Berkeley: University of California Press.

Khafagy, Fatma. 1984. "Women and Labor Migration: One Village in Egypt." *MERIP Reports*, June, 14–21.

Kupferschmidt, Uri M. 1987. "Reformist and Militant Islam in Urban and Rural Egypt." *Middle Eastern Studies* 23: 403–418.

Lazreg, Marnia. 1988. "Feminism and Difference: The Perils of Writing as a Woman on Women in Algeria." *Feminist Studies* 14 (Spring): 81–107.

————. 1994. *The Eloquence of Silence: Algerian Women in Question*. London: Routledge.

Lerner, Gerda. 1986. *The Creation of Patriarchy*. New York: Oxford University Press.

Lesch, Ann M. 1985. "The Impact of Labor Migration on Urban and Rural Egypt." UFSI Reports, no. 39. Hanover, N.H.: Universities Field Staff International.

———. 1989. "Democracy in Doses: Mubarak Launches His Second Term as President." *Arab Studies Quarterly* 11 (Fall): 87–107.

MacLeod, Arlene Elowe. 1991. *Accommodating Protest: Working Women, the New Veiling, and Change in Cairo.* New York: Columbia University Press.

Madan, T. N. 1989. Foreword in *Society from the Inside Out: Anthropological Perspectives on the South Asian Households,* ed. John N. Gray and David J. Mearns, 9–12. London and New Delhi Park: Sage.

Makram-Ebeid, Mona. 1989. "Political Opposition in Egypt: Democratic Myth or Reality?" *Middle East Journal* 43 (Summer): 423–436.

Mattoon, Scott. 1993. "Terror Makes Its Mark." *Middle East Journal* 47 (June): 4–10.

Mernissi, Fatima. 1991. *The Veil and the Male Elite: A Feminist Interpretation of Rights in Islam.* Reading: Addison-Wesley.

Middle East Watch. 1991. "Egyptian Authorities Clamp Down on Dissent." *Middle East Watch,* February 13.

———. 1992. "Egypt: Court Upholds Closure of Women's Organization." *Middle East Watch,* June.

———. 1993. "Egypt: Human Rights Abuses Mount in 1993, U.S. Policymakers Should Hold President Mubarak Accountable." *Middle East Watch,* October 22.

Mohanty, Chandra. 1988. "Under Western Eyes: Feminist Scholarship and Colonial Discourses." *Feminist Review* 30 (Autumn): 61–88.

———, Ann Russo, and Lourdes Torres. 1991. *Third World Women and the Politics of Feminism.* Bloomington: Indiana University Press.

Moore, Henrietta L. 1988. *Feminism and Anthropology.* Minneapolis: University of Minnesota Press.

Nader, Laura. 1986. "The Subordination of Women in Comparative Perspective." *Urban Anthropology and Studies of Cultural Systems and World Economic Development* 15 (Fall–Winter): 377–397.

———. 1989. "Orientalism, Occidentalism and the Control of Women." *Cultural Dynamics* 2: 323–355.

Naggar, Said El-. 1989. "Privatization and Structural Adjustment: The Basic Issues." In *Privatization and Structural Adjustment in the Arab Countries,* ed. Said El-Naggar, 1–17. Washington, D.C.: International Monetary Fund.

Netting, Robert McC., Richard R. Wilk, and Eric J. Arnould, eds. 1984. *Households: Comparative and Historical Studies of the Domestic Group.* Berkeley: University of California Press.

Papenek, Hanna. 1990. "To Each Less Than She Needs, from Each More Than She Can Do: Allocation, Entitlements, and Value." In *Persistent Inequalities: Women and World Development*, ed. Irene Tinker, 162–181. Oxford: Oxford University Press.

Post, Erika. 1987. "Egypt's Elections." *MERIP Middle East Reports*, July–August, 17–22.

Posusney, Marsha Pripstein. 1993. "Irrational Workers: The Moral Economy of Labor Protest in Egypt." *World Politics* 46 (October): 83–120.

Ramadan, Abdel Azim. 1993. "Fundamentalist Influence in Egypt: The Strategies of the Muslim Brotherhood and the Takfir Groups." In *Fundamentalisms and the State: Remaking Polities, Economies, and Militance*, ed. Martin E. Marty and R. Scott Appleby, 153–183. Chicago: University of Chicago Press.

Redclift, Nanneke. 1985. "The Contested Domain: Gender, Accumulation, and Labor Process." In *Beyond Employment: Household, Gender, and Subsistence*, ed. Nanneke Redclift and Enzo Mingione. Oxford: Basil Blackwell.

Reed, Stanley. 1993. "The Battle for Egypt." *Foreign Affairs* 72 (September): 94–107.

Rogers, Barbara. 1980. *The Domestication of Women: Discrimination in Developing Societies*. London: Tavistock.

Roy, Delwin A. 1990. "Egyptian Debt: Forgive—or Forget." In *The Political Economy of Contemporary Egypt*, ed. Ibrahim M. Oweiss, 161–176. Washington, D.C.: Center for Contemporary Arab Studies.

Rugh, Andrea. 1984. *Family in Contemporary Egypt*. Syracuse: Syracuse University Press.

Sadowski, Yahya M. 1991. *Political Vegetables? Businessman and Bureaucrat in the Development of Egyptian Agriculture*. Washington, D.C.: Brookings Institution.

Saeed, Javaid. 1994. *Islam and Modernization: A Comparative Analysis of Pakistan, Egypt, and Turkey*. Westport: Praeger.

Said, Mohamed, El-Sayed. 1990. "The Political Economy of Migration in Egypt, 1974–1989." West Asia and North Africa Regional Papers, no. 36. Population Council, Cairo.

Sayed, Moustapha K. El- 1990. "The Islamic Movement in Egypt." In *The Political Economy of Contemporary Egypt*, ed. Ibrahim M. Oweiss, 222–239. Washington, D.C.: Center for Contemporary Arab Studies.

Scott, James C. 1985. *The Weapons of the Weak*. New Haven: Yale University Press.

Sen, Amartya. 1990. "Gender and Cooperative Conflicts." In *Persistent Inequalities: Women and World Development*, ed. Irene Tinker, 123–149. Oxford: Oxford University Press.

Sharma, Ursula. 1986. *Women's Work, Class, and the Urban Household: A Study of Shimala, North India*. London: Tavistock.

Sherif, Khaled Fouad, and Regina M. Soos. 1992. "Egypt's Liberalization Experiment and Its Impact on State-Owned Enterprise." In *Privatization and Liberalization in the Middle East*, ed. Iliya F. Harik and Denis J. Sullivan, 60–80. Bloomington: Indiana University Press.

Shorter, Frederic. 1989. *Cairo's Leap Forward: People, Households, and Dwelling Space.* Cairo Papers in Social Science, no. 12. Cairo: American University in Cairo Press.

Singerman, Diane. 1995. *Avenues of Participation: Family, Politics, and Networks in Urban Quarters of Cairo.* Princeton: Princeton University Press.

Sivan, Emmanuel. 1985. *Radical Islam: Medieval Theology and Modern Politics.* New Haven: Yale University Press.

Sullivan, Denis J. 1994. *Private Voluntary Organizations in Egypt: Islamic Development, Private Initiative, and State Control.* Gainesville: University Press of Florida.

———. 1995. "Bureaucracy and Foreign Aid in Egypt: The Primacy of Politics." In *The Political Economy of Contemporary Egypt*, ed. Ibrahim M. Oweiss, 125–160. Washington, D.C.: Center for Contemporary Arab Studies.

Taylor, Elizabeth. 1984. "Egyptian Migration and Peasant Wives." *MERIP Reports*, June, 3–10.

Tesche, Jean, and Sahar Tohamy. 1994. "A Note on Economic Liberalization and Privatization in Hungary and Egypt." *Comparative Economic Studies* 36 (Summer): 51–72.

Thorne, Barrie, and Marilyn Yalom. 1982. *Rethinking the Family: Some Feminist Questions.* New York: Longman.

Timwell, Stephen. 1993. "Egypt: Let the Fight Begin." *The Banker* 143 (July): 47–50.

Tinker, Irene, ed. 1990. *Persistent Inequalities: Women and World Development.* Oxford: Oxford University Press.

Tinker, Irene, and Jane Jacquette. 1987. "UN Decade for Women: Its Impact and Legacy." *World Development* 15: 419–427.

Toth, James. 1991. "Pride, Purdah, or Paychecks: What Maintains the Gender Division of Labor in Rural Egypt?" *International Journal of Middle East Studies* 23: 213–236.

Wallerstein, Immanuel. 1984. "Household Structure and Labor-Force Formation in the Capitalist World Economy." In *Households in the World Economy*, ed. Hans Deiter-Evers, Joan Smith, and Immanuel Wallerstein. Beverly Hills: Sage.

Waring, Marlene. 1988. *If Women Counted: A New Feminist Economics.* San Francisco: Harper & Row.

Waterbury, John. 1982. "Patterns of Urban Growth and Income Distribution in Egypt." In *The Political Economy of Income Distribution in Egypt*, ed. Gouda Abdel-Khalak and Robert Tignor, 335–337. New York: Holmes & Meier.

Wilk, Richard R. 1984. "Household in the Process: Agricultural Changes and Domestic Transformation among the Kekchi May of Belize." In *Households: Comparative and Historical Studies of the Domestic Group*, ed. Robert McC. Netting, Richard R. Wilk, and Eric J. Arnould. Berkeley: University of California Press.

Wood C. 1981. "Structural Changes and Household Strategies: A Conceptual Framework for the Study of Rural Migration." *Human Organization* 40: 338–344.

World Bank. 1984. *World Debt Tables: External Debt of Developing Countries.* Washington, D.C.: World Bank.

———. 1987. *World Debt Tables: External Debt of Developing Countries.* Washington, D.C.: World Bank.

———. 1989. *World Tables: From the Data Files of the World Bank, 1988–1989.* Baltimore: Johns Hopkins University Press.

Yanagisako, S. J. 1979. "Family Household: The Analysis of Domestic Group." *Annual Review of Anthropology* 8: 161–205.

Yang, Lihua. 1994. "The Economic Reform in Egypt." *Beijing Review,* October 24, 46.

Zaytoun, Mohaya A. 1991. "Earnings and the Cost of Living: An Analysis of Recent Developments in the Egyptian Economy." In *Employment and Structural Adjustment: Egypt in the 1990s,* ed. Heba Handoussa and Gillian Potter, 219–257. Cairo: American University in Cairo Press.

Zurayk, Huda, and Frederic Shorter. 1988. "The Social Composition of Households in Arab Cities and Settlements: Cairo, Beirut, Amman." Regional Papers. Population Council, Cairo.

DEVELOPMENT, CHANGE, AND GENDER IN CAIRO

1

SURVIVAL STRATEGIES AND
THE POLITICAL ECONOMY OF
LOW-INCOME HOUSEHOLDS IN CAIRO

HOMA HOODFAR

HOUSEHOLDS DEVISE VARIOUS survival strategies based on their assessment of the resources they can mobilize and the options open to them.[1] The broad goal of these strategies is to maximally incorporate the households into the life of their community as best as possible. Failure to achieve this goal by a sizable number of individuals and households in a given society can have serious social and political consequences.[2] The strategies that households adopt to generate income (in cash or any other form) probably represent the most important aspect of the survival strategies, given the context of increasingly commercialized economies. Research in both developing and developed countries indicates that households generate their income through combinations of activities in cash and subsistence (including domestic and child care) economic domains (Goldschmidt-Clermont 1987, 1982). Thus the incorporation of non-market economic activities in our studies is essential if we are to develop a more thorough understanding of the choices people make in regard to the political economy of their households. This is particularly significant if the focus of the study is low-income households, in which the flow of cash and other forms of income is limited and the survival of the household may be at stake. Incorporation of these factors also would enable us to understand the rationales for the choices women make in their contributions to their household economies.

Earning a livelihood is one aspect of survival strategies, as is its disposal and allocation within the household. Since human beings are social, beyond a minimum basic level of satisfaction of physiological needs people give priority to reproducing themselves socially (Douglas and Isherwood 1978; Philibert 1984), and this priority strongly influences the choices they make in regard to the allocation of resources. Despite the significance for human and social development of the cost of social reproduction, this factor has commonly been neglected in studies of survival strategies.[3] Material culture and consumption, whether it involves the use of modern medicine, education, food, or other products, is one of the most important means by which households incorporate themselves into the life of the wider society (McCracken 1990; Csikszentmihalyi and Rochberg-Halton 1981). In fact, the chief liability of a low income from an economic viewpoint is that it excludes people from participating in mainstream consumption practices that are vital to social reproduction (Douglas and Isherwood 1978).

A thorough understanding of household economies and survival strategies depends on our ability to develop and deploy a holistic theoretical framework to study social and economic rationales for income acquisition, consumption priorities, and their allocation within the household. A comparison of trends in potential and actual income contribution and distribution will make it possible to delineate the forces that encourage individuals to remain in their household units and cooperate with other members despite conflicts. Moreover, such an approach will make it possible to examine whether socioeconomic changes reproduce, exaggerate, or modify household inequalities.

In this chapter, after broadly defining sources of household income, I examine the factors which influence individual and household choices with respect to participation or nonparticipation in the market economy in the context of low-income neighborhoods. Concerning the prevailing sexual division of labor, I argue that women's differential response to the labor market is not due to traditionalism and "Islamic" ideology but is economically rational and is determined by their much higher opportunity costs when compared with those of men. ("Opportunity cost" refers to the process of cost benefit analysis that individuals go through when they are deciding about participating in the labor market or changing employment.) Both men and women make economic decisions with reference to their own economic function and position in the household, and both try to maximize the return on their economic endeavors regardless of whether the yields are monetary or nonmonetary.

Furthermore, I examine both the social and the economic elements which influence consumption patterns of low-income households. My data show that the eagerness of low-income families to accumulate household goods stems from their desire for financial security and that indeed there is often a social or economic rationale behind much of what appear on the surface to be irrational consumption patterns.

The Neighborhoods

I began the fieldwork for this study at the end of January 1983, and by March 1986 I had lived and carried out intensive anthropological research in three low-income, newly urbanized neighboring districts in Cairo.[4] Since then I have paid short visits (in 1988, 1992, and 1994) to update my data and expand the research. Here I present the data I collected on the households using 1986 as the baseline and weaving in new developments as I discuss the issues.

Until the last couple of decades, the neighborhoods of the study were primarily agricultural land which produced vegetables for Cairo's markets. As the city expanded, an influx of rural migrants transformed these agricultural lands and villages into densely populated areas of Greater Cairo. Presently, though one may still meet original inhabitants, the majority of the population of the neighborhoods consists of first- and second-generation migrants.

All three neighborhoods had electricity. Only one had running water, though it was introduced into a second neighborhood in 1986. The people in the third neighborhood were eagerly anticipating city water by the mid-1990s. Homes in these neighborhoods were one- or two-room dwellings. Most dwellings with two rooms were self-contained apartments, although only a few contained kitchens. Many families lived in one-room dwellings and shared cooking and bathroom facilities with other households.

During my stay in these neighborhoods, I developed a wide network of friends in many households. Seventy-eight households formed the core of my sample, though for the purpose of this chapter I have concentrated on sixty-two households, the majority of whom were still in their family-building cycle. The majority of the adult population, particularly women, were illiterate. Some of the women had some schooling, but since they never used their skills, they quickly forgot them. On the other hand, many men could read and write although they had never attended school. Their friends and colleagues at work taught them the rudimentary skills which were required in their jobs.

The Family in Its Cultural Context

Marriage and family are the basis of formation of households in Egypt. It is rare for individuals to form a household outside family, kin, or marriage relations (Shorter 1989; Shorter and Zurayk 1988). Rights and obligations of husbands and wives within marriage are defined by Islamic law, the sexual division of labor, and Egyptian cultural practice.[5]

A Muslim marriage gives a wife the unconditional right to economic support from her husband regardless of her own financial resources. She also remains in control of her property, including inheritance or earned income. Her rights, as will be discussed later, have a profound impact on the way in which women assess labor market opportunities and the management of their wages. However, in case of divorce, the former wife is only entitled to three months' alimony and to those possessions which she brought with her at the start of the marriage or those she acquired with her own income, as well as any portion of her *mahr* which is due her. *Mahr* is a sum of money or durable property which, according to Islamic practices, a husband agrees to pay to his bride at any time prior to or during the marriage or upon divorce.

In return for the unconditional economic support of his family, a husband has certain rights within the marriage, the most important of which is the right to restrict his wife's physical mobility, which has often been interpreted as the right to prevent his wife from working outside the home. He also has the unilateral right to end the marriage without the consent of his wife. And in case of divorce, the husband has custody of the children.[6] Recently, though, legislation has curtailed some of these rights. Cultural practices such as cross-cousin marriages and sizable sums of *mahr* have evolved to protect women and counterbalance these unequal rights in divorce.[7] However, the relatively low incidence of divorce in Egypt, particularly after children are born, suggests that marriage is a stable institution.[8]

The traditional responsibility of a man to provide for his family is further strengthened by the modern capitalist ideology in which a man is regarded as the "breadwinner"; it has remained not only a principle of Egyptian beliefs but one of the major factors shaping modern family legislation. However, the contributions of the wife and other members of the family are taken for granted by both traditional and modern ideologies. Furthermore, reality has always been much more complex than expressed in ideology. Women and children have always played a very active role in the fulfillment of what are believed to be men's responsibilities (Tucker 1985). Nevertheless, the prevailing gender ideology, even when it does not correspond with practices, has an impact on perceptions and the way in which options are prioritized and valued. Perhaps the most significant manifestation of this ideology is the way in which male and female children are trained and equipped with skills they are expected to utilize in later life.

The Household Economy

Recent studies of survival strategies, subsistence, and informal economies both in the West and in developing societies have documented that the real income of a household is generated by a variety of market and nonmarket activities (Goldschmidt-Clermont 1982, 1987; Pahl 1984; Waring 1988). A narrow focus on market transactions results in underestimation of the contribution women (and to a lesser extent men) make to the household economy through nonmarket activities.[9] The standard of living of a household is therefore determined by several factors: "income"—whether in the form of cash or goods and services derived from nonmarket production such as housework or home produced foodstuffs; appropriation of public goods and services (such as subsidized goods and free hospital care), which can constitute a considerable part of a household's income in Third World cities; rent and transfer of goods and services through gift exchange and inheritance; management ability in allocating available resources to satisfy both immediate and long-term needs of the family while minimizing the need for scarce resources such as cash. Therefore I have adopted broader and more encompassing definitions of *economic activity* and *economic contribution* to include all those activities which bring direct or indirect material benefit to the household.

Market Activities

The Egyptian labor market is characterized by three distinct features which are pertinent to this study. First, as a result of the lingering policies of state socialism instituted during the Nasserist era (1956–1967), the state and public sector account for a very large share of formal employment, even after two decades of applying structural adjustment policies under the guidance of the International Monetary Fund and the World Bank. Many of those employed by the state are workers in low-ranking clerical or blue-collar jobs (Abdel-Fadil 1980). This group includes all my informants who were employed in the formal sector. Second, the massive international migration of semiskilled and unskilled labor, though in decline since 1985, and the introduction of the Open Door Policy (market economy) have probably been the most influential factors in the recent restructuring of the labor market, especially benefiting those who in the past were at the bottom of the labor market hierarchy.[10] Third, despite the lack of reliable statistics, scholars and policy makers agree that a very dynamic informal sector absorbs a large percentage of employment (Abdel-Fadil 1983).

The occupation composition of my informants reflected the diversity of job opportunities in an urban setting, ranging from casual work to semiskilled jobs in both the formal and the informal sectors of the economy (see Table 1). Occupations included plumbers, construction workers, and those in personal services, such as drivers and cooks. Self-employment, including petty trading, was one of the most important ways of earning an income for those without education, technical skills, or social networks. There also were a number of low-grade clerical and blue-collar workers, such as messengers, cleaners, and so on, particularly in the oldest neighborhood of the study. It is, however, only in rare cases that it is possible to classify a person in one job category. Many had changed occupations many times in the course of a couple of years. Many were engaged in several professions simultaneously. For the table, I have classified my informants under those professions in which they generated the largest income during 1986, the last year of the extended field research.

The informants' employment histories reveal the extent to which recent changes in the labor market have affected the occupational choices, albeit differently, for men and women. The majority of the male government employees in the sample were middle-aged. In the past, the high degree of job security and good wages had made government work the most desired occupational option. However, after the introduction of a liberal economy, salaries in the public sector did not keep up with the high rate of inflation. The wages of low-ranking employees were insufficient to support a family. In contrast, wages in the private and informal sector increased considerably, making that sector a more attractive option for men despite the lack of job security. The availability of high-paying jobs in the Arab oil-rich countries has also made migration to those countries a popular choice.

Accessible jobs in the private and informal sectors are generally manual, requiring little formal education. Thus boys who are viewed as the breadwinners of their future households are no longer encouraged to stay in school; they are sent out to the labor market as apprentices at an early age to learn skilled crafts. Occasionally, where the opportunity exists, they enter vocational schools. Abu Waᶜil, himself a low-grade government employee, expresses such a change of attitude.

> I will send Waᶜil [his son] after his elementary education to a technical school to learn a skill. A man needs to earn money to provide for his family. All those who have spent years in educational institutions at great cost to their parents

Table 1. Cash-Generating Activities of the Sample Households

Type of Occupation	Male[*]	Female
Government and Public Sector		
White-collar (junior clerk)	9	8
Blue-collar	16	3
Wage Workers		
Driver	6	–
Cook	2	–
Construction worker	4	–
Imam of mosque	1	–
Plumber	3	–
Semiskilled construction worker	4	–
Casual worker	6	–
Maids and handperson	1	4
Self-Employed		
Carpenter	1	–
Butcher	1	–
Petty trader	7	9
Home produce for the market	–	3
Unpaid family worker	–	7
Total	61	34

[*]In one household the male had never contributed any cash at all; he does not appear in this table. Neither do unmarried children who may be engaged in cash-generating activities.

now cannot earn enough money to rent a flat, or to marry. Times have changed and one has to be alert. Under Nasser, education was the most important means, but under Sadat and Mubarak it is skills which earn money.

In families with limited resources, education is seen not as a luxury but rather as an investment toward acquiring a better-paying job. Those households with few material resources to spare tend to be very alert to changes in salaries and job prestige.[11] Ironically, the withdrawal of sons from school has made more resources available for investment in the education of daughters, facilitating their acquisition of white-collar public sector jobs.

Besides wage levels, factors such as status and especially job security influenced employment choices as people strived for an equilibrium. Thus low-paying government jobs still had an appeal, given the absence of an effective social welfare system. None of the government employees, despite their bitter complaints about low pay, had resigned or even planned to resign from their jobs. Many pointed out, by way of example, people in the community who had once earned high wages in the private sector as young skilled workers but now had to sell vegetables in the local market to survive in their old age. Abu A'zza had been approached by an acquaintance who offered him a relatively attractive job in a workshop. He was offered a wage almost three times his salary, but he refused. He told me:

> I know that is a very good wage and we need the money very much but I have four children and have to think of their future. Suppose I have an accident tomorrow or get permanently sick. If I am a government employee at least they are paid a minimum, enabling them to eat. But if I work in the private sector at best they will have the employer's sympathy.

In addition, the shorter effective working hours and the low level of energy expenditure in the public and government sectors allowed employees to acquire a second job to supplement their low pay. Thus Abu-A'zza's wife agreed with him:

> He has had more than ten years with the government and it would be foolish to lose all that. The government income is very low but they do not have to work hard and they can find another job to supplement the family income. They can get leave without pay and migrate to the Gulf for a few years and improve the family condition.

Both the low pay of the public sector and job insecurity in the private sector encouraged people to engage in more than one source of cash-earning activity. In fact there was tremendous social pressure on all men working one shift to engage in a second or even a third job. Men, particularly married men, are expected to invest all their time and energy in cash-earning activities. Those who fail to comply with these standards are accused of laziness and their wives and children are pitied. Umm Habah complained that she had lost all her friends and few women visited her because her husband stayed home:

> My husband works in a government factory and comes home at three o'clock and stays home until seven or eight in the evening when he leaves for the coffeehouse. He is lazy and although we are very poor he refuses to find a second job. He does not care that we have to live in one room and eat poorly and there is nothing I can do.

After she had left, Umm Shadia added in sympathy with her:

Poor Umm Habah. She was not lucky in finding a good man. Poverty is terrible but it becomes unbearable when you have a lazy and useless man who does not like working hard—poor Umm Habah and her children.

Those who were wage earners in the private sector viewed unemployment as inevitable once they were older, since employers always looked for energetic younger workers. They therefore planned and hoped one day to open their own workshops or a small corner shop. It was, however, rare for a wage earner ever to save enough money to open his own shop. The few who had managed to establish a small workshop of their own were returning migrants.

Hence petty trading was the most obvious source of employment for many who could not find jobs elsewhere, or for women who could not accommodate fixed working hours in factories or offices. Their capital ranged from a couple of pounds to a few hundred. With the exception of those with larger businesses, most self-employed men engaged in other cash-earning activities whenever the opportunity arose. Men's businesses were, in fact, family ones and were locally based. For instance, many government employees had established a small business, often with the collaboration of their wives. Abu Ahmed, talking about his employment history, explained:

> I used to be a construction worker until I grew older and few people were prepared to employ me. Then my wife and I sold our television and a few other items and opened this small shop and started to make and sell pickles. Now we earn little but at least we don't starve. I supplement our earning with occasional wage work which I may be offered in the neighborhood.[12]

Even though the participation of women in running family businesses was regarded as essential by their husbands and many of the women regularly invested long hours there, few of these women were considered "working" women by their husbands, neighbors, or even themselves. This attitude has made it difficult to collect information on women's unpaid family work (Ibrahim 1983; Beneria 1982, 1992).

Many women in the low-income neighborhoods were engaged in a wide range of cash-earning activities. Their economic activities in the nonmarket domain greatly influenced the choices women made when considering employment opportunities. The sexual division of labor has assigned different tasks and responsibilities to men and women. Since women are expected to attend to domestic and child-care responsibilities, their opportunity cost is much greater. These activities are crucial to the household, and to hire or arrange replacement labor is often economically not a viable option for unskilled wage workers, since it can claim a considerable part of their wages, which are very small to begin with. Therefore men and women, when faced with similar opportunities in the labor market, may make different employment decisions on the basis of their different opportunity costs.

Unskilled women with little or no education tended to opt for informal economic activities, such as petty trading or production, which offered flexible hours and did not require long hours away from home. Factory work, with its small income and rigid long hours, was considered suitable only for unmarried young women who had few responsibilities at home. That is because even when the inconveniences to the women and their children caused by long hours are discounted, the immediate financial cost of these jobs outweighs their benefits.

Zaynab was complaining of the difficulties of having to manage and provide for her family (her unemployed husband and her two sons) on her income from selling soaked beans in the market. I asked her why she did not return to the position she had in a factory before her marriage. She explained:

> Factory work is hardly the answer to my problems. The income from such work is about thirty pounds. I have to take my children and leave them with my mother who does not live near me. I also have to pay for their food because my parents are also very poor and cannot feed my children all the time. Then I cannot buy inexpensive or subsidized food which the cooperative shop sells occasionally. Working also includes other costs such as bus fare and food. When you account for all the expenses, a woman with children is worse off in those jobs.

Zaynab is typical of many other women in the neighborhoods who had resigned from their factory work after marriage or after their first child was born. National statistics indicate that despite an overall increase in the rate of female labor force participation, the percentage of women in the blue-collar categories has consistently decreased since the 1967 census.[13] This indicates that Zaynab's and her friends' assessment of the market may be a universal trend. Women did not feel that access to such jobs was difficult but that their small wages made the jobs undesirable for them.

Among my informants, all but one woman with more than nine years of formal education were white-collar government employees.[14] Both male and female informants universally saw government jobs as more suitable for women than private sector jobs because of the policy of generous maternity leave and other allowances made for female state employees. For instance, women in white-collar public sector jobs, over and above three months of paid maternity leave, are entitled to two years' leave without pay for each of their first three children. They may also occasionally take a day off to attend to sick children or household emergencies without fear of losing their jobs.[15] Though women regretted that the real wages of government employees had not kept up with inflation, their preference for these jobs remained the same.

Migration

After 1973, migration to the Gulf became an important option open to unskilled and semiskilled male workers (Amin and Awny 1985; Fergany 1987). Migration has had a profound effect on wage levels in Egypt, particularly for the waged and artisan workers: on one hand, remittances have encouraged investment in enterprises and trade, which heightens the demand for additional workers; on the other hand, migration has limited the supply of labor in Egypt. This situation has enabled many unskilled and semiskilled workers, whose wages were very low in the past, to renegotiate their position in the labor market and demand higher wages. Some of the informants had experienced as much as an elevenfold wage increase during the last decade.

Many men in the low-income neighborhoods had exploited this opportunity in order to raise cash.[16] Many others were hoping to be able to migrate; however, they recognized that the opportunities have shrunk as a result of economic recession in oil-rich countries. Migration was viewed as a short-term strategy to raise cash for the household, although many migrants had been abroad for more than fifteen years. The decision to migrate was influenced by the structural position of men or women in their household, the availability of information about the job market, and access to some social network in the host country. Most commonly, men migrated before marriage or after they had fathered several children, because their wives preferred to start building a family at an early stage of marriage.[17]

Nonmarket Activities

Nonmonetary contributions to the political economy of the household account for a considerable part of the household's livelihood. For most households, wages alone do not cover immediate expenses, much less long-term needs. Wages must be supplemented by income from other forms of productive activity. For example the cash income of a household is supplemented by home production for self-consumption and by funneling public goods and services, including subsidized goods and free medicine, to the household. Similarly child care and housework are essential activities of wage supplementation, although their value is rarely incorporated into family income. Accounting for these contributions is particularly important among the low-income stratum of any society; in these households such multiple contributions are essential, for they do not merely improve the level of household welfare but often represent the margin of survival (Goldschmidt-Clermont 1987). Though men contributed to households in this fashion, in Egypt, as in most other societies, it was women's labor which accounted for most nonmonetary contributions.

Domestic Work

The concepts domestic work, housework, and child care clarify little if one is actually interested in the nature of household tasks and how they change over time. These tasks have been treated in the literature as transhistorical and cross-cultural; this approach ignores the fact that the nature of housework and childrearing activities is affected by such factors as the level of socioeconomic development, ecological conditions, and the cultural values of a society, as well as by the extent of resources available to the household (see Davidson 1982 for the impact of technology on housework). For instance, in many developing areas, housework includes carrying water and fuel from miles away, processing food, and cooking and cleaning with very primitive equipment. This hardly resembles the work of a middle- or working-class housewife living in London.

Domestic work is the most underestimated aspect of subsistence activities in modern societies (Waring 1988; Oakley 1974; Folbre 1986). Until recently, it had rarely featured in any discussion in the social sciences, whether in economics, family studies, or other areas. To a large extent, this neglect is a consequence of emphasizing the cash economy. In Egypt, traditionally domestic tasks were valued and considered important contributions to the household. However, modernization and Westernization in the last three decades, by stressing the importance of market achievements, have devalued domestic contributions.

All married women in my study spent several hours each day attending to washing, cleaning, and cooking tasks, although they all agreed that the load of housework had decreased as a result of modernization, urbanization, and the expansion of public provisions. Many tasks, such as baking bread and making jam or pickles, which were traditionally performed by women as part of their housework have become commercialized. Moreover, in contrast to the past era, men who mostly worked all day outside the local community rarely ate at home, thereby reducing the burden on women of cooking elaborate meals. However, women remained ambivalent about these changes: on one hand, they welcomed them and eagerly tried to obtain modern electric household appliances; on the other, they resented the fact that they had become more dependent on their husbands' cash income to fulfill their share of responsibilities.

Child care, all the women pointed out, was becoming increasingly demanding, mainly owing to higher expectations. One elderly woman explained:

Children these days remain children until they are seventeen, nineteen, and sometimes older. In my time we became adult once we were seven or eight and were expected to accept responsibilities.

Another woman said:

When we were children we were clothed and fed and sent off to play in some field or street. No one bothered about what we did or how dirty we looked. But now I have to change my children every day, take them to school, and feed them nutritious food. Although I am illiterate, I still have to sit and watch over them while they do their homework. My mother was a good mother but she was not expected to do all that.

Many were quick to point out that urban life had robbed them of their kin support, since they often lived in different parts of the city, isolated from relatives. Ironically, while the tasks of child care increased, public recognition of child care as an important contribution to the household and society has considerably decreased (Hoodfar 1986). As one middle-aged informant pointed out with some resentment,

In my mother's time we only heard about good mothers and how much everyone was indebted to their mothers. In our time, though we do so much more, we only hear about bad mothers, negligent mothers, bad mothers.

Men rarely participated either in child care or housework; nor were they expected to. All women, regardless of their cash-earning activities, expressed strong opposition to such participation by their husbands. Women, by publicly teasing men who showed interest in these tasks, reinforced the traditional division of labor. This attitude, however, did not stem from their internalization of the patriarchal ideology or from the alleged traditionalism and conservatism of Muslim women. Rather it reflected strategies women consciously adopted to protect their own interests. By retaining control over the domestic

domain, women resisted further male encroachments on their power and authority. Umm Wa'il's views in this regard are typical of many other informants:

> I would never have my husband touch anything around the house. I will see
> to all his needs. He only occasionally eats at home and I send his clothes to be
> laundered because I cannot wash suits or iron them. If I also expect him to
> make his own tea and help tidying up and look after children, why would he
> want me or pay for me? God has made women for home and men for the mar-
> ket. It is not wise to change this order.

These women were conscious that the new social order had tipped the interdependent balance of husband and wife in favor of men. Even those women
in secure jobs felt much the same as nonearning wives with regard to their husbands' participation in housework. It was this particular contribution of domestic work that legitimized their claims on the husbands' income. Nismah, a
white-collar worker, explained her views at a gathering of her colleagues:

> If I am not well or if the children are sick and need help, of course I appreciate
> his help but I am perfectly capable of attending my housework. If ever I felt I
> could not do both I would give up my job and stay home. After all a woman's
> prime responsibility is her home and not her job. If I let him do the housework
> today, tomorrow he will demand that I pay for the household expenses. If I
> want him to take over my role he would want me to take over his role. There
> is wisdom in the traditional division or else God would not endorse it in the
> Qur'an.

Neither religion nor religiosity could account for these women's behavior.
None of the young married women were very religious. None of them said their
daily prayers or read the Qur'an, even when they could read; they simply used
the legitimacy of religion to defend their interest and privileges. If they attended to their responsibilities at home they could legitimately expect their
husbands to attend to traditional and religious responsibilities and provide for
the family. The women's adherence to Islamic doctrine would also prevent their
husbands from laying claim to the wives' income (Hoodfar 1988). The common
attitude of both the waged and unwaged women in this respect also strengthened the grounds for solidarity among them.

Cash Economizing and Home Improvement

Studies of the urban household economy often overlook a wide range of
cash economizing measures which are beyond the definition of housework.
Both male and female informants participated in these kinds of activities with

the conscious intent of improving their standard of living. However, as we will discuss, it appeared that the development of commoditization has had a differential impact on such activities among male and female informants.

When the household's supply of cash is limited, its efficient allocation is very important, since cash resources have to be stretched to their fullest with efficient, skilled shopping and management. Keeping track of complex and temperamental pricing of goods in the open and government-controlled markets demands constant attention and is not a trivial task. The unpredictable pattern of distribution of goods, particularly of subsidized and rationed goods in Cairo, further complicates even those simple shopping tasks.

In Cairo, obtaining subsidized goods can save as much as one-third of the daily food budget among low-income households (Khouri-Dagher 1986). Since women increasingly do more of the shopping, their absence from the neighborhood would inflict financial losses on the household. This is an important factor in discouraging unskilled women, whose wages would be meager anyway, from joining the labor market. Yet the same fact encouraged other women who had to generate cash to work locally in preference to those better-paid jobs elsewhere. Umm Sabah, who sold green vegetables in the local market, had a capital of three to four Egyptian pounds and earned one Egyptian pound or less per day. She explained:

> I earn little by selling watercress and parsley but because I am here in the vicinity I learn when there is meat, chicken, eggs, or other items in the *gam'iyya* [government food cooperative] and I can always leave my basket either for my children or a friend here and run to the queue. Sometimes other people queue for me so that I can attend to my business. This way we can buy items which otherwise we could never eat. If I was working in the factory, since I am illiterate I would earn only ten pounds or so more, but I would have to buy more clothes since I could not go in my *gallabiyya* [traditional dress]. I would have to pay bus fare and then when I came home I would have to purchase food at the free-market price, wasting as much as fifteen to twenty pounds monthly.

As noted, two of the neighborhoods in the study, like many low-income neighborhoods in Cairo, lacked piped water to the houses, and residents had either to purchase water or to carry it from public taps. No household in my study bought water, and women carried the water home daily. Carrying water is a task universally performed by women, though the water dealers are often men. The market value of water in different neighborhoods in Cairo (when purchased) was estimated at £E19.20 per month (Shorter 1985). Within the budget of a low-income household, a savings of £E19 per month represents a substantial sum.

Traditionally, urban men had little chance of contributing anything other than cash to the household. This has changed in recent years, as men spend much time performing tasks that in the past would have been referred to a specialist, such as construction, painting, and decorating. Such a change may be more universal than has been recognized. Studies in Western Europe have indicated a similar pattern (Pahl 1980; Gershuny 1979). Abu Sa‘d, a blue-collar worker in the public sector, explained his economic rationale as he was painting his apartment:

> At first I wanted to ask a decorator, Naqash, to come and paint the flat because it was very dirty, but he gave me an estimate of at least 120 pounds. I could not afford his price because I only earn 35 pounds a week from both my jobs. Therefore I applied for leave from my jobs and I am doing it myself. This way I save a lot of money while my children live in a clean and neat flat.

On another occasion, Hamid, a former migrant who had become an unskilled worker in the public sector, had obtained a second job as a doorman, and had managed to build a flat for his family, explained:

> I took three weeks of my yearly holiday and with the help of my two eldest sons finished building the first room. Of course we had to employ skilled people for certain tasks but we did whatever we could because it is so expensive to employ skilled workers. They demand five or six times more than what I earn in a day. Once the room was finished my family moved here and I gradually built a second room and a kitchen. Now I am working on the second floor whenever I have time and the money to buy the materials. I think that in a year or two I can finish the second floor too.

The normative sexual division of labor holds men responsible for house improvements and other kinds of repairs. My data indicate that male cash-economizing tasks tended to increase as the household's material resources increased, while women were affected in the opposite way. For example, women no longer preserved food, since they saved little money, if any, in the process. Many, however, still raised chickens, rabbits, geese, pigeons, or sheep for the household's consumption and sometimes sold them for cash. Where women had cash income of their own, however, they preferred to invest their money in household goods, which would be recognized as their own property.

Utilizing Public Institutions

With urbanization and modernization, societies concurrently develop complex systems of communal consumption of goods and services, systems which are essential for work and reproduction in an industrial society. Although government control has substantially declined in the 1990s, the Egyptian state still has substantially more control over the consumption and distribution of a wide range of goods and services than the governments in many other developing countries. Thus bureaucracy in Egypt has expanded to cope with the demands of state control. Lack of sufficient resources and organizational inefficiency, common to many developing countries, make any transaction with the state a laborious and time-consuming task. Citizens must spend days in the corridors of government buildings trying to collect signatures, filling out forms, buying stamps, and paying bribes under different pretexts in order to obtain the proper papers enabling them to take advantage of public goods.

Despite bureaucratic difficulties, the low-income household cannot afford to overlook the benefits that the state offers. Since such provisions are rarely delivered to one's doorstep, consumers must invest time and energy to direct these benefits to their households. As the men in the study were often away at jobs, it was often the women who developed the networks and the expertise required to deal with these institutions. Their varied missions included taking the children to public hospitals or health centers, obtaining free baby milk, acquiring a ration card (Khouri-Dagher 1986 and chapter 5 in this volume), registering the children at school, dealing with housing or tax authorities, applying for passports and permission to migrate, and many other bureaucratic errands.

While material scarcity in the neighborhoods has brought about practical changes in the division of labor by gender, ideological changes lag behind practice. Men traditionally were responsible for all those tasks beyond the physical compound of home. Thus women performed these tasks under the auspices of their husbands, and they perceived themselves as helping out their husbands. As a result, neither they, their husbands, nor their community credited them for their contribution in this field. The major exceptions in this respect were the wives of migrants, who in the absence of their husbands were compelled to see themselves as heads of their households and publicly demanded recognition and credit for their contributions (see chapter 3 in this volume).

Expenditure Strategies

Consumption and material possessions, in addition to satisfying physiological needs, are important channels through which a household integrates itself into the life of the wider community. The careful planning of allocation and disposal of income is affected by a variety of social and economic considerations. For instance, the social and material position which members of the households in my study envisaged for themselves in the matrix of their immediate and the wider society was a prominent factor. The power relations, the degree of sharing between husband and wife, and to a lesser degree the influence of children and other members of the household are further elements.

The major part of the household's income was allocated to meet recurring needs such as food, clothing, rent, education, medical bills, and other small expenses. People weighed their consumption needs against those of other households they considered their equals in social rank. All households in the neighborhoods tended to keep daily expenses to a minimum in order to make accumulation of durable household goods possible. Some households, particularly those of government employees, used the securest part of their cash incomes to meet these needs and channeled all other cash from overtime, second jobs, and such to buy household assets. Women were particularly eager to reduce recurrent expenses so that more cash could be allocated for the acquisition of household goods. They encouraged their husbands to seek extra employment and engaged in any feasible cash-earning activities themselves in order to finance the accumulation of these items.

This pattern of expenditure within the lower-income stratum was very recent and was the result of the booming Egyptian economy and new socioeconomic conditions. Traditionally, women's dowries included all the essential items that they needed for the household and they rarely expected to acquire more furniture in the future.[18] The history of the informants' household inventories (see table 2) suggests a significant change between 1975 and 1985. Items such as television sets and electric washing machines used to be categorized as luxuries and were obtained only by the middle and upper classes. Now they are widespread in low-income homes.

When ranking their expenditure priorities, all my informants placed better housing as the most important one (see table 3 for sizes of informants' dwelling units). Those persons without a permanent or secure job counted establishing a business as the next most important priority, and only then did they mention

Table 2. Inventory of Electrical Appliances Owned by the Sample Households

Item*	Years of Ownership				Households	Total
	1–3	4–7	8–10	More	Without	
Stove	14	21	12	5	7	59
Refrigerator	12	17	6	3	21	59
Television	16	26	13	1	4	59
Washing tumbler	16	26	10	1	6	59
Fan	21	15	7	—	16	59
Cassette player	15	15	20	—	14	59

*I have excluded such items as beds and wardrobes which all households possessed and have focused on items that only since the late 1970s have come to be considered standard electrical household goods in low-income neighborhoods.

Table 3. Size of the Dwelling Unit among the Sample Households

Number of Rooms	Frequency
1	18
2	30
3	11
4	2
5	1
Total households	62

improving the day-to-day living conditions by investing in modern appliances, better clothing, and more nutritious diets. To an outsider, such an account may appear contradictory to the practices in low-income neighborhoods, where people seem to invest in household goods above all other elements, but a closer examination would prove to the contrary.

Improving housing or establishing a business required a substantial amount of capital, and in the absence of the possibility of loans from financial institutions or saving of remittances, persons in these neighborhoods had to deploy other long-term saving strategies. However, the chronic shortage of cash to finalize the financing of their marriage, together with a cooperative spirit toward their neighbor's problems, made saving cash very difficult. There was always the neighbors' sick child who needed the immediate attention of a physician or a niece or nephew who was in desperate need of cash for a wedding.

The importance of one's social network and the great value placed on sharing with and helping each other prevented people from saving. Furthermore, once they parted from their cash they were unlikely to receive it back in a lump sum, at least not for a long time, particularly when a substantial sum was involved. The very high inflation rate that Egypt has experienced during the last decade has also increased unexpected financial emergencies and discouraged saving cash.

In these circumstances, the best strategy was to spend whatever was available, or what might become available, on goods that retained their value even though their use might be freely shared with friends and neighbors. All neighbors were welcome to watch the color television, put their meat in the refrigerator, or borrow ice. Generosity of this nature brought status and power to a household, and no one was expected to sell their possessions in order to pay the neighbor's bills. Equally, in times of need, these items could easily be sold for cash with little loss in their value (due to high inflation). Thus, in the cultural context and circumstances of these neighborhoods, acquiring these items should not be viewed as simple consumption. Accumulating assets was the most viable saving strategy for households. On my visit to Umm Habah in her new two-room flat, which she was excited and extremely happy about, she told me:

> Everybody thought with five children I would never be able to move to a better residence. When I bought the television and the radio and all the other things on hire purchase, against my husband's wish, everybody thought I was in the wrong. But when I became aware of this vacant flat, through a friend, I went and talked to the landlord and reached an agreement with him on key money. Then I talked to my husband and he agreed to apply for two hundred pounds on loan. I sold every household item and we raised the one thousand pounds to pay to the landlord. I know I have to start to buy the appliances again but everybody agrees that the most important thing is the flat. I know in a few years I can replace the items in the same way.

As further evidence of this very practical and rational strategy of saving, in 1992 I learned that three more households had managed to buy small pieces of land by cashing in their household goods and the few modest pieces of gold which are the only worldly possession women have in their own names. Similarly, two other households had made down payments toward future ownership of small flats in a low-income housing project.

Furthermore, the possession of these items indicated to their community and the wider society that they approved of and aspired to enjoy, when they could, what modern technology had to offer. Simultaneously, these assets extended the power and influence of their owners through the sharing of the use of the appliances with neighbors, making the neighbors indebted to them. Contrary to the assumption of some social critics, members of low-income communities have not been transformed into mindless consumers; rather, it is their shrewd understanding of their socioeconomic circumstances that dictates such patterns of expenditure.

The aspirations of the low-income households in the neighborhoods of the study generally corresponded with those of the middle classes. However, in contrast to many middle-class and richer households, the low-income stratum had to employ different strategies in order to fulfil the same kind of needs. Moreover, some households lacked the means to fulfil their top priorities of better housing and establishing a business, but they could satisfy their more modest goals. There was no reason why this should preclude them from finding opportunities to satisfy their less immediate needs: even if the family of one household lives in one room, it might enjoy, and benefit from a television or a modern stove.

To recapitulate, although most studies of survival strategies concentrate on earning a living, in this chapter I have argued that a broad and encompassing definition of income, along with inclusion of the cost of social reproduction, would enhance our understanding of the choices people make in regard to the allocation of the resources at their disposal. Households rely on a much broader range of resources for their survival than just their cash income. Nonmonetary contributions such as domestic work, child care, cash-saving activities, and appropriation of public goods and services constitute a considerable part of a household's income, and despite their absence from the national accounting system, they are essential to the planning of survival strategies of low-income households. Moreover, because in Egypt, as in most societies, a larger share of women's contributions tend to be in the nonmarket domain, adoption of a broader definition of household income is particularly helpful in understanding women's choices.

Men and women as members of their households allocate their labor power to the domain which yields the highest utility (whether in cash or otherwise). Thus, after examining the context of daily life and women's economic activities, I have suggested that their absence from the lower echelons of the formal labor market is best explained not by traditionalism and their adherence to the Islamic ideology but by the high opportunity cost of such jobs. Similarly, women's preference for the informal cash economy is influenced by its flexible work conditions, which allow them to combine their domestic responsibilities and cash-earning activities. Men, on the other hand, are expected to invest more time and energy in fulfilling the amplified need for cash. This often means that men work long hours away from home while diversifying their sources of employment. Many migrate to the Gulf countries for months or years at a time.

Despite the vitality of the services that women perform for the survival and well-being of their households, the commercialization of many goods and services has left women more dependent on their husbands' cash contributions. In order to prevent the loss of more ground to men, women actively discourage the participation of men in domestic tasks. A further response of women to this situation has been to stress their Islamic right to economic support by their husbands and to defend the traditional division of labor, which they view as the basis for interdependence of the sexes. Therefore, at least in part, the roots of women's increasing public support for the Islamization of their society should be found in the way in which development and social change have devalued their contributions without offering them viable alternatives.

Consumption is a means through which both the physiological and the social needs of people are fulfilled. Low-income households are basically concerned with strategies which enable them to reproduce themselves biologically and socially at the highest possible level. Given the prevailing socioeconomic conditions and job insecurity among low-income households, investing in durable domestic appliances is the most appropriate strategy for accumulating savings. Much of the criticism of the consumption patterns of low-income people in Egypt is fueled by misconceptions about their conditions of life. Such criticism fails to recognize that the tendency of the poorer households to consume more than their monetary income allows does not arise from their lack of consideration for future or unforeseen needs. On the contrary, their eagerness to collect possessions is motivated by their concern for such eventualities. After all, they know through experience that in times of hardship they can rely only on themselves and perhaps on the sympathy of their neighbors. Their assets are not luxury items; they represent security.

NOTES

An earlier version of this chapter appeared in the *Journal of South Asian and Middle Eastern Studies* 13 (Summer 1990).

1. *Household* here is defined as a group that ensures its maintenance and reproduction by generating and disposing of collective income (Wood 1981). For a discussion of the concept of strategy, see Crow (1989).

2. This failure may lead to their disenchantment with the social and economic system, making them receptive to the idea of alternative sociopolitical organization.

3. See, for instance, Schmink 1982; Roberts 1978; Dinnerman 1978.

4. For more details on the fieldwork, see Hoodfar 1994.

5. Marriage among different religious minorities is governed by their respective religious laws.

6. Among the poorer classes it is rare that a father demands custody if the mother does not demand money for the upkeep of the children. It is generally accepted that children, particularly daughters, are better off remaining with their mother. Men with low incomes, once they start a second family, cannot support two families even if they wish to.

7. In cousin marriages, the alliance of the extended families gives the wife a greater degree of protection in marriage. Also the sizable *mahr* makes it difficult for men to divorce their wife or make life difficult for her because she can demand the *mahr* at any time during the marriage or at the time of divorce.

8. The rate of divorce has remained relatively low at 2 percent (1986 census). This figure does not include deserted wives who, for convenience, consider themselves as married.

9. For a review of the literature on this point, see Folbre 1986.

10. For a review of the literature, see Amin and Awny 1985.

11. Critics have blamed migration and the absence of fathers for the high rate of school dropouts. What they have not appreciated is that education beyond the primary school has been viewed as a means of access to better jobs. The new situation has changed the labor market conditions, and it is the skilled and technical jobs which are the more remunerative. Therefore young men choose to join the labor force at an early age to be trained as skilled workers.

12. Abu Ahmed did not consider his wife, who made the pickles and worked with him, as a "working" wife. His use of the first-person plural pronoun here (when he said that "we" earn little) was in accordance with the view that men's income is family income.

13. See *ILO Yearbook of Labor Statistics* for 1970–1986.

14. This educated woman married while looking for a job and became pregnant immediately. She then took over the management of her husband's local shop while attending to her child. However, she intended to find a white-collar job as soon as her children grew older.

15. The government implicitly recognizes that a woman's first priority is her domestic responsibilities and, accordingly, has introduced certain concessions. See Sullivan 1981.

16. Although many women, including those in their family-building phase, have migrated (with or without their husbands) as teachers, maids, hairdressers, etc., migra-

tion has remained predominantly a male option. In the neighborhoods included in this study, it was usually the elder women who migrated as maids, although I knew a few young women who migrated as teachers, hairdressers, and nurses.

17. See Hoodfar's essay on the impact of male migration in this volume (chap. 3).

18. For more discussion of this point, see Nadim 1985.

WORKS CITED

Abdel-Fadil, Mahmoud. 1980. *The Political Economy of Nasserism: A Study of Employ-ment and Income Distribution Policies in Urban Egypt, 1952–1972.* Cambridge: Cambridge University Press.

———. 1983. "Informal Sector Employment in Egypt." In *Urban Research Strategies for Egypt,* ed. Richard Lobban. Cairo Papers in Social Science, no. 6, Monograph 2. Cairo: American University in Cairo Press.

Amin, Galal, and Elizabeth Awny. 1985. "International Migration of Egyptian Labor: A Review of the State of the Art." International Development Research Center, Ottawa. IDRC Manuscript Report, no. 108E.

Beneria, Lourdes. 1982. "Accounting for Women's Work." In *Women and Development: The Sexual Division of Labor in Rural Societies,* ed. L. Beneria, New York: Praeger.

———. 1992. "Accounting for Women: The Progress of Two Decades." *World Develop-ment* 20 (November): 1547–1560.

Crow, Graham. 1989. "The Use of the Concept of 'Strategy' in Recent Sociological Lit-erature." *Sociology* 23, no. 1: 1–24.

Csikszentmihalyi, Mihaly, and Eugene Rochberg-Halton. 1981. *The Meaning of Things: Domestic Symbols and the Self.* New York: Cambridge University Press.

Davidson, Carolyn. 1982. *A Woman's Work Is Never Done: A History of Housework in the British Isles, 1650–1950.* London: Chatto and Windus.

Dinnerman, Ina R. 1978. "Patterns of Migration among Households of U.S.-Bound Mi-grants from Michoacan, Mexico." *International Migration Review* 2, no. 4: 485–501.

Douglas, Mary, and Baron Isherwood. 1978. *The World of Goods: Towards an Anthropol-ogy of Consumption.* London: Penguin Books.

Fergany, Nader. 1987. "Differentials in Labor Migration: Egypt (1974–1984)." Occasional Paper, no. 4. Cairo Demographic Center, Cairo.

Folbre, Nancy. 1986. "Cleaning House." *Journal of Development Economics* 22: 3–40.

Gershuny, Jonathan. 1979. "The Informal Economy: Its Role in Post-Industrial Society." *Future* 11, no. 1: 3–15.

Goldschmidt-Clermont, Luisella. 1982. *Economic Evaluation of Unpaid Household Work: A Review of Economic Evaluation Methods.* Women, Work and Development Series 14. Geneva: ILO.

———. 1987. *Economic Evaluations of Unpaid Household Work: Africa, Asia, Latin America, and Oceania*. Women, Work and Development Series, no. 14. Geneva: ILO.

Hoodfar, Homa. 1986. "Childcare and Child Survival in Low-Income Neighborhoods of Cairo." Regional Papers. Population Council, Cairo.

———. 1988. "Patterns of Household Budgeting and Management of Financial Affairs in a Lower-Income Neighborhood in Cairo." In *A Home Divided: Women and Income in the Third World*, ed. D. H. Dwyer and J. Bruce. Stanford: Stanford University Press.

———. 1989. "Survival Strategies among Lower-Income Households in Newly Urbanized Neighbourhoods of Cairo, Egypt." Ph.D. diss., Kent University.

———. 1994. "Situating the Anthropologist: A Personal Account of Ethnographic Fieldwork in Three Urban Settings: Tehran, Cairo, and Montreal." In *Urban Lives: Fragmentation and Resistance*, ed. Vered Amit-Talai and Henri Lustiger-Thaler, 206–226. Toronto: McClelland and Stewart.

Ibrahim, Barbara. 1983. "Strategies of Urban Labor Force Measurement." In *Urban Research Strategies for Egypt*, ed. Richard Lobban. Cairo Papers in Social Science, no. 6, Monograph 2. Cairo: American University in Cairo Press.

Khouri-Dagher, Nadia. 1986. "Food and Energy in Cairo: Provisioning the Poor." Report prepared for the Food and Energy Nexus Program, United Nations University, Cairo.

McCracken, Grant. 1990. *Culture and Consumption: New Approaches to the Symbolic Character of Consumer Goods and Activities*. Bloomington: Indiana University Press.

Nadim, Assad, Nawal el-Messiri Nadim, and Sohair Mehanna. 1980. *Living without Water*. Cairo Papers in Social Science, no. 3, Monograph 3. Cairo: American University in Cairo Press.

Nadim, Nawal el-Messiri. 1985. "Family Relationships in a Harah in Cairo." In *Arab Society: Social Science Perspectives*, ed. Nicholas S. Hopkins and Saad Ibrahim. Cairo: American University in Cairo Press.

Oakley, Ann. 1974. *Housewife: High Value Low Cost*. London: Allen Lane.

Pahl, Jan. 1989. *Money and Marriage*. London: Macmillan.

Pahl, Ray E. 1984. *Division of Labor*. Oxford: Basil Blackwell.

Philibert, Jean Marc. 1984. "Affluence, Commodity Consumption, and Self-Image in Vanuatu." In *Affluence and Cultural Survival*, ed. Richard F. Salisbury and Elisabeth Tooker. American Ethnological Society.

Roberts, Brian. 1978. *Cities of Peasants: The Political Economy of Urbanization in the Third World*. London: Edward Arnold.

Rugh, Andrea. 1984. *Family in Contemporary Egypt*. Syracuse: Syracuse University Press.

Schmink, Marianne. June 1982. "Women in the Urban Economy in Latin America." Working Paper, no. 1. Population Council, New York.

Shorter, Frederic. 1985. "Preliminary Analysis of Manshiet Nasser Study." Population Council, Cairo. Report.

————. 1989. *Cairo's Leap Forward: People, Households, and Dwelling Space.* Cairo Papers in Social Science no. 12, Monograph 1. Cairo: American University in Cairo Press.

————, and Huda C. Zurayk. 1988. "The Social Composition of Households in Arab Cities: Cairo, Beirut, Amman." Population Council, Cairo. Paper.

Singerman, Diane. 1995. *Avenues of Participation: Family, Politics, and Networks in Urban Quarters of Cairo.* Princeton: Princeton University Press.

Smith, Joan. 1984. "Nonwage Labor and Subsistence." In *Households and the World Economy,* ed. Joan Smith, Immannuel Wallerstein, and Hans-Dieter Evers. London: Sage.

Sokkari, Myrette Ahmed El-. 1984. *Basic Needs, Inflation, and the Poor of Egypt.* Cairo Papers in Social Science, no. 7, Monograph 2. Cairo: American University in Cairo Press.

Sullivan, Earl L. 1981. *Women and Work in Egypt.* Cairo Papers in Social Science, no. 4, Monograph 1. Cairo: American University in Cairo Press.

Tekçe, Belgin, Linda Oldham, and Frederic C. Shorter. 1994. *A Place to Live: Families and Child Health in a Cairo Neighborhood.* Cairo: American University in Cairo Press.

Tucker, Judith. 1985. *Women in Nineteenth-Century Egypt.* London: Cambridge University Press.

Waring, Marilyn. 1988. *If Women Counted: A New Feminist Economics.* San Francisco: Harper.

Wood, Charles. 1981. "Structural Changes and Household Strategies: A Conceptual Framework for the Study of Rural Migration." *Human Organization* 40, no. 4: 338–344.

2

TRANSFORMING WOMEN'S IDENTITY
The Intersection of Household and Workplace in Cairo

ARLENE ELOWE MacLEOD

CLASSIFYING WOMEN'S LIVES as "traditional" or "modern" seems an enduring tendency in portrayals of women in the developing world. Traditional women, it is assumed, live within the household, while modern, and by implication emancipated, women have left this realm behind and venture out into the workplace. Yet the lives of most women are difficult to place in either the traditional or the modern category; instead we see housewives who run businesses from their kitchens, professional women who juggle careers, cleaning, and child care, and workers who bring household tasks or small children to the offices. We need to refocus our attention toward the intersection of these areas, the political space in which the interactions women face as both female family members and participants in paid employment are acted out.

Thinking more carefully about the trade-offs and choices women make at the intersection of household and workplace leads us to a better understanding of the politics of the "double load" women carry in most societies and the complicated choices women must make to participate both in the home and in the workplace. By examining this area of intersection, where negotiations necessarily take place, we can begin to understand the experience of lower-middle-class women in Cairo with their transition to "modernity." Indeed, it is only when this space of interaction is investigated that a very important and difficult tension appears—one that shapes women's feelings about working outside the home and the responsibilities and joys of work within the home and that leads women to ambivalence about working and other activities Western women might assume are progressive. While this study highlights the challenges faced by a specific group of women in Cairo, it also pushes our more general understanding beyond the distorting categories of tradition and modernity and toward a more subtle understanding of how constraints are structured and opportunities created in times of social transition.[1]

Changing Patterns of Women's
Work in Lower-Middle-Class Cairo

What does it mean to be a lower-middle-class woman in Cairo? What kind of work do women of this class do in the home and outside? These questions plunge us into controversy. The first point of controversy stems from the assumption by many Western women that in the home women are housewives, relegated to a private world and excluded from public life, important decisions, and financial independence. Yet this is essentially untrue in Cairo, where the household is the key economic unit and often the political arena in which important negotiations initiate through informal financial and political networks (Nelson 1974; Singerman 1995). When I first went into the field and asked women whether they worked, they always corrected me: "Do you mean do I work outside the home? Certainly I work, all women work, inside the home is just as important as outside." Certainly in Cairo the family must be viewed as an important arena of decision making rather than a lesser privatized world excluded from the central decisions of the society. While the middle-class family in Cairo has changed considerably in the last century, moving from the extended-family toward the nuclear-family model, the importance of family in ideology and as an institution has remained constant (Nawar et al. 1994).

A second point of controversy centers on the way women construct their family histories; women in these families portray the past as a time when women worked in the home and the present as an era "when everyone works outside the home." Yet this picture clouds the historical reality that women in Cairo have often worked outside the home—in factory jobs, as domestics, as street peddlers (Tucker 1976, 1985). However, young women working outside the home in lower-middle-class Cairo are generally the first in their families' recent histories to pursue formal employment and their memories of the parameters of women's lives become the key to constructions of women's role, and the crucial marker that, for them, separates their lives from those of older women.

These lower-middle-class women belong to families in which the parents are recent migrants to the city, coming from peasant villages and lacking formal education. They live in apartments of two or three tiny rooms, with very limited plumbing and few amenities. The fathers of these families usually work as unskilled laborers, and often they are far away working as migrant laborers in the oil-rich states of the Middle East. Mothers work in the home, as housewives and by bringing resources to the family through constructing important networks of friends, relatives, and contacts who are called on in times of need or expensive celebration. Women are expected to contribute through this economic and emotional labor, as well as through income-producing activities such as raising ducks, sewing for friends, and cooking for neighbors. Therefore, the change to daughters working in paid formal employment must be evaluated in the context of trade-offs of sources of income, prestige, and daily routines. Such trade-offs create a much more complex picture than observers might first expect.

These lower-middle-class families are distinguished from lower-class families by their success at educating their children. During the Nasser era, reforms provided free schooling and guaranteed work in the government bureaucracy upon gaining a degree, a policy that encouraged lower-class families to keep their children in school, with the goal of secure employment in a government office. This policy proved particularly attractive for daughters, given the need for respectable employment which would not harm family honor, and ultimately created the overcrowding that now characterizes government offices. Typically, four or five women work in a tiny room performing clerical tasks of various sorts for the government bureaucracy. Obtaining these jobs makes an immense difference to their families, for they leave the lower class and climb to the very bottom rungs of the middle class based on the small but secure incomes and the higher prestige accorded this office work. Indeed, economically, these families may be on the same level as lower-class families, but they perceive themselves as "people of the middle level" because of these more prestigious occupations (Wikan 1985). Lower-middle-class women carefully distinguish their families from those of the "poor," the "*fellahiin*," the "rough" and "uncultured" masses who are not "modern" or "civilized." "Poor women," one woman commented, "are ignorant and uneducated, so they cannot find suitable jobs." Yet lower-middle-class women are also firmly divided from the middle and upper ranks of the middle class, and certainly from upper-class women, by the distinction between public and private sectors in post-*Infitah* Egypt (Mohsen, 1985). Private companies require better education, skills, and connections, and they pay several times the salary of government jobs, but it is seldom possible for these women to secure such work. These immediate social distinctions, from families just below and just above, are most important for understanding some of the choices about work that lower-middle-class women and families make.

Women's Work Experience outside the Household

How can we understand and evaluate these women's experience with changing patterns of work? Their feelings about working outside the home can best be termed ambivalent; while most see paid employment as a major change which differentiates their lives from the lives of women of their mother's generation, they are unsure that this change should be designated as progress. Weighing the benefits and the costs, many remain undecided about which way the scale ultimately tips.

On the positive side, the obvious material benefit of earning income of their own is cited by all these women as very important. These clerical workers labor primarily because they and their families need the extra money, although the women mention socializing, keeping busy, the challenge, and finding a husband among their reasons for valuing work. As lower-level clerks and secretaries, they generally earn around 45–60 Egyptian pounds a month. These women value the ability to earn and are proud of their capacity to contribute to the family's resources. Furthermore, earning their own salaries gives these women and their children greater financial security, as they can now purchase food and basic necessities themselves, rather than relying on husbands who might keep some of their earnings for personal indulgences like coffee, films, and cigarettes.

These women work the typical six-day week, with Friday, the Muslim holy day, off. Usually they are expected to be in the office between eight and nine in the morning, and they leave around two in the afternoon; this adds up to a work week of approximately thirty hours. As they work in the government bureaucracy, they benefit from protective labor laws, which bar discrimination on the basis of sex in hiring, benefits, and salary. Additionally, their workplaces offer maternity leaves and often provide child care. Women value the flexibility, shorter hours, and easier work these jobs offer when compared with alternative employment. "Working here is not too bad," commented one of these women, "because I can easily do my work and relax so I'm not so tired for all I have to do this afternoon." Nevertheless, many of these women feel disappointed and complain that the salaries they earn are very low; they often earn less for the clerical tasks they perform than other workers earn in factories, or certainly in private firms. This forms a point of conflict with the state; because women's incomes are still generally regarded as supplementing family incomes, low salaries are considered justifiable. These women occupy an underpaid subclass of jobs in which the wages have not risen with the inflationary spiral and there is little incentive on the part of the state to raise salaries. Yet according to these women, the government has a responsibility to pay them enough so that they can buy those foods and household goods they consider necessary and indeed those goods which signify the promised middle-class status. This perception of the welfare responsibilities of the state, which derives from the socialist rhetoric of the Nasser era, shapes lower-middle-class feelings about the failures of the Sadat and Mubarak governments to fulfill the promise of a better way of life.

In this context, it is important to note that these women's salaries are spent predominantly on family needs. The young, single women generally spend most of their funds to purchase the household goods they will need once they are married. They also spend money on clothing and hairstyling designed to attract a future husband's eye, but the bulk of their salary goes to this trousseau of household goods, which would otherwise have to be purchased by the parents of the couple. With the married women the picture is even clearer; their income goes into the family budget and is expended on food, rent, educational expenses, health costs, and commuting. In general, these women do not retain any of their earnings separately for personal spending.

Typically these women are responsible for making a household budget for the month. A normal budget for a young couple of about 150 Egyptian pounds (including bonuses and informal earnings) is generally expended on rent, food, commuting, clothes, medicine, and private tutoring for the children. Rents require a disproportionate amount of these families' income as the housing shortage in Cairo continues. Given the lower-middle-class concern with finding a suitable apartment which will reinforce family status, these housing costs are relatively inflexible. Typically, a young couple finds an apartment to rent after the formal engagement party and before the final marriage celebration, a period of perhaps two or three years. They plan to stay in this home for their entire future, barring drastic swings in family fortunes. Apartments which cost their parents about three to seven pounds monthly (because of rent control) will cost these young couples between forty and sixty pounds. In addition, key money, which renters must pay initially to acquire an apartment, often amounts to 3,000–6,000 pounds—clearly a crippling expense for families with only 1,400 to 2,000 pounds in expected annual income. Utilities—electricity, water, gas—further strain the budget. Food costs vary with family size and are spent on a diet which is heavy on starches, principally rice, macaroni, and bread. Chicken or fish is eaten about once a week, often on Friday or when visitors are expected. Meat is consumed less frequently because of its high cost. Fava beans, goat cheese, eggs, vegetables, fruits, and sweets round out the diet. Commuting by bus or tram adds to the regular expenses for many workers. Any remaining funds are used for clothing, holiday expenditures, medical emergencies, tutoring children, and savings for expensive celebrations.

In the past, the husband's earnings were sufficient to cover the necessities of housing and food, while the wife's earnings could be used to supplement that income, purchasing those appliances which make life easier and more enter-taining. Women envisioned purchasing washing machines, refrigerators, fans, tapedecks, televisions, and the ornate gold-painted furniture that signifies middle-class status. Increasingly, however, the wife's wages are required to cover basic needs, especially rent and food, creating tensions within the family and between these families and the state. All told, these women see their in-comes as the basic reason they choose to work outside the home but complain that their pay is so low it barely encourages them to continue in their jobs.

In addition to concerns over low salaries, these women focus on changes in their everyday routines when asked about the costs and benefits of working outside the home. One point they make centers on the unfortunate reality that many find the jobs themselves quite disappointing. To get these jobs, most women have at least completed secondary school and often attended a higher institute or college, where they studied commerce, secretarial skills, social work, or liberal arts. Very few of these skills are utilized in their offices. These women operate copy machines, record appointments, work as cashiers, stamp documents, or type. Besides being underemployed, they seldom learn new skills at the office, where the work is usually repetitive and boring. These women complain of the tedious hours, and they occupy the time chatting, since the work itself requires so little attention. Usually four or five women hold similar positions and can easily cover for one another while one slips out to shop, pray, run an errand, or go home to visit a sick relative. While the time to do these chores is useful, it is also clear to women that they are not doing truly necessary labor. Some even suggest that the state should pay them their salaries and simply let them stay home, where they could take care of their chil-dren, a much more useful and important task in their eyes. There are a few women who stand out as exceptions and occupy more responsible positions, perhaps supervising their department, a job which holds their interest and keeps them busy. Some opportunity does exist for women who are willing to put the extra efforts in time and creativity into their jobs, and these women state that they have the same rights and opportunities at work as the men in their departments. When asked why men fill the upper layers and women the lower, they commonly respond that women have other duties and only put half their time into the office, while men, with little else to occupy their time, are able to advance. Most saw this as a natural outcome of women's divided responsibilities and not as a social problem. Although they do not perceive legal impediments should they wish to rise in their jobs, it is certainly arguable that the government could not absorb a significant number of such women, since the interesting jobs are few and generally occupied by men or higher-class women.

Another factor that figures in women's accounting of the costs and benefits of working outside the home is mobility. Traditionally, both men's and women's lives centered on the home and the neighborhood. In more recent years it has become increasingly common for men to go out of the neighborhood to work while women remained inside. While older women are limited to shopping at nearby markets accompanied by their children or occasionally to venturing out to visit relatives in other areas of the city, their working daughters' lives provide new challenges and valued opportunities. For instance, each day women must commute, often long distances, to their offices. Most prefer to meet with friends and make the commute together, but they are alone for at least part of the trip. This traveling to and from work gives these women a knowledge of the city they never had before; they gain the ability to master the bus systems, memorize the winding streets, and acquire the know-how that makes them more successful in dealing with the bureaucracy. On the other hand, they are also exposed to annoyances, out on the streets alone or in the company of female fellow workers, away from the protective family. Men walking down the streets or sitting in sidewalk coffee shops compliment and comment; they attempt "accidental" touching and pinching. Women are bothered in this manner as they walk the crowded sidewalks and are squeezed overenthusiastically and often unnecessarily on the overloaded buses. Learning to deal effectively with these situations without the help of family members is crucial for maintaining one's reputation and avoiding more difficult situations. Typically, women cluster in groups on the buses and stroll arm in arm on the streets, signaling that they have no wish for other company. They will walk far out into the street to avoid passing right in front of a sidewalk café and to show that they are not loose women, but moral. While the necessity of avoiding such situations is annoying, the ability to take care of oneself becomes a source of great pride and self-respect for many.

While traveling about the city in this manner and in the workplace itself, these lower-middle-class women are exposed to a variety of customs, dress, attitudes, and behavior. The neighborhood can be a reasonably homogeneous place; people vary in income or style of family life, but there is consensus on appropriate behavior and reasonable goals. Out in the city, women see people from all over the world—villagers from the Sudan, rich sheikhs from Saudi Arabia, miniskirted tourists from Europe and America. They notice other nationalities and classes; they observe different lifestyles. Women acquire an awareness of the particular nature of their own customs and the knowledge that in other areas of the city, or of the world, people often live quite differently. For instance, one woman's mother asked in the midst of a discussion of religion: "Where do American people go when they go on the *hagg* [pilgrimage]?" Her daughter quickly answered her, explaining that Americans do not go on these pilgrimages; she was aware that Christians in America differed from the Muslims or even the Copts of Egypt. These women take pride in the uniqueness of their own customs, and learn tolerance for the customs of others. Further, at the workplace, they meet new people every day. They spend long hours chatting over steaming cups of sweet tea with fellow workers, male and female, from other sections of the city. They make friends outside the *harah* and the family; they sometimes go to visit these friends in their homes just as they would visit relatives. Arguing over questions of marriage, child care, veiling, weddings, and prices, they encounter new opinions rather than being restricted to the sentiments available in their own homes. This opportunity to see a wider world gives these women a feeling of self-confidence in their ability to understand and act on changing conditions.

These women also meet men, possibly future husbands, in the workplace. Traditionally, young women married cousins, more distant relatives, or neighbors who knew the family. These marriages were arranged, and the couple might or might not know each other before the marriage. Now women have added the workplace to the list of possible sources for future partners. Men and women at work sit and talk, joke, even mildly flirt with each other. Through mutual friends they learn about the other's family and consider the potential for becoming partners. The man might then call on the woman's family and be considered for marriage. Usually, a woman will meet with her future husband once or twice for an extended conversation in which they discuss their wishes for the future. Children, working, finances, and hopes are all considered as each decides whether the other would be a good partner. After reaching a mutual decision, the formal engagement party and lengthy engagement period of two or three years commences; in this time the husband earns the money to set up the new household, often working in one of the wealthy Gulf states, while the wife works to buy the household goods to help furnish their new life. Meeting a husband at the workplace widens a woman's opportunity to know her husband better before committing herself to marriage and gives her more autonomy to choose.

Despite these women's increased mobility and visibility, some traditional patterns continue to hold. For instance, although the women leave the house each morning, traverse the whole city, and return from work each afternoon, they still generally ask for permission to leave the house for any other reason, such as for shopping or for visiting. And men have the right under Islamic law to say no. According to most women, a good husband seldom will, for he assumes his wife is involved in proper activities and gives his permission for whatever she wishes, but he will occasionally impose his right. Particularly in the first few years of marriage, these women commented, when young and insecure, men tend to apply this right more often, and this causes marital disagreements and occasional divorce. Men also hold the right to allow wives to work outside the home. For example, one of these women, Aida, finally broke her engagement because the man she was to marry steadfastly refused to allow her to work and she was very committed to retaining a job, which she said was a challenge, kept her from being bored, and was fun. Another, Nadia, was less fortunate, as her husband decided after they were married that the idea of his wife working out of the home was not in accordance with Islam and forced her to quit her job.

These women see real advantages in working which cause them to stay in the offices in large numbers. Yet, the heavy associated costs make many claim they want to quit and virtually all to express disappointment. Working seems an ambivalent step for these women rather than an example of completely progressive change. This ambivalence is particularly unsettling as they had extremely high expectations for leaving the home to work and its potential benefit for their lives. Their families often sacrificed considerably to enable them to stay in school, and women expected their jobs to bring them financial security, challenging tasks, new social contacts, and especially, firm middle-class status. Many of these expectations have not been met. Yet despite this ambivalence, these women's assessments of the value of working stress the expansion of opportunities created by the chance to explore outside the realm of the home, and especially the value of increased mobility, a gain they firmly intend to keep.

The Intersection of Workplace and Household

That women find working an ambivalent rather than progressive step in lower-middle-class Cairo pushes us to think more carefully about the trade-offs between work and family. In fact, focusing on their ambivalence allows an important double bind to emerge, one which helps us understand the recent growth of Islamic symbolism, and especially the wearing of Islamic dress, in this group as well. The *higab*, or Islamic dress, forms a highly visible and controversial symbol of the negotiations women face in a changing urban environment. Not limited to Cairo, but a movement throughout the Muslim world, the new veils nonetheless have local meaning that requires investigation. The assumption that veils are automatically equated with oppression and that the new veiling signals a return to a medieval and reactionary version of Islamic politics and roles for women needs to be carefully questioned; indeed, I have argued that for these women the new veils are a mode of negotiation and protest rather than a reactionary concession to conservative politics (MacLeod 1991, 1992). Veils are often perceived in the West as the premier symbol of women's subordination in Islamic societies; yet in the Muslim world veils serve a wide range of social and symbolic purposes, expressing kinship relations, class status, nationalist politics, and personal qualities as well as negotiating women's space and arenas of control in the larger society (Antoun 1968; Papenek 1973; Murphy 1970; Makhlouf 1979; Pastner 1972; Abu-Lughod 1986). In Cairo, traditional dress was composed of long dresses of colorful flowered cloth and headscarfs, covered with a black cloth, but younger middle-class women changed their dress several decades ago to Western-style clothing (Rugh 1986). Many are now changing this dress again in a voluntary movement to the more modest clothes of the *muhaggaba*, or covered woman (El Guindi 1981, 1983; Williams 1979; Zuhur 1992). In this context, it is important to note that women are not reverting to the dress of their mothers or grandmothers but inventing a new form of Islamic clothing, clearly distinguishing them from older women and from traditionally dressed women of the lower classes. While this new veiling could be seen as an expression of Islamic militancy, I believe the new veils in this class setting have more to do with the tensions at the intersection of workplace and family and the related roles of worker and wife/mother than with fundamentalist Islamic politics.

When we examine these tensions more carefully, the most obvious problem is the double load of duties women now confront. In the home, women take care of virtually all housework and child care; and in Cairo, where automated appliances and convenience stores are nonexistent or extremely expensive, women must do most work by hand. Typically, shopping for food is done daily; women or children go out to nearby vegetable stands and select the best produce for the money. Meals, generally stewed vegetables and macaroni or rice, are cooked every other day and leftovers from the first meal are saved to be served again. This practice is possible when families own a refrigerator, but not possible, given the heat, before they can afford to buy one. One day a week is set aside for washing, which involves scrubbing clothes in the sink in cold water and hanging them out to dry on clotheslines suspended outside the windows of the house. Another day is for general cleaning; floors are swept and furniture is dusted. Children are often the focus of the home, and everyone helps to play with them, feed them, and dress them. The men of the household, including male children, very seldom help out in any substantial way with this housework. They may help when a woman is sick or especially busy for some reason, or they may stop for bread on their way home or get up to make their own tea once in a while, but these duties are all considered women's responsibility.

In families where both husband and wife work, this traditional pattern has altered, but not dramatically or uniformly. Husbands are usually not pleased that it is necessary for their wives to "help out" with the earning of income. An irate and discouraged husband complained to me: "In the old days, when I was living at home with my mother, I would go out to work and come home tired at the end of the day. My mother would have a beautiful dinner waiting for me as soon as I walked in the door. Now, times are hard and everything has changed. You see me now, I am tired and I sit here and must wait for dinner." He and his wife had just returned home from full days at the office and she was busy in the kitchen preparing a hot meal as he sat in the living room. Even men who recognize the extra burdens on their wives feel there is really little they can do to remedy the situation; men simply cannot do such tasks. Women cope as best they can. They send one person from the office out to do shopping for all. They buy eggs and bread on the way to and from work. They leave their children at the child-care center or with relatives while they work.

However, with the recognition that women will probably be working outside the home for some time, if not permanently, some families are altering these housework roles. Perhaps half of the men admit, with some embarrassment, that they do in fact help their wives with some of the housework. Usually they help with the food shopping or light cleaning, yet very seldom will men perform such tasks in front of guests. One husband, newly married, actually helps cook and serve dinner in front of friends; he explains that since his wife helps him provide for the home, he must in turn help her with her tasks in the house. However, such an understanding is rare and most women complain: "I don't know why he doesn't help me at home. I am very tired when I come home in the afternoon and still I must cook the meal and have everything in place or he will be upset with me."

Male members of the lower middle class often take on an additional outside job and work one job from about eight to two and then take a second job until about eight in the evening. When a man has a second job, however, he generally puts the income from one into the family budget but keeps the second for his personal expenses, such as buying cigarettes, coffee, or sandwiches or going to a movie. Unfortunately, the wife's second job, caring for the house and family, does not provide extra cash to make personal purchases. As a result, women have far less discretionary income, even when they earn a salary equivalent to that of their husbands. This financial situation means that they acquire the duties of an equal breadwinner in the home but are left without some of the privileges this status entails for men. Several women explained that although they worked to provide extras for the home, their husband had no right to expect this from them and that they had the right to control and save their own money. A few, mostly younger married women without children, said they followed the more traditional pattern in which they actually kept their earnings apart and their income did not contribute to the household budget (Hoodfar 1988). Once children enter the scene, however, this financial autonomy is difficult to maintain. Furthermore, the women's new status as breadwinners is difficult for these families, for it is the men, according to Islamic doctrine, who are the designated breadwinners, and women often resent having to help out once children appear and the work becomes much heavier.

Another consideration which appears when household and workplace are considered together is that a woman's labor in the workplace is largely unappreciated, while her work in the home is highly valued. The work these women do at the office is regarded as simple and boring, unchallenging, and unimportant; on the other hand, the work they do at home is considered challenging and important. Indeed, in a culture where family and household are the centers of economic, political, and social activities, it is quite reasonable that work done at the government offices would be seen as less useful than that accomplished in the home. As the government bureaucracy has become more and more bloated, the prestige of these jobs has suffered along with the salaries. The end result is a devalued workplace and sense of personal accomplishment. Sons and husbands, however, all appreciate that women work hard in the home. They praise the woman with the clean and peaceful home, the good cook, the thrifty shopper, the loving and responsible mother. Indeed, some women resent a husband's efforts to help out in the home, despite the difficulties of the double load of work, because they then lose the prestige and informal power this labor can bring. In this context, the reality that many women prefer the idea of quitting work and staying home, if they could afford this move, becomes quite reasonable. Furthermore, to be a breadwinner is not a social achievement for women. With her spouse, a woman enters a new and uncharted relationship, causing tensions and sometimes unhappiness. Typically, the relationship of complementarity has been the Muslim goal; now women are entering men's realm and men who cannot fully provide for their families feel diminished. As a result, women's status in the household becomes unsettled.

Another point which arises at the juncture of workplace and household relates to the question of the political atmosphere each embodies. Working involves women's moving from the sphere of the household into the workplace—moving from home life in which women are very much in charge to the legalistic space and bureaucratic atmosphere of the office. This move is probably not correctly characterized by the Western ideas of the switch from the private into the public spheres. Home life in the Middle East has many public aspects; women are involved in organizing the economic and social resources of a large family. They prepare the budgets, purchase goods, grow chickens for sale, participate in *gamʿiyya* arrangements, organize engagements and weddings, and help in the children's education. Family life in Cairo is firmly tied into informal networks of larger economic, social, and political import. In the workplace, most women hold low-ranking jobs where they follow orders rather than organize and instruct themselves; they must punch in on a time clock and ask permission to go on errands or take time off. Indeed, women have gradually transformed office atmospheres as a way to resist this imposition, and many offices in the Cairo bureaucracy now have a very informal feeling, with the women workers sometimes shelling peas and sorting eggs as well as typing and chatting over tea. In this way, women seek control over their time and labor; evading the authority of the office and the legalistic demands it tries to impose becomes a game of resistance related to women's higher status in the home. Despite their relative success (especially as their numbers in these office buildings grow), women resent these losses in personal authority.

Finally, women feel the loss of informal power in their lives as they transfer time and attention to the workplace. In the home, women rely heavily on family and neighborhood networks to support them financially and emotionally through crises or simply through the tribulations of everyday living. These networks are crucial for women and their families in the attempt to cover basic needs and for special occasions such as engagements and weddings (Singerman 1995). By leaving the household for long hours each day, women lose access to these informal but crucial sources of power, and the time spent in the office offers little compensation for this important loss. Women with sisters, mothers, or cousins who remain at home may still be able to call on these networks through other female relatives, but increasingly women workers find themselves cut off from a traditional source of influence, material resources, and personal pride.

These disappointments which appear at the intersection of household and workplace account for the ambivalence women feel toward working and demonstrate the tensions women feel in their new roles. Women feel pulled in conflicting directions, toward the workplace and the home, and troubled by the necessity to play two roles, that of worker and that of mother and wife. This dilemma of identity and role which emerges from the cross-currents of the sea changes occurring in lower-middle-class Cairo places women in an untenable double bind.

The Worker and Wife/Mother Double Bind

Women are caught in a double bind, for they feel the need to satisfy two conflicting ideologies in this subcultural context; essentially, the economic ideology of Cairo's lower middle class pushes women into the workplace, but the gender ideology strongly opposes this move. Women, trying to play the two parts of worker and wife/mother, find themselves at an impasse; it is virtually impossible to play both roles well, and they find their position inherently compromised.

Among the poor, or the lower class, in Cairo, women often do not labor outside the home, despite the extra income this would bring to their families. Instead, they tend to participate in informal labor activities: sewing, raising poultry, cooking, or shopping for neighbors. However, most women of the lower middle class work because they need the income to obtain economic advantages, and owing to the advantage of their education, they can gain secure government jobs. Families of the lower middle class are striving for more than subsistence; they have a clear idea of the type of life they want to lead, and they have hopes of achieving these goals through sacrifice and hard work. They cite the need to pay expensive rents, to save key money for a flat or to buy good food for children, as reasons for working. These families believe government promises that they can rise in Cairo's social and economic ladder. They are willing to commit family resources toward advancement, and the women work hard to help attain these desired ends. These heightened levels of expectation are politically and personally important and form the center of an economic ideology that values hard work, ambition, and the prestige and standards of a middle-class life. As a result, the economic ideology of this class becomes particularly compelling as a standard for decisions about women's work patterns.

In this lower-middle-class environment, while the jobs these women secure in the government bureaucracy provide little money, they add substantially to straitened budgets as well as ensuring a reasonable level of status. To send one's daughter or wife out to work on the streets or in someone else's home would be regarded as a last resort, but sending women members of the family to government offices actually advertises their educational achievements and promises prestige and marriageability. The ambitious orientation toward gaining secure middle-class status is often defined as the proliferation of consumer goods such status entails. Yet these desires, realizable in the professional upper middle classes, may be very difficult for these families to even begin to attain, let alone consolidate. Since they exist on the very margins of the middle class, their entire class position rests on their ability to realize at least some of these hopes. These economic desires have been fueled by government policies dating from the Nasser regime. The Nasser era reforms were designed in part to encourage social mobility through education and work in the government bureaucracy. However, the result has been an enormous swelling of the government bureaucracy, producing a most inefficient system which gives jobs to many but satisfying work only to the highest-ranking officials. Not surprisingly, as the status of these jobs has fallen, lower- and lower-middle-class men often migrate to other nations or perform blue-collar work, which pays better. Women, however, remain in the government ranks, as alternatives such as factory labor are considered unsuitable. Today, even these jobs are in jeopardy as newspaper articles point out that men with families to support could be holding these jobs.

During the Sadat era, the Infitah, or Open Door Policy, was designed to promote foreign investment and economic development. Its unintended consequences included an inflationary spiral of rising prices which were not matched by rising wages, an influx of foreign luxury goods accompanied by aggressive advertising to promote conspicuous consumption, and a rise in class disparities due to the growth of a newly wealthy upper middle class working in the private sector. The inflationary increase has been partially offset by an extensive food subsidy program, which keeps the prices for goods such as bread, oil, sugar, rice, tea, and clarified butter relatively low. However, food prices have not remained constant, and unsubsidised goods, such as housing, have more than kept pace with the inflation rate. The lower middle class is hard pressed to maintain its status. At the same time, advertising and the lifestyle of the upper middle class promote the attainment of luxury goods—cars, jewelry, perfumes, clothes, expensive appliances. Lower-middle-class men and women generally do not participate in the private sector jobs the open door has created; as a result, their expectations are raised but their ability to achieve their goals is reduced. Inflationary pressures, coupled with their ideology of hard work and ambitious goals, lead to an explosive mixture.

The lower middle class now finds its position most precarious. Indeed, members of this class are losing ground relative to other classes in the society; the upper middle class is getting richer by comparison, and even the lower class is better off—men who migrate can send home large sums of money which are used to buy appliances and household furnishings, making lower-class flats better equipped, even though smaller, than many lower-middle-class homes. The relatively modest goals of lower-middle-class people are in jeopardy. In short, the economic ideology which initially encouraged the entrance of women into government offices, fueled by hopes of increased purchasing power and the chance to securely gain middle-class position, now obliges these women to stay working to barely maintain their class standing. The reference groups these women use to measure their gains and losses demonstrate to them that they are increasingly squeezed; they need the income of two earners to support a household with any pretensions to middle-class status, and they have little hope at all of getting ahead. As a result, the issue of women working has assumed even greater salience.

However, in the lower-middle-class subculture there is another relevant ideology which counters the push of economic ideals, an ideology of gender roles. In this sector of Cairene society, male and female roles are regarded as set by nature, not as alterable social roles. Furthermore, men and women have complementary parts to play, and household harmony and economic well-being depend on each fulfilling his or her duties well. This gender ideology strongly opposes women leaving the home to work.

Gender constructions in the lower middle class are similar, but not identical, to those of other classes in Cairo society, and are based in part on Islamic beliefs about male and female roles. While Islamic ideals are certainly important, it must always be remembered that they are filtered and altered through local needs and that they change over time (Ahmed 1992; Keddie and Baron 1991). The Qur'an considers the role of women in a number of passages, some specifically concerned with women's place in society, some dealing with women's unique nature, and some including women within the general congregation of believers. Considerable controversy surrounds the question of women's status even within the context of Islamic orthodoxy. Some claim that women are considered equal as believers within Islamic doctrine: "O mankind! Be careful of your duty to your Lord Who created you from a single soul and from it created its mate and from them twain hath spread abroad a multitude of men and women. Be careful of your duty toward Allah in Whom ye claim (your rights) of one another . . . " (Fernea and Bezirgan 1977); others argue that women cannot achieve any clear emancipation within Islam because of the distinct denigration of women as second-class believers: "Men are in charge of women, because Allah hath made the one of them to excel the other, and because they spend of their property (to support women). So good women are the obedient . . . " (Fernea and Bezirgan 1977). Controversies over these texts continue today in numerous newspaper and media disputes over the true interpretation of these original texts and others found in the Islamic traditions (Mernissi 1991).

Beyond these controversies over contradictory religious texts, gender beliefs are influenced by numerous local concerns, which can be derived from conversations, stories, myths, media portrayals, and language. In general, men and women are seen as biologically different, a natural and not socially constructed dichotomy which cannot and should not be eradicated. Men and women both emphasize the difference and, further, the complementarity of the sexes. Women are characterized in two main roles, inside and outside the family (Sabbah 1984; al-Messiri 1978). First, women are portrayed in their linked role as wife and mother. The importance of family in Egyptian culture elevates this role to great heights; women as mothers are respected and even idolized. Typically, mothers are portrayed as "self-sacrificing," "caring," "nurturing," and "indulgent to their children." They are perceived as centering their lives on rearing their children, deriving their pleasures, structuring their routines, and gaining their most important identity from this role. Their duties within the home, caring for and educating their children, are not only women's most important responsibilities and the culmination of their linked role as wife; they are also highly appreciated tasks in the societal context as a whole. Acting appropriately and competently as a mother is a woman's highest ideal attainment.

The second major image and role constructed around women is that of woman as sexual temptress, outside the family boundaries. Women are perceived as having a strong sexual nature which needs to be controlled for society to retain any order. This overpowering appetite is controlled by various rituals, customs, and traditions to ensure that women's sexual urges and women's power to disrupt society will be constrained (Sabbah 1984). Veiling, seclusion, economic constraints—these are all examples of society's checks on women's unruly nature. Women cannot be trusted on their own; they must be controlled by outside forces, for women by nature can be weak, crafty, and malicious, although within the family they would naturally be kind, generous, and strong. The corollary of this image of women's sexual nature is a view of man, who also cannot control himself; if he sees a woman, by his very nature he wants her. So she must not be seen, because the man inevitably will be tempted and she inevitably will be unable to control her actions.

These contradictory images of women within and outside the boundaries of family make the role of wife particularly difficult and particularly important to the society. Society deals with the problem by making a division between women who "belong" to a certain man and those who do not. Women in one's family are due respect and appreciation and a measure of dignity; women outside the family are fair game. The contests of honor between men, with women's reputation as the center of the competition, can range from simple challenges and teasing on the streets to serious feuds involving entire extended families. Women are thus honored and protected within the family but vulnerable, in reputation and reality, once outside its confines.

Changes in this gender ideology have occurred as women increasingly leave the home for work. Many of the women I spoke with cited the example of Aisha, daughter of the Prophet Muhammad, as a woman who left the boundaries of the home and performed public services as she sought to turn the Islamic community in the right direction. This Islamic role model provides justification for women's need to leave the home to labor today in a time of family or public need. Yet other women I spoke with admitted, with some discomfort, that they felt working was wrong; modern times, they said, can make you do things which go against religion. Controversy over women's role is prevalent, but the centrality of family has helped to secure gender constructions from significant change. Certainly both men and women feel that women are by nature different than men and that these differences are positive. Men are suited to going out in the world, thus they are responsible for providing financially for the family. Women are suited to remaining within family boundaries, creating and caring for the home, the children, the husband. And both women and men agree that family life is essential to develop one's nature as a full person within society. The family structure emerges as all-important in this account, creating an ordered society and moral lives. Family roles of both men and women are fundamental in maintaining the entire societal structure; therefore, gender constructs are highly sensitive, pointing to women's staying in the home, strongly opposing women's working outside and abandoning their key role.

Women in this context are torn by the push and pull of cross-cutting ideological pressures, and face a difficult dilemma. They face an economic ideology linked to their class position and strongly supporting women's going outside the home to work by focusing on women's responsibility to help the family in its ambitious push toward firm middle-class status. Yet, this new role of "working woman" is not supported, and indeed strongly opposed, by subcultural ideas about women's nature which locate women's place within the home. This push and pull of contradictory ideological forces confronts these lower-middle-class women with a classic double bind—by definition, working out of the home and being a good wife/mother are simply at odds. At the center of this tug of war, these women face compromising choices, and as the economic situation in Cairo has deteriorated, this conflict has intensified.

It is in this troublesome context that many lower-middle-class women have started to wear the *higab* in recent years. For these women, covered dress expresses the double bind they find in a changing Cairo and offers some practical alleviation of the resentment and problems they discover as they venture into uncharted experiences. By emphasizing women's identity as virtuous wives and Muslim mothers, the *higab* allows women to reclaim traditional respect, even while moving into new realms. The new veiling offers a powerful and public signal of women's distress at their ideological double bind, and their determination to retain and advance the gains they have made by essentially creating a new way to be good Muslim women (MacLeod 1991, 1992).

Negotiating at the Intersection

This exploration of women's changing work patterns in lower-middle-class Cairo shows that women face difficult choices and complex trade-offs rather than a clear path of progressive change. Recent work has altered our assump-

tions about household and workplace, making the equation of household/
tradition and workplace/modernity problematic and raising important questions about the relationship between women's work and the alleviation of subordination. Early arguments to the effect that working outside the home is necessary for women's "liberation" have given way to more subtle discussions of
the gains and losses involved as women move from the household to participation in both paid and household labor. The realities of class position and its
influence on the kinds of gains and losses women will experience has also been
detailed. Yet where do these revisions lead us in terms of the question of the
negotiation of women's powers? If we do not promote working for women, are
we simply conceding to cultural constructs which advocate an inferior, or at
least circumscribed, role? The assumption that women could leave the "traditional" household and its constraints behind and enter the "modern" workplace, gaining power and prestige, while naive, remains compelling in part because it avoids some of the troubling implications of these questions. This
theoretical ambivalence is reflected in women's expressions as well; many comment that they do wish to retain some aspects of the working experience—the
mobility, the chance for social encounters, the challenge of new opportunities.
Women's feelings about these positive aspects of the working experience mean
that a simple recourse to advocating staying at home is as problematic as suggesting that all women should leave the home for paid labor. These questions
are further complicated by controversies over the proper path for feminist
progress in Third World societies; should all goals advanced by women be considered feminist? How can such disputes be settled given the unresolved questions about cross-cultural understanding and cultural differences (Mohanty
1991; Lazreg 1990)?

Yet the fact remains that Cairo, like many Third World urban areas, is un-
dergoing tremendous change; women necessarily face the ambiguities of negotiating a future within this ferment. Theoretical assessments will have to deal
with these ambivalent and uncertain interactions, portraying the ambiguities
and trade-offs rather than searching for grand solutions to women's subordi-
nations which overlook the subtleties of women's problems and opportunities
in a particular setting (Probyn 1990). Detailed explorations of the interactions
taking place at the intersection of household and workplace are an example of
the work needed in order to understand, in each unique circumstance, the factors which provide sources of power for women and those which serve as constraints.

A second point we learn from this case study is that competing ideologies can produce especially difficult tensions for women. In Cairo, the ideological conflict intensifies controversy over the construction of women's identity, preventing women from realizing some of the advantages of working outside the home. How competing ideologies interact, reinforcing or contradicting each other, even within one particular class setting, is clearly important for how women will perceive and attempt to act on their options. This study suggests that more work, located in particular subcultural settings, on how different ideologies interact to structure spaces for potential resistance and to create constraints on consciousness and action is certainly very important in the attempt to understand potential changes in women's status (Beneria 1987; Cott 1987).

Finally, the example of the adoption of the new veils in lower-middle-class Cairo offers an inspiring example of the imaginative capacity of ordinary women. The new Muslim woman they have created may work outside the home, but she never forgets or neglects her family. The new veils symbolize women's protest of a compromising double bind and show the innovative capacity of ordinary women to create a new role and new identity for a changing world. They provide a wonderful example of imaginative negotiation—the emergence of symbolic resistance and the creation of alternatives in a time of crisis.[2]

The rise of militant Islamic politics in Egypt tempts us to consider the Islamic symbolism of the veils as part of this "fundamentalist" militancy against the state. Yet to say the new veils are a symbol of the rise of Islam is certainly to raise more questions than we answer. Islam, in this context, must be viewed as the language of political opposition, a language which allows competing positions on social issues to be articulated, not simply as a dogma supporting a fundamentalist state. The question becomes: what exactly are women protesting, and advocating, by using the Islamic symbol of the veil in this innovative fashion? Women in these families certainly question the ability of the state to make good on its economic promises, and they question the virtues of adopting the morality of the Western world wholesale. In this sense they advance oppositional politics. But for these families, involvement in national politics is to be avoided, and the strenuous routines of everyday life more than occupy their energies; as we might expect, their concerns and their political negotiations are closer to home. The task of constructing a new identity suited to a modern, yet Islamic, Cairo begins with families (Mernissi 1987, 1992), and women are taking the lead in suggesting a new form of community that avoids the extremes of wholesale Westernization or of fundamentalist Islam.

NOTES

1. I thank Diane Singerman, Homa Hoodfar, Frederic Shorter, and Barbara Ibrahim for their helpful and insightful comments on earlier versions of this chapter. I also benefited from discussions with the participants in the "Research on Cairo Households" seminar held in Cairo. The American Research Center in Egypt provided the initial support to conduct research in 1983–84; Yale University funded study in 1986; and Bates College funded further research in 1988 and 1991. I appreciate the support from these institutions. My deepest gratitude must be expressed to the women in Cairo who are the subjects of this study. This chapter is based on a larger study on lower-middle-class women in Cairo entitled *Accommodating Protest* (MacLeod 1991).

2. For an intriguing case study highlighting the difficulties in creating an alternative identity and the negotiations between the dominant and emergent identities, see Young 1990. For a wide-ranging discussion on unusual forms of resistance and oppositional politics, see Scott 1990. And for a case study among the Bedouin in Egypt, focusing on the dangers of the "romance" of resistance, see Abu-Lughod 1990. The new veiling, while an imaginative and empowering example of symbolic politics, must be viewed in the context of an ongoing negotiation over women's identity, as an "accommodating protest" (MacLeod 1991, 1992).

WORKS CITED

Abu-Lughod, Lila. *Veiled Sentiments: Honor and Poetry in a Bedouin Society.* Berkeley: University of California Press, 1986.

———. "The Romance of Resistance: Tracing the Transformations of Power through Bedouin Women." *American Ethnologist* 17, no. 1 (1990): 41–56.

Ahmed, Leila. *Women and Gender in Islam.* New Haven: Yale University Press, 1992.

Ait Sabbah, Fatna. *Women in the Muslim Unconscious.* New York: Pergamon, 1984.

Antoun, Richard. "On the Modesty of Women in Arab Muslim Villages." *American Anthropologist* 70, no. 4 (1968): 671–698.

Beneria, Lourdes, and Martha Roldan. *The Crossroads of Class and Gender.* Chicago: University of Chicago Press, 1987.

Cott, Nancy. *The Grounding of Modern Feminism.* New Haven: Yale University Press, 1987.

Elshtain, Jean Bethke. *Public Man, Private Woman.* Princeton: Princeton University Press, 1981.

Fernea, Elizabeth, and Basima Qattan Bezirgan, eds. *Middle Eastern Muslim Women Speak.* Austin: University of Texas Press, 1977.

El-Guindi, Fadwa. "Veiling Infitah with Muslim Ethic: Egypt's Contemporary Islamic Movement." *Social Problems* 28, no. 4 (1981): 465–487.

———. "Veiled Activism: Egyptian Women in the Contemporary Islamic Movement." *Femmes de la Méditerranée, Peuples Méditeranéens* 22, no. 23 (1983): 79–89.

Hoodfar, Homa. "Patterns of Household Budgeting and Financial Management in a Cairo Neighborhood." In *A Home Divided*, ed. Daisy Dwyer and Judith Bruce. Stanford: Stanford University Press, 1988.

Keddie, Nikki, and Beth Baron. *Women in Middle Eastern History*. New Haven: Yale University Press, 1991.

Lazreg, Marnia. "Feminism and Difference: The Perils of Writing as a Woman on Women in Algeria." In *Conflicts in Feminism*, ed. Marianne Hirsch and Evelyne Fox Keller. New York: Routledge, 1990, 326–348.

MacLeod, Arlene Elowe. *Accommodating Protest: Working Women, the New Veiling, and Change in Cairo*. New York: Columbia University Press, 1991.

———. "Hegemonic Relations and Gender Resistance." *SIGNS* 17, no. 3 (1992).

Makhlouf, Carla. *Changing Veils: Women and Modernization in North Yemen*. Austin: University of Texas Press, 1979.

Mernissi, Fatima. *Beyond the Veil: Male-Female Dynamics in Modern Muslim Society*. Bloomington: Indiana University Press, 1987.

———. *Islam and Democracy*. Reading: Addison-Wesley, 1992.

———. *The Veil and the Male Elite*. Reading: Addison-Wesley, 1991.

Al-Messiri, Sawsan. *Ibn al-Balad: A Concept of Egyptian Identity*. Leiden: E. J. Brill, 1978.

Mohanty, Chandra, Ann Russo, and Lourdes Torres, eds.. *Third World Women and the Politics of Feminism*. Bloomington: Indiana University Press, 1991.

Mohsen, Safia. "New Images, Old Reflections." In Elizabeth Fernea, ed., *Women and Family in the Middle East*. Austin: University of Texas Press, 1985.

Murphy, Robert. "Social Distance and the Veil." In *Peoples and the Cultures of the Middle East*, ed. Louise Sweet. New York: Natural History Press, 1970, 290–315.

Nawar, Laila, Cynthia Lloyd, and Barbara Ibrahim. "Autonomy and Gender in Egyptian Families," *MERIP Reports* 24, no. 5 (1994): 18.

Nelson, Cynthia. "Public and Private Politics." *American Ethnologist* 1, no. 3 (1974): 551–563.

Papanek, Hannah. "Separate Worlds and Symbolic Shelter." *Comparative Studies in Society and History* 15, no. 3 (1973): 289–325.

Pastner, Carroll McC. "A Social, Structural and Historical Analysis of Honor, Shame and Purdah." *Anthropological Quarterly* 45, no. 4 (1972): 248–262.

Probyn, Elsbeth. "Travels in the Postmodern: Making Sense of the Local." In *Feminism and Postmodernism*, ed. Linda Nicholson. New York: Routledge, 1990, 176–189.

Rugh, Andrea. *Reveal and Conceal: Dress in Contemporary Egypt.* Syracuse: Syracuse University Press, 1986.

Sabbah, Fatna A. *See* Ait Sabbah, Fatna.

Scott, James. *Domination and the Art of Resistance.* New Haven: Yale University Press, 1990.

Singerman, Diane. *Avenues of Participation: Family, Politics, and Networks in Urban Quarters of Cairo.* Princeton: Princeton University Press, 1995.

Tucker, Judith. "Egyptian Women in the Workforce: A Historical Survey." *MERIP Reports* 50 (1976): 3–9.

———. *Women in Nineteenth-Century Egypt.* New York: Cambridge University Press, 1985.

Wikan, Unni. "Living Conditions among Cairo's Poor." *Middle East Journal* 39, no. 1 (1985).

Williams, John Alden. "A Return to the Veil in Egypt." *Middle East Review* 11, no. 3 (1979): 49–54.

Young, Alison. *Femininity in Dissent.* London: Routledge, 1990.

Zuhur, Sherifa. *Revealing Reveiling: Islamist Gender Ideology in Contemporary Egypt.* Albany: State University of New York Press, 1992.

3

EGYPTIAN MALE MIGRATION AND URBAN FAMILIES LEFT BEHIND

"Feminization of the Egyptian Family" or
a Reaffirmation of Traditional Gender Roles?

HOMA HOODFAR

LARGE-SCALE INTERNATIONAL labor migration from Egypt to the Arab oil-producing countries has been characterized by the predominance of unskilled and
semiskilled male workers unaccompanied by their families.[1] This feature is a
result partly of the migration policies of the host countries and partly of the
clandestine nature of migration for less-skilled and less-educated workers, but
a major reason is the cost of moving the family.[2] To take the family would defeat
the purpose of migration, which is often adopted as a short-term strategy to
generate more cash and improve a household's standard of living (Fergany
1987, 18).

As a result, many families have been transformed temporarily into de facto
female-headed households. Although this unconventional phenomenon and its
implications for women, children, and family in Egyptian society have received
much attention, at least within Egypt, it has been the focus of little scholarly
research, particularly in urban settings (Amin and Awny 1985, 155–99; Brink
1991). Data from rural Egypt and other countries in the region have suggested
that migration can often lead to a nuclearization of the family (Khattab and
El-Daeif 1982; Khafagi 1984) and greater decision-making power for the wife,
usually at the mother-in-law's expense. Other questions, such as whether wives
acquire greater power vis-à-vis their husbands or within the wider community
and, more important, whether the changes that occurred during the migration
would be permanent in nature, have remained much more controversial. This
last question is particularly pertinent, because Egyptian migration to the oil-
producing countries has been overwhelmingly on a short-term basis.

The evidence from my anthropological field research in urban Cairo indicates that while the impact of male migration on children in low-income communities is more positive than a reading of the literature would suggest, its impact on women is more diverse. My findings indicate that contrary to commonsense expectations, traditional and less-educated wives managed to improve their position within the household and vis-à-vis their husbands both during and after the migration. In contrast, better-educated wives, particularly those who had been white-collar workers, lost much ground to their husbands. Moreover, my data confirm that many of the changes tend to be permanent. However, not only have I found no evidence that migration has led to reversals in conventional gender roles in Egypt, but instead my observations indicate that the essence of traditional gender roles was strengthened. Though in one sense male migration may have "feminized the Egyptian family" (Ibrahim 1982, 92) and at the same time extended the realm of contributions some women make to their households, in another sense this migration, by creating a large gap between male and female cash earnings, has mitigated against the possibilities of acceptance of fundamental changes in prescribed gender roles, which depict men as breadwinners and women as homemakers.

The Research

The data presented here are based on extensive anthropological fieldwork during 1983–1986 and several subsequent field visits (1988, 1992, 1994, 1995) to forty-two households living in three adjacent low-income neighborhoods of greater Cairo-Giza.[3] Forty-seven percent of the sample comprised households of current migrants;[4] 28.5 percent comprised returned migrants; and 23 percent belonged to a control group of nonmigrant households. The three groups were equally divided between those households whose wives were gainfully employed and those who had no income of their own (see table 1).

More than half the wives, as compared with a quarter of the husbands, were illiterate; 45 percent of the husbands and 38 percent of the wives had finished primary schooling or equivalent; while 23 percent of the husbands and 9.5 percent of the wives had graduated from high school.

The couples in the study had been married from three to twenty-six years, with a majority clustering between ten and fifteen years. The households included 133 children still living at home. The number of children per household ranged from zero to eight, with a mode of three children and a mean of 3.17. The majority of the children were under fourteen years of age.

Nuclear households are the norm in low-income neighborhoods (Shorter

Table 1. Occupations of Wives and Husbands in the Study Sample (%)

	Wife	Husband*
Homemaker	50.0	0.0
White-collar (government employee)	9.5	19.0
Blue-collar	7.1	26.4
Professional (semiskilled)	9.5	38.0
Petty trader	16.5	14.3
Casual worker	7.1	2.3

N = 42 households.
*For households of current migrants, the jobs are those held prior to migration.

1989), particularly in the newly urbanized neighborhoods whose residents are mostly first- and second-generation rural-urban migrants. Although some of the informants lived very close to, or in the same building as their kin, only one household in my sample had lived as an extended family prior to the migration.[5]

Decision to Migrate

The reason for migration, the process of decision making, and the extent to which it was a unilateral decision of the husband rather than a joint decision of the couple, all set the scene for the postmigration situation. Therefore an assessment of these processes can provide important insights into the impact of the migration.

Male and female informants unanimously agreed that economic reward was the only motivation for migration, which they viewed as the only option open to low-income social groups to raise their standard of living and improve opportunities for their children.[6] The informants generally recognized the importance of macro factors, such as the differential wage structure between Egypt and many of the oil-rich countries, and political situations, such as government-to-government relationships in opening possibilities to migrate.[7]

Within this setting, the decision to migrate was frequently linked to certain stages of the family cycle, which were an important indicator of who might migrate and who might stay behind. Generally, two groups of men were considered eligible for migration. First were those of marriageable age who needed to finance their marriage, which even in low-income neighborhoods can cost a considerable sum (see Singerman 1995). The second group included those married men with at least two or three children.[8] Otherwise, only under exceptional circumstances was it legitimate for a husband to migrate before building a complete family.

Men felt that once a marriage was consummated it was not right to leave a young bride before the marriage ties had strengthened. "After all, migration is to improve our life not to separate us more," said one young man in explaining why he had turned down his friends' offers of assistance in migrating. Generally, men and women in the neighborhoods agreed that young women had the right to demand that their husbands postpone plans for migration.[9] Once a woman had two or three children, her marriage and her relationship with her husband were considered secure and therefore geographical distance was less threatening to the stability of the marriage. At this stage "it is the children that we have to think about"—a point made repeatedly by many of the informants, particularly the younger wives. Their emphasis on this point, however, belied their own unvoiced personal interest. For many young wives, the migration of their husband at an earlier stage of their marriage would mean the end of their newly gained independence, probably the most valued gift of the marriage, since they would have to move and live either with their parents, their in-laws, or other relatives.

There was a striking consistency among my informants in viewing migration as a period of hardship. A husband's willingness to migrate to the Gulf was considered the best proof of his devotion to his family, and many wives were quick to recount the difficulties of their husbands or other migrants as evidence.[10] Many wives remarked that men from Saudi Arabia and Kuwait came to Cairo for fun, since there was so little amusement in their own country. Then they would point out that Egyptian men went to such places to work only for the sake of their family. "There is nothing there except hard work, loneliness and harsh treatment by the authorities," many women repeatedly reminded me. Only after long years of migration which brought financial improvement and if the husband had the possibility of employment in Egypt might a wife raise complaint and expect the husband to return. However, these conditions were hard to meet among less-skilled workers, whose wages were relatively low even in the host countries.

While the final decision on migration was made by the husband, the practical and emotional support of wives and friends had a considerable influence on them. Wives of many migrants were eager for their husbands to work

Table 2. Sources of Financing of Migration among the Sample

	Number of Households
Sale of gold and household goods	11
Loan from wives' relative	4
Loan from husbands' relative	8
Loan from other source	7
Savings	2
All	32

abroad and played an active role in making the departure arrangements. Many of the wives, in spite of their illiteracy, had taken upon themselves to obtain their husbands' passport, a formidable task given the complexity of the Egyptian bureaucracy. Many others encouraged their relatives to give loans to their husbands to cover the initial cost of migration (see table 2). Others sold their gold and household items in order to raise the necessary cash.[11] Fargany's study indicated that, in the urban setting, spouses have by far the most important influence over the decision to migrate, (1987, 19). However, when asked directly, despite this evidence, all migrants in my sample, and often their wives, unequivocally declared that the decision to migrate was the husbands'.

Residential Status

Previous studies of migration in Turkey and rural Egypt have indicated that migration accelerates the process of nuclearization of a household and usually affords more autonomy to the wife (Khattab and El-Daeif 1982; Khafagi 1984; Taylor 1984; Kiray 1976; Abadan-Unat 1986). In the Cairo setting, where nuclear families are the norm, however, the reverse is often the case. After the husband's migration, their young wives may temporarily return to the extended family setting. Culturally it is not acceptable for young women to live on their own; nor do they want to.[12] Thus, young wives with no children often have to return to live with relatives, a move all wives agreed was unpleasant because it meant the loss of the autonomy which they had gained through marriage. Generally, low-income families live in overcrowded accommodations; few households can accommodate another family. On rare occasions, however, a wife's brother, mother, or other close kin might move in with a young wife during the husband's absence.[13] In fact, in the course of discussions with both men and women it became evident that the major underlying reason for men to postpone their migration to a later phase of family building was that once a woman had two or three children she was perceived as a matron and could continue to live independently in her own residence.

When a wife did have to move, her first choice was to join her own parents if that option was available. Most husbands, as well as people of low-income neighborhoods generally, considered this choice both legitimate and appropriate.[14] The exceptions tended to be where a woman had married into a family of a much higher socioeconomic status. The result was that her husband and his family had more influence and control over the wife during the early years of the marriage. Within my sample, three young women had moved in with their parents and only one woman had to move to her mother-in-law's for the duration of their husbands' migration. The other twenty-eight wives continued to live in their own independent households.

The Daily Life of a Migrant's Household

Except when wives joined other households, the departure of husbands transformed their households into de facto female-headed ones. In addition to their usual tasks, the wives had to shoulder much of their husbands' responsibilities. Skillful management of the financial affairs of families with limited cash resources was essential for the survival of the households. Many of the wives had to learn to budget for daily expenses, educational costs, and unexpected expenses. They had to improve their managerial and shopping skills, extend their old networks, and weave new ones in order to gain access to information and support that would assist them in protecting their households' interests. Thus, the early months after the husbands' departure for all wives, particularly those not engaged in cash-earning activities, were colored with anxiety until they grew accustomed to the new situation.

The households' finances were the most immediate worry, especially for less-educated wives who did not enjoy the security of a permanent job. Though many women had encouraged their husbands to migrate and some had sacrificed a great deal to finance the migration, they nevertheless worried about the possibility of their husbands' failure to find a job in the host country.[15] These worries occasionally encouraged the wives who did not have independent incomes to seriously contemplate or engage in cash-earning activities, usually petty trading in the local market. Generally, though, on the eve of migration the non-wage-earning wives were often entrusted with some cash to manage their households with the hope that the husband would send more shortly.

Cash-earning wives were simply expected to manage their households on their own incomes, often without any specific arrangement as to whether or not the husbands would send money. As a financial arrangement, this represented a major shift for many of these households, since according to the Islamic code and Egyptian customs it is the husband who is responsible for meeting the day-to-day expenses of the family, regardless of his wife's income. The most common and preferred budgeting practice is for wives to spend their income on household goods or on those extras for which husbands manifest little enthusiasm (Hoodfar 1988; Nadim 1985). Only under exceptional circumstances would women willingly spend their income on the basic needs of the family. To their dismay, many wives in this group came to realize that the reversal of this budgeting pattern was permanent.

In contrast to the increase in their managerial responsibilities, most wives in the study agreed that their daily domestic chores had decreased as a result of their husbands' absence. However, although they felt less obliged to cook more elaborate meals, it was mostly the flexibility of their schedules that made them feel less pressured. As one wife explained,

> the advantage of not having him [her husband] around is that I can do all my washing or cook in the middle of the night if I feel like it and sleep late. When he is around I have to give him food and tea and keep the children quiet after he comes home from a twelve–fourteen-hour workday.[16]

The exceptions were those few wives who had had to move in with their parents or their parents-in-law: they complained that their work load had increased, since, as young women, they had to serve everybody in the household and attend to the guests. They eagerly looked forward to the day they could move back to their own homes. Thus the urban situation was clearly different from the rural one where wives and children often had to perform additional farming tasks after the husbands' migration (Khafagi 1984; Taylor 1984; Muaty 1984).

Impact of Migration on Parent-Child Relationships

The high average number of dependent children among the migrants' households in Egypt (Fergany 1987, 10) and in Turkey (Kiray 1976; Yasa 1979) has led some scholars to argue that the economic needs of such large households are an important factor encouraging migration. In Egypt men often migrated alone to keep the expenses to a minimum.[17] The temporary nature of Egyptian migration and job insecurity among less-skilled migrants also mitigates against families migrating collectively. Moreover, many of the Arab host countries have adopted migration policies which discourage family reunification. Often, however, the social restrictions and the inferior educational systems in many of the Arab host countries discouraged even those middle-class Egyptian migrants who had the option of taking their families from doing so.

Despite the fact that leaving children behind is a widespread practice, there has been little scholarly research focused on the impact of migration on children. In Egypt, impressionistic analysis of the phenomenon has been primarily negative (Ibrahim 1982; Muaty 1984). This negative view has been influenced at least partly by the findings from Turkish migration to Western Europe, where often both parents migrate and leave their young children in the care of others (Kiray 1976; Kagitcibasi 1984). In Egypt, however, the case is very different in that few young children are left without at least one parent present, usually the mother.

The view that children need both parents as role models (Ibrahim 1982) has also influenced opinion about Egyptian migration. This position implicitly assumes that, first, the fathers spend a reasonable amount of time at home and are active in the day-to-day affairs of their children and that, second, the absence of a father is equivalent to the absence of all males. My observations suggest that in the case of low-income households at least, a great majority of fathers with underage children spend almost all their time away from home and neighborhood, at the workplace, as they try to meet their family's financial needs.[18] On the other hand, in Egypt in general and among the low-income communities in particular, there is much interaction with the neighbors and with kin, which provides the children with other male role models.

The urban situation differs from rural settings where the fathers are always in the vicinity and take part in disciplining and bringing up their children (Khafagi 1984; Muaty 1984). Many of my informants pointed out that their husbands' absence had little effect on children's upbringing, since the father's role, beyond an economic one, was minimal. However, some women claimed that their husbands' presence lent them moral support in raising their children and that any wife should be able to demand such support. According to most migrants' wives, it was this loss of moral support which was the greatest sacrifice they had made in trying to secure a better life for themselves and their children.

I did not find any evidence that children in migrant households were given more work and responsibilities than children in other households, as has been reported for rural Egypt (Khafagi 1984; Muaty 1984). Customarily in these neighborhoods, daughters aged fourteen or older actively participated in the daily chores of the household. Although these responsibilities sometimes interfered with their studies if they were students, daughters generally enjoyed them because it often brought them some say within their households. They took such work as an indication of their impending adult status, especially since daughters in general had few ways of occupying themselves, lacking as they did the freedom of movement that their brothers enjoyed. These young women in migrant households often had more decision-making power, became closer to their mothers, and were more frequently rewarded for their efforts with little presents than their counterparts in nonmigrants' households.

In lower-income neighborhoods, sibling rivalry over limited financial resources was a constant source of conflict between parents and their elder children. There was never-ending discussion, arguments, and tears over money for books, money for tutorials, money for clothes, and so on. Often remittances alleviated some of these tensions.[19] The conditions of life in these neighborhoods dictated a type of interaction between a father and his children which was very different from the ideal middle-class model. Fathers didn't (couldn't) spend much time with their children because they had to spend their energy earning cash for the family. When children witnessed their parents exerting extra effort and enduring hardships so that they could have a better life, the children felt loved and wanted. None of the children from the migrant families expressed hostility at the idea of their fathers' absence. Children often explained with much zeal that their fathers had migrated in order to provide a better life for them.[20] Many times I heard children publicly praise their fathers for enduring hardship in order to give them a better future. Magda, who was the only female university student in my sample, said, in discussing the financial hardship of a neighboring family:

> I remember we were as poor as they are, even worse, because there were seven of us living in one room. But my father went to Libya and there he worked twelve hours a day every day of the week for four years and slept in a room with many other Egyptians and didn't eat much. Finally he bought the land and saved enough to build two rooms. Then we moved here and gradually built a second floor and bought a TV. He still has to work at two jobs but he is happy because he never went to school and still has managed to send me to university. My elder brother and sister have finished high school. Many of our neighbors don't have money to send their children to school.

The high dropout rate for boys from secondary school during the eighties was sometimes blamed on migration and the absence of fathers. My observations, however, suggest that there was a change in the way parents assessed the importance of their sons' education. In the past, education was the single most important means of gaining access to well-paid and secure jobs. Introduction of the Open Door Policy (Infitah) and the possibility of migration to the Gulf radically changed the Egyptian wage structure. While the wages in the private and informal sectors rose rapidly, the wages in public and governmental jobs barely kept pace with rising prices.

While the value of education remained generally high in low-income neighborhoods of Cairo (see K. R. Kamphoefner's essay in this volume, chapter 4), people preferred that their sons learn a trade or, if possible, enroll in a technical school after their initial six to nine years of schooling. Thus, in many households, the eldest son had graduated from high school or even university, while the younger ones had only had a few years of education, after which they had taken up an apprenticeship in a trade such as plumbing, mechanics, etc. Many other households were actively seeking workshops which would accept their sons as young as eight or nine years old as apprentices during the summer in the hope that they would learn a trade (*hirfa*) as soon as possible. People with few material resources were very alert to economic realities and swift in their response to the changing conditions of the labor market.[21]

Male children were eager to count the reasons why education was not the answer to their future financial needs (as a father and husband). Hassen, who at age eighteen was a good plumber and earned from 200 to 250 Egyptian pounds per month, was eager to complete his military service and open a shop jointly with his older brother, who was a university graduate working as a high school teacher and earning less than 100 pounds. Hassen explained to me:

> At first my mother wanted me to be educated like my brother, but when she saw that it took him about eight years to save enough money to get married, she thought it was best that I learn a trade. She asked around and then sent me to work with a friend of her brother's. . . . Now my educated brother is going to leave his job and work with me because a man has to earn money for his family. . . . What is a degree worth if your pocket is empty?

Ironically, the withdrawal of sons from school meant there were more funds available for daughters to finish high school (twelve years of schooling) and try to find jobs in government offices.[22] Government jobs, despite their low pay, were still considered the most suitable jobs for women, primarily because of legal concessions made to married women in order to enable them to combine their role as wives and mothers with their professions.[23] Many parents, particularly mothers, were keen for their daughters to have some kind of financial security in case their marriage went wrong.

Interhousehold Relations

The help and support that neighbors provide one another, both on a daily basis and at times of crisis, is significant in low-income quarters of Cairo (Singerman 1995; Hoodfar in this volume, chap. 1). Many of the informants pointed out that as kin are increasingly forced to spread across the city,[24] neighbors acquire even more importance. It is primarily women who develop the neighborly network because, in contrast to the old neighborhoods of Cairo, few men work in, or spend much time in, the newly urbanized quarters. Generally, much of women's interaction with one another takes place in the absence of their husbands, whether they have migrated or not. Migrants' wives had freer schedules for socializing and their homes provided a more suitable center for women to assemble to perform collective activities such as sewing, baking, preparing vegetables, or simply watching television. Most wives and their neighbors viewed their acquired freedom as a compensation for their loneliness.

Similarly, the interaction of wives with their own kin intensified when they lived in close proximity. They often developed closer ties and exchanged services much more readily with their mothers or sisters and sometimes their brothers. This stood in sharp contrast to a diminishing of relations with the husbands' kin after the husbands' migration. Often there was almost a deliberate tendency for migrants' wives to publicize their differences with their husbands' kin, to air complaints of a lack of support. However, my observations repeatedly made it clear that it was the wives themselves who actively tried to curtail these interactions and offers of help. This stemmed from the wives' assessment that any help, moral or otherwise, which the husbands' kin provided would legitimize their expectation of a handsome present once the husbands returned. Umm Mona, whose husband had been a migrant for four years, always complained that with four children nobody helped her and that her own family lived far away. On an occasion when her sister-in-law offered to stay with the children while she took the youngest child to the hospital, she flatly refused and told her that the children were naughty and she did not wish to bother her. During the whole visit the sister-in-law was treated very formally. Later, when I asked why she did not accept her kind offer, she said:

You do not understand. They want to do some small thing and then write to my husband to tell him how much they help me so as to encourage him to bring them expensive presents. My husband and I suffer the hardship of migration and they want to benefit from it. If you don't believe me ask Umm Hassan [her neighbor] whose husband's relatives fought with her and took the best of what her husband had brought. I know better. I have my own friends and can manage without them.

Later in the week I came across Nadia, her sister-in-law, who lived in the same neighborhood. Without much hesitation she started to complain about Umm Mona's attitude:

Can you believe that before my brother migrated she was very friendly to me and acted as if we were sisters. Now did you see how she treated me and rejected my offer to help. Then she goes around and complains to everybody that we do not help her or call on her. She sends messages of complaint to my brother, too. Do you know why? Because she is worried that my brother may bring presents for us. She wants to keep everything for herself and her own family, but we don't care about presents.

Such incidents were not uncommon. Many of the migrants' wives adopted strategies that alienated the husbands' families.[25] This is because customarily the immediate members of a husband's family of origin can raise a claim to his earnings, particularly if they are poorer than he. For instance, brothers or unmarried sisters and parents can expect financial assistance from their better-off sons or brothers. Such assistance is not in the form of straightforward returnable loans; rather it is expected in return for providing help and assistance as and when needed.[26] Failing to fulfill their responsibilities, for example, not being available and willing to help a brother's family during his absence, would remove the legitimate grounds for laying claim on his remittances or receiving a considerable gift. Therefore the wives are often consciously engineering situations which make it hard for their husbands' kin to expect much generosity on the husbands' part.

Both returned migrants and those on home visit to Egypt tended to side with their wives and blame their kin. One returned migrant, in justifying the cold reception he gave to his brother and nephew, told me:

I do not want brothers who only want me when I am rich. Where was he when I was away and my children were sick? How often did he come to bring some cake and presents for my children? They now come to visit me because my nephew is getting married and they want me to act as an uncle and give him a lot of money.

The limited remittances of migrants encourages them to limit their responsibilities to their own immediate families. Similar situations have been reported for rural Egypt, where disagreements between the wife and the parents-in-law often lead to the establishment of a nuclear family (Khattab and El-Daeif 1982). These developments are not limited to the migrants' households, but migration clearly hastens the process and provides the wives with opportunities to play active roles in restructuring family social interactions to their own advantage.

Management and Investment of Remittances

The role wives played in deciding how to allocate remittances varied greatly. Contrary to commonsense expectations, the less-educated wives played a more significant role in the management and investment of remittances than the better-educated wives. The latter had little knowledge of the amount of the remittances and did not expect to have much of a say in their disposal. In fact, since all educated women in the study were government employees, their husbands did not send money for housekeeping regularly (Hoodfar 1995). They would deposit their earnings in their own bank accounts or make investments whenever they returned to Cairo to visit the family.

Though these husbands often bought household goods and generous presents for their families, wives often complained about their lack of participation in decisions about the investment of remittances, which they viewed as a family matter. They often pointed out that before migration they used to plan the family budget with their husbands and, in fact, several of the wives in this group had been the financial managers of their households and had allocated their husbands' earnings as they saw fit. However, after the husbands' migration they effectively lost control over and access to their husbands' income and remittances. To make the husbands resume payment for daily household expenses, which in the Islamic and Egyptian context is an unequivocal responsibility of a husband, many wives had to adopt strategies such as taking a leave without pay from their government jobs under the pretext of attending to their home and children; or, less frequently, they bought household goods on installment and committed all their wages to pay the installments (see Hoodfar 1995).

The less-educated wives, even if they were engaged in cash-earning activities, often received remittances to spend on day-to-day needs. Depending on the level of remittances, the wives often tried to invest in durable goods as assets for their households. Those with more resources purchased pieces of land on installment and hoped to build one- or two-room dwellings and move their families there at some future time. Generally, the improvement of housing conditions was the most important goal of the migrants' households, though many migrants' wives knew that with their meager remittances their chances of achieving that goal were very slim. Among my informants, seven out of thirty-two households had managed to buy land on the outskirts of Cairo and four had built or were in the process of building dwelling units.[27] One household managed to rent a better flat in the same neighborhood. A few other wives whose husbands were still away were hopeful that they would be able to buy land before their husbands returned.

Wives were often actively involved in gathering information on the availability and price of land and in discussing the terms of land transactions.[28] In four of the seven households that had managed to buy land, it was the wife who was the sole or principal agent in negotiating and concluding the sale contracts. Three of these women were illiterate. In all cases, however, the land was bought in the name of the husbands, whether or not the wife had contributed financially. One woman bought the land in her husband's name with her own savings and the savings from the housekeeping money her husband had sent, even though her husband knew nothing about the transaction. She explained to me:

> I did not tell him because, who knows, he might not have agreed or stopped sending me money. Men do not always have the best sense of how to invest the money. But of course I could not buy the land in my own name. My husband and the neighbors would think I stole his money.

Among the less-educated people of the neighborhood, particularly people of the Nile Delta region, women were generally viewed as shrewder and more realistic than men on issues related to investment and stretching a limited income.[29]

Another woman, once she was assured that her husband had found a job, sold her gold (what she was given at the time of her wedding and what she had inherited from her mother) and those household goods which belonged to her in order to pay the first installment on land she bought in her husband's name. When asked why not in her own name, she said that it was not right for a house or land to be in a wife's name, especially since the remaining installments would be paid out of the remittances the husband would send.

Investing in a business, especially for those who did not have a secure or permanent job, was the second most important goal among migrants, even though very few expected to succeed. Among the better-educated migrants, one had saved enough to buy a secondhand taxi, which he drove in the afternoons, and another had invested in a chicken farm along with a few other returned migrants. The income from these investments supplemented income from their regular office jobs. Neither of the wives, both of whom were educated, had any influence over these investment strategies. Among these semiskilled migrants only two had saved about 1,500 Egyptian pounds, and with the help of their wives, they established very small corner shops. Another three older men had bought small kiosks to sell sweets and vegetables. Their wives also worked in these businesses.

Since the savings for a majority of the less-skilled migrants were too small to be invested in land or businesses, obtaining durable household goods, such as refrigerators, was the most common method of investing.[30] This strategy, unlike many depictions of migrants in the media, was not an example of conspicuous consumption and extravagance but in the context of life in these neighborhoods an economically rational investment decision. First, it meant a higher standard of living for the family. Second, the families drew prestige and power by sharing the use of these items with the neighbors and other members of their social network. Third, and most important, they could sell these items for cash when the need arose, especially since electric goods did not lose their value during periods of high inflation.[31]

Impact of Migration on the Wives' Labor Market Participation

Among urban low-income households, women's engagement in the cash market often facilitated the husbands' migration, since their income eliminated worries about the day-to-day needs of the family. Moreover, migration in some cases had encouraged some wives to engage in cash-earning activities, albeit temporarily until the husbands could send money. The ultimate desire of many women in low-status jobs, however, was to give up their cash-earning activities, especially since these jobs provided no security, health insurance, or old-age pension. The loss of cash for the family was often compensated for by more efficient shopping and management of the family resources (Hoodfar forthcoming). Leaving the labor market also often meant that women gained greater access to their husbands' incomes, while at the same time they did not have to carry double workloads.[32] Moreover, such a move was a public declaration of the household's success and an indication of its higher socioeconomic position.

However, in all cases where the families had managed to invest their remittances in establishing small corner shops or kiosks, the wives played very important roles in running the business, whether or not they had had prior experience. In two cases, the husbands returned to their jobs abroad while the wives took over the business. In other cases the wives' services were indispensable to the husbands, who held other jobs in addition to their businesses, as is prevalent among men in Cairo. Though the wives were not directly paid, they became their husbands' business partners, which afforded them more decision-making power and greater access to the households' cash income.

Those wives employed in the formal sector remained employed despite their complaints about low government wages. Because many of their husbands had stopped contributing housekeeping money on a regular basis, even after their return, those women who were eligible took one or two years of leave without pay in order to force their husbands to resume responsibility for the everyday expenses of the family. They often justified their action by claiming that they needed to devote more time to their husbands and children. Once they had established a new pattern of budgeting under which the husbands resumed their financial support of the household, they would return to their jobs. Although no woman in this group had given up her employment, these wives felt that migration had a negative impact on their roles in the households. Prior to the migration, they felt, their wages, which were in many cases comparable to their husbands', had given them status equal to their husbands'. However, migration had increased the income and resources which husbands brought into the household, rendering their wives' contributions insignificant.[33] Many wives in this group felt that migration had afforded their children and themselves a higher standard of living but at the cost of their status. Many of the younger, educated wives were discouraged; they questioned whether men and women could be equals and whether education and employment had really changed their position in comparison to their mothers, after all.

Changes in Gender Roles and Power
Relations within the Household

Distribution of power within the household in any society is influenced by factors beyond the household. The power and status that husbands and wives enjoy in the wider society influence their relationships within the household. Since the balance of power within the household is partly constrained by factors beyond the wife's and husband's control, this area is a complex field for social investigation (McDonald 1980; Dube et al. 1986).

Nonetheless, it has been demonstrated that in many societies there tends to be a positive correlation between those more concrete aspects of power, such as access to household resources, and those recognized material and nonmaterial contributions made by individuals to their household (Sanday 1981). The evaluation of an individual contribution to one's household is influenced by at least three different but overlapping factors. The first and most commonly recognized is the actual utility of a contribution. Second is the ideological value that a society attributes to a particular contribution. For instance, in most modern societies a cash contribution, regardless of its actual utility, is given much more importance than subsistence production or child care, which in many societies still plays a more significant role in the material well-being of households (Goldschmidt-Clermont 1982, 1987). The third factor, which is related to the second, is the value that the contributor attributes to his or her own contribution and the extent to which the contributor demands recognition for it. It is in the interplay of these factors, as well as in the actual level of contributions, that I have looked for evidence of change.

Most women in the neighborhoods were socialized to see themselves as inherently domesticated and to underestimate their ability to perform tasks beyond the boundaries defined as domestic. They were encouraged to see motherhood, within marriage, as their most valuable and relevant social role and their source of power, security, and status.[34] Consequently, from early childhood they strove to become and to acquire the reputation for being a good marriage partner. They were educated to avoid violating norms of gender roles as well as to be honorable, compromising, and supportive of the male head of household.

Since a woman's chastity had a crucial influence on the honor of both her own family and her husband's, she was, as a general rule, prevented from going beyond her neighborhood unaccompanied. I often heard men publicly praise young women who knew, or more often pretended to know, nothing of the world outside the four walls of their home and who acted hopelessly unable to perform any task beyond the traditional female domain. Other women expressed fear or unease at the idea of having to leave their familiar environments to enter into an alienating and unfamiliar outside world.

As in most urban neighborhoods, this general picture was somewhat disturbed by regional diversities and the fast pace of social change. Clearly, women of the Delta, particularly women from Old Cairo, were expected to be much more assertive and aggressive in defending their household's interest—though within their traditional roles as wives and mothers (Tucker 1985; El-Messiri 1978)—than their counterparts from central and upper Egypt. In recent times, schooling and employment had taken some women to the wider world, opening up other alternatives to the more conventional female roles.

The conventional mentality, however, came increasingly into conflict with the reality of daily life in lower-income neighborhoods. More and more, public and formal domains had impinged on the private. Families needed to interact with not only kin and friends but also with state institutions that were geographically distant. Since the men of low-income groups were principally engaged in meeting their families' cash needs, women were forced to assume other responsibilities. Thus many urban married women, even prior to their husbands' migration, had acquired some ability to deal with hospitals, government co-ops, schools, and so on. Often they viewed this as only helping their husbands.

The absence of husbands for months and years at a time created a new situation. Not only did wives have to take on many new duties but they had to accept responsibility for the decisions and direction of their households. Those husbands who sent money to their families sent it directly to the wives and in their names. Several women had to deal with banks and post offices for the first time. One woman said that the first time she went to the post office she didn't know which way to look. Another woman, from a rural background, managed to obtain a ration card, a task her husband had failed at despite many attempts. She explained to me:

> Everything is so expensive at market price, and it was getting harder to manage the household after my husband migrated. I had no choice but to spend days going to the police station and many other offices until I finally got the ration card.[35]

Many women had to find ways to overcome their inability to read and write and had to learn how to manipulate the system. Some of the informants proudly claimed that they had learned everything, and that all the women from the neighborhood came to them for advice.

Despite some confusion during the initial period of adjustments, most informants, particularly the less-educated women, were amazed to find themselves more capable than they had imagined. Their self-perception had changed, and this change had influenced their relationships with their husbands, children, and the broader community. The words of Umm Ahmad, a thirty-two-year-old illiterate woman who had to learn to deal with hospitals, the post office, the police, and the Ministry of Education, summed up this new attitude:

> I was brought up to be a "woman," but nowadays everyone has to be a "man." I learned the hard way, but I'm raising my daughters to be "men" so that they can take care of themselves and not be dependent on others.

All informants recognized that the change had not been easy, but none regretted it. Male migration, particularly among the less-skilled and less-privileged migrants, had brought the significance of a wife's contributions to the attention of the husbands, the community, and the wives themselves, thus shifting the power equation somewhat in favor of wives.

Most men in Egypt have always lived with their families and have been provided with domestic services, first by their mothers and then by their wives. These services often go unappreciated. But when men went to work in the Arab oil-producing countries, for the first time they had to take care of themselves. Returned migrants were full of stories about how things went wrong when they first made tea or tried to cook or wash their clothes.[36] The experience of less-skilled migrants was much more acute than that of the middle classes and the more educated, who were often provided with housing and other facilities and whose higher income made it possible to buy such services. To minimize the cost of living, the unskilled Egyptian worker usually lived in a group of at least four in one small room with few or no facilities.[37] Such conditions forced him to recognize and appreciate his wife's services and the pleasures of family life. As one migrant told me,

> The work was so hard and people treated us so badly. Not that work was easy here but Egyptians do not treat people as disrespectfully as the Saudis and Libyans. Often as I went to my place, tired and exhausted, I dreamed of coming home and children greeting me and Umm Ahmad [his wife] calling Nahed [his older daughter] to bring me tea and the young ones coming to see if I have any sweets or fruit for them.

This phenomenon, which I have termed the "recovery of forgotten assets" on the part of husbands, coincided with women's higher self-confidence and boosted their position within the household. The result, as many of the wives pointed out, was the improvement of the husband-wife relationship and the prevalence of a more cohesive atmosphere at home.

The small group of educated and employed women had a different experience. Prior to the migration of their husbands, educated women had already achieved many of the characteristics which less-educated and more conventional women attained during the migration process, positive self-awareness particularly. Migration had often meant only more responsibilities for them. The educated women had hoped for and expected a different kind of marriage than that of their mothers and their less-educated counterparts. "Modernist ideology," which underlay formal education, had suggested to them a more equal partnership and companionship in marriage. However, migration had undermined this aspect of their marriage, partly because of the geographical distances but more importantly because it created a large gap between the wives' financial contributions and those of their husbands, upsetting the balance in favor of the husbands. Some of the wives, hoping to enter a marriage which was more of an equal partnership, had carefully assessed this balance and at the time had rejected richer and better-educated suitors in favor of suitors whose credentials were closer to their own. In trying to explain how her relationship with her husband had changed after migration, Umm Abiir, at a gathering with two colleagues from different neighborhoods whose husbands had also migrated, explained to me:

> Not that he did a lot of housework before. You know, men in our part of the world do not help their wives very much. But we often came home at the same time and he was considerate and would ask me if I needed anything from the shop or if I liked him to make a salad or set the table. He knew I was working like he was. But now he comes home and announces he is hungry and expects me to get the food ready for him immediately. If I complain, he says if you can't look after your home and work, give up your work. Moreover, then, everything we wanted to buy we would talk it over and decide together but now I don't know how much he earns or has in his savings account. One day he comes home with a new tape recorder and the week after, he may bring a new dress for our daughter without ever asking me if that is what she needs.

Her guest Umm Samir added:

> You know, the problem is that we cannot complain about this to anybody but ourselves. Because if we tell others they think we have to be grateful that he buys us anything at all. Other men go and marry a second wife or things like that. They are not educated and do not understand the kind of relationship we had and we hope to continue to have in our marriage.

Though the educated wives recognized that with the considerable changes in the economic conditions in Egypt, migration was the only possible way to compensate for the low pay of government jobs and to improve their standard of living, they regretted the change nevertheless.

Cultural Impact of Migration

The cultural impact of migration has been a preoccupation of many social scientists (Ibrahim 1982; Furnham and Bochner 1986). The question is whether, and to what degree, the cultural practices of the host countries might influence the values and social practices of the migrants while they are in the host countries and when they return to their homeland. In the case of Middle Eastern countries, these preoccupations have focused particularly on women's roles and codes of behavior. For instance, it has been suggested that Turkish migration to Western Europe might encourage more positive attitudes among the migrants toward women's education and participation in the labor market (Abadan-Unat 1986; Brouwer and Priester 1983). By inference, migration to the Gulf countries, particularly Saudi Arabia, where a severe sexual segregation and restrictive behaviorial code in the name of Islam prevails, could encourage similar values in countries which export Muslim labor. The data have been inconclusive, however.[38] Brouwer and Priester (1983) found that among Turkish families living in Amsterdam, many of the women were employed but their movements and social interaction were more controlled by their husbands than when they lived in Turkey. In addition, they had lost the support of their kin and the women's networks which they traditionally enjoyed back in Turkey. On the other hand, Myntti (1984) has observed that in North Yemen the wives of successful migrants to the Gulf countries adopted a more secluded lifestyle.

My data from Egypt, however, suggest that the impact of other cultures is primarily a function of the immigrants' position in their home country. Many married migrants returning from Saudi Arabia considered the strict segregation and code of conduct surrounding women to be very unnatural. As one informant put it, "Perhaps it is good for them but we are Egyptians and we have our own ways." Another migrant told me:

> If the Saudis were poor they would have a very hard time. I cannot imagine what I would do if my wife was as *useless* as the Saudi Arabian women are. How could I leave her in charge of the family and children and migrate to earn money? God forbid that a Saudi woman lose her husband and brothers; she would have to lie down and die. She cannot shop or work or take her children to the hospital. She cannot even talk to a man. . . . I think we are lucky that our women are *almost* as capable as men.

However, the younger men who had migrated to earn enough money to marry had a more positive response to the new practices. One young and educated man who had returned from Saudi Arabia after four years said:

> God has put men in charge of women and they should remain in charge of them. Saudis have obeyed God's rule and they have been blessed with so much oil they do not have to work like us.

He tried to force his two sisters to wear the veil. After a period of tension, his mother intervened and said that the girls would not have to veil until they found suitors, and the brother finally agreed. However, he chose a wife who, by neighborhood standards, was considered very modern and was working in a fashionable boutique. A week after the engagement he accompanied his fiancée on a trip with her family to Alexandria to buy a bathing suit, although when I talked to him later he still believed women should cover themselves and stay home.

I learned of several other cases of young men returning to marry in Egypt and demanding that the brides take the veil. A suitor with enough cash to marry fast rather than having to wait for years while accumulating the necessary funds is hard for many marriageable young women to refuse. They often agree to marry but find ways of accommodating to the new demands. A bride who initially had resisted veiling explained her change of heart by saying that "obviously he was responsible and family-oriented because he already had suffered for a few years to provide a good life for his future wife." However, it is not clear that such demands on the part of returned migrants are the result of their exposure to the more segregated Gulf society, since many other men who were not migrants made similar demands (Hoodfar 1991). What seems to lead grooms to make such demands is their much greater material contribution to the marriage, to the establishment of the new household, and to the upkeep of the family.

Male Migration, Women's Power, and Traditional Gender Roles

Studies of the impact of male migration on the position of women must take into consideration other important variables such as age, social class, education, rural versus urban context, and the duration of migration. My data indicate that contrary to commonsense expectations, the less-educated and more traditional wives tended to gain more decision-making power over family resources, notably their husbands' income, as a result of their husbands' migration. It afforded them an opportunity to extend the domains in which they can contribute to the household, while remaining financially dependent on their husbands. Their new managerial skills and their experience outside the immediate domain of the family gave the more traditional women a new self-confidence and a new status which affected their position in the household positively. However, such changes should not be taken as synonymous with a fundamental change in perception of gender relations within the wider society.

Such transformations occur only when the changes have worked their way into the commonsense knowledge and world view of the society at large.[39]

In contrast, the more educated women, all white-collar employees with incomes often comparable to those of their husbands prior to migration, not only lost access to their husbands' incomes but experienced a sharp decline in participation in family decision making. These women had hoped for and in many cases had managed to establish marital unions which afforded them more equal relationships with their husbands. Their claim to equality, however, had been based on their cash contributions and did not embrace any other major changes in the domestic division of labor. Migration had changed the balance of cash contribution in favor of their husbands, who after years of geographical separation often did not feel the same affinity for their wives as they did before the migration. These changes were a source of regret on the part of these wives despite their recognition of the material advantages of migration.

Ironically, male migration, which had put women in the unconventional position of heading their own households, regardless of whether it resulted in more or less power for the wives, has also strengthened the more traditional marriage ideology in which the husband remains the unequivocal breadwinner and the wife the financially dependent mother and homemaker. This situation has raised doubts in the minds of many young women about whether it is possible at all or even wise for women to aspire and strive for a different and more flexible sexual division of labor than the traditionally ascribed one. Migration may have resulted in the "feminization of the Egyptian family" (Ibrahim 1982, 92), but it has also reaffirmed the essence of the traditional gender ideology, which perpetuates the situation in which women are financially dependent upon their male folk, despite some superficial changes in the realm of activities they may perform.

NOTES

1. A shorter version of this chapter was published in *Sociological Bulletin, Journal of the Indian Sociological Society* 22, nos. 1 and 2 (Fall 1993). I have benefited greatly from the comments of Dr. F. C. Shorter, Dr. Roger Owen, Dr. M. N. Panini, and Dr. B. Baviskar.

2. There are no reliable figures as to the actual number of Egyptian migrant workers. Fergany (1987) estimates that 2.8 million Egyptians participated in migration for employment purposes during 1974–1984. He also reckons that 23.7 percent of migrants are accompanied by some or all members of their family (p. 23). For an overview

of the literature on Egyptian migration, see Amin and Awny (1985). For more recent debates and perspectives, see El-Sayed Said (1990) and Sell (1988).

3. This study was part of a larger project on the survival strategies of lower-income Cairene women, the partial result of which is discussed in chapter 1 of this volume. As is the rule with many anthropological studies, snowballing was a major method of meeting my informants. During my residence in the neighborhood, I met many more migrant families, but for the purpose of this study I focus mostly but not entirely on households in the early or middle stages of their family cycles.

4. In this study I have defined a migrant's household as one whose husband had been out of the country in search of employment for at least twelve months.

5. Many households may temporarily or occasionally permanently incorporate kin, including mothers-in-law, who live under the auspices of the husband and the wife. Therefore in terms of power structure, these households resemble nuclear rather than the conventional patrilocal extended households, where the younger couples live under the control of the husbands' mothers and fathers.

6. Fergany's nationwide study has confirmed the universality of this view (1987, 18).

7. Many informants mentioned that the Gamal Abdel Nasser government had not been interested in bringing dollars to the country but wanted to be the big brother of the Arab countries. In contrast, Anwar Sadat had realized that Egypt and Egyptians needed dollars to improve their lives, and therefore made it possible for all educated and noneducated persons to work. Interestingly, many respected Nasser for his view and his nationalism but thought Sadat had been more realistic and agreed with him. As well, they rarely failed to mention that the Libyan government had expelled thousands of Egyptian migrants every time a conflict arose between the governments of Egypt and Libya.

8. Fergany's national study indicates that almost 60 percent of urban migrants were married, with an average of 3.65 dependents (1987, 10).

9. Marriages of two couples who had not had children before migration broke down while I was in the field. Of three couples who had only one child, one lived through a period of uncertainty before their differences were finally patched up after migration. The second wife, whose husband had been away for five years, was not sure if her husband was ever going to resume their marriage, though she thought he would pay for her and her daughter's upkeep.

10. There were many troubling stories about the hardships and problems that migrants faced and their frequent abuse at the hands of the authorities. There is no national institution which protects the rights of Egyptian migrants in the host countries.

11. Among women of low-income social strata, a few precious items, usually a piece or two of gold jewelry which they acquired at the time of marriage, are the only property they possess and to part with them signifies a great sacrifice.

12. Both men and women are socialized to view living on one's own as very undesirable. For women, however, the situation is more complex, because living alone often means a much more restricted life under the watchful eyes of the community.

13. This too is a mixed blessing, because the guests would not be expected to contribute to the cost of his/her own upkeep, thereby making it difficult for the family to save much (which is the logic behind male migration in the first place).

14. Brink (1991, 205–206), who worked in a village near Cairo, alludes to a similar pattern there. These findings contradict the common assumption that within the patrilineal family structure, in the absence of a husband, his wife has to live under the supervision of his close kin.

15. A considerable number of less-educated migrants from low-income neighborhoods migrated without a secure job in the host country.

16. The desire for flexibility stems in part from these women's living conditions. For instance, even in a neighborhood which was theoretically connected to the main water supply, due to shortages the water ran usually only at night and not every night. As well, very often they experienced power outages during the day and early part of the evening.

17. In fact, it is not uncommon for both older and younger women who are well trained and can earn more than their husbands to migrate alone, leaving their families behind. While in the field, I came to know a nurse who had left her husband and six-month-old baby and migrated for a year to Kuwait. Another woman had gone to Saudi Arabia as a hairdresser, leaving her three children of six, eight, and twelve years with her husband. I also learned of a few other married women who had spent time abroad on their own as teachers and maids.

18. Many fathers leave at six in the morning and do not return until nine or ten in the evening. Given the low wages and the state of job insecurity they face, many of them work even on Fridays, which is their religious holiday.

19. The father's absence in some cases had resulted in a more democratic family structure, where the mother was more open with the adolescent children about the family finances and the children responded with more understanding and support for their mother's position.

20. My observations in Egypt diametrically oppose those of Kudat (1975, 90), who in studying the Turkish case wrote that alienation occurs between parents and children left behind, since children come to view their parents not as providers of love and affection but as providers of goods. While such an interpretation may apply at higher levels of living, it is hard to relate it to the life of low-income families in Cairo.

21. Some researchers have suggested that in the countryside the children, particularly the sons, are kept home to shoulder some of the responsibilities of their absent fathers (Khafagi 1984; Muaty 1984). This may explain part of such a tendency, but the fact remains that education beyond reading and writing is no longer a means of access

to better-paid jobs. Moreover, the rate of boys' dropout above the primary school level is a national phenomenon.

22. National data show a sharp increase in women's rate of high school completion during the eighties (CAPMAS 1986).

23. For instance, married women who were government employees were entitled to take two years' leave of absence without pay for each of the first three children born to them, and married women could demand to work at the office nearest their home. Many women did utilize these rights.

24. Two major factors prevent the kin from living nearby, a traditional preference. First, the shortage of housing in old quarters of Cairo forces the younger generation to move to the outskirts of the city at the time of establishing their own households. Second, many of the inhabitants of the neighborhoods were rural migrants with many of their kin still living in the countryside.

25. The exceptions were when the husbands and wives were close relatives, i.e., cousins.

26. Traditional Egyptian mores and Middle Eastern mores in general do not specify a period within which people need to return a favor. The return may be delayed sometimes for a generation or two.

27. These lots were normally five by eight meters or less in size. The land was composed of farmland and village lots one or two hours' travel time from Cairo proper which were divided and sold informally. The price of the land decreased in inverse relation to the distance from Cairo. The prices in 1985–1986 ranged from 2,000 to 5,000 Egyptian pounds.

28. Information about exchange rates and channels for getting the best prices had become part of these wives' casual conversation.

29. On this point, see Wikan (1985) and Khattab and El-Daeif (1982).

30. The migrants often returned with small electrical items, but they generally preferred to buy the cheaper Egyptian-made stoves, refrigerators, etc. This often meant that women had a say or, more likely, that they made the purchase.

31. The critical view of the consumption patterns of the migrants' households is at least partly fueled by the fact that many of these electrical household goods, until a decade ago, were considered middle-class markers. However, the remittances as well as higher labor wages, which are at least partly caused by curbing the supply of labor through external migration, have made these items more widely available and therefore have blurred these class boundaries. In fact, Fergany (1987, 25–30), in his nationally representative survey of migrant households, found that expenditure patterns in migrant households are similar to those in nonmigrant households in the same income bracket.

32. As participants in the informal market they all could resume business if their financial situation deteriorated.

33. The husbands of these wives were also among the better-educated and more successful migrants.

34. For boys the roles of father and provider go hand in hand, so they are encouraged to find ways of earning money in order to be good fathers.

35. Reissuing a ration card involves a complicated bureaucratic procedure (Khouri-Daghar 1986), and many families who had moved from other regions to Cairo had given up hope of ever getting their ration cards transferred. Therefore they could not take advantage of subsidized food.

36. Other researchers have reported similar cases (Khattab and El-Daeif 1982; Khafagi 1984).

37. The experience of Gulf migrants differs from that of migrants to Europe, where launderettes and other facilities are more available. Moreover, migrants to Europe have, at least theoretically, easier access to leisure facilities, and their segregation from the host society is less overt.

38. For a short review of the Egyptian studies, see Amin and Awny (1985, 59–187). For a review of Turkish studies, see Keyder and Aksu-koc (1988, 129–134) and Abadan-Unat (1986).

39. By common sense, I am referring to the part of collective knowledge and shared world view based on the experiences of a people or a social group.

WORKS CITED

Abadan-Unat, Nermin. 1986. *Women in the Developing World: Evidence From Turkey.* Monograph Series in World Affairs. Denver: University of Denver.

Amin, Galal A., and Elizabeth Awny. 1985. *International Migration of Egyptian Labor: A Review of the State of Art.* Ottawa: International Development Research Center (1DRC-MR 108e).

Brink, Judy H. 1991. "The Effect of Emigration of Husbands on the Status of Their Wives: An Egyptian Case." *International Journal of Middle East Studies* 23: 201–211.

Brouwer, Lenie, and Marijke Priester. 1983. "Living in Between: Turkish Women in Their Homeland and in the Netherlands." In *One Way Ticket: Migration and Female Labor,* ed. Annie Phizlackea. London: Routledge & Kegan Paul.

CAPMAS (Central Agency for Public Mobilization and Statistics). 1986. *Statistical Yearbook: Arab Republic of Egypt, 1952–1985.* Cairo: CAPMAS.

Dube, Leela, Eleanor Leacock, and Shirley Ardener, eds. 1986. *Visibility and Power: Essays on Women in Society and Development.* Delhi: Oxford University Press.

Fergany, Nader. 1987. "Differentials in Labor Migration, Egypt (1974–1984)." Occasional Paper, no. 4. Cairo Demographic Center, Cairo.

Furnham, Adrian, and Stephen Bochner. 1986. *Culture Shock: Psychological Reaction to Unfamiliar Environments.* London: Methuen.

Goldschmidt-Clermont, Luisella. 1982. *Unpaid Work in the Household: A Review of Economic Evaluation Methods.* Women, Work and Development Series, no. 1. Geneva: ILO.

———. 1987. *Economic Evaluations of Unpaid Household Work: Africa, Asia, Latin America and Oceania.* Women, Work and Development Series, no. 14. Geneva: ILO.

Hoodfar, Homa. 1988. "Patterns of Household Budgeting and Management of Financial Affairs in a Lower-Income Neighbourhood in Cairo." In *A Home Divided: Women and Income in the Third World*, ed. Daisy Dwyer and Judith Bruce. Stanford: Stanford University Press.

———. 1991. "Return to the Veil: Personal Strategy and Public Participation in Egypt." In *Working Women: International Perspectives on Labor and Gender Ideology*, ed. Nanneke Redclift and M. Thea Sinclair. London: Routledge.

———. 1995. "The Impact of Male Migration on Money Management and Domestic Budgeting: Egyptian Women Striving for an Islamic Budgeting Pattern." Manuscript.

———. Forthcoming. "Women in Cairo's (In)visible Economy: Linking Local and National Data." In Richard Lobban, ed., *Women in the Informal Economy*, Gainesville: University of Florida Press.

Ibrahim, Saad Eddin. 1982. *The New Arab Social Order: A Study of the Social Impact of Oil.* Boulder: Westview Press.

Kagitcibasi, Cigdem. 1984. "Alienation of the Outsider: The Plight of Migrants." Paper presented at the conference "Urban Alienation: The Search for De-Alienation Strategies," Columbus, Ohio.

Keyder, Caglar, and Ayhan Aksu-Koc. 1988. *External Labor Migration from Turkey and Its Impact: An Evaluation of the Literature.* Ottawa: International Development Research Center (MR 185e).

Khafagi, Fatma. 1984. "Women and Labour Migration: One Village in Egypt." *MERIP Reports*, June, 17–21.

Khattab, Hind Abou Seoud, and Syada Greiss El-Daeif. 1982. "Impact of Male Migration on the Structure of Family and the Roles of Women." Regional Papers, no. 16. Population Council, Giza.

Khouri-Dagher, Nadia. 1986. "Food and Energy in Cairo: Provisioning the Poor." Report prepared for the Food-Energy Nexus Program, United Nations University, Paris.

Kiray, Mubeccel. 1976. "The Family of the Immigrant Worker." In *Turkish Workers in Europe, 1960–1975*, ed. Nermin Abadan-Unat. Leiden: E. J. Brill.

Kudat, Ayse. 1975. "Structural Changes in the Migrant Turkish Family." In *Manpower Mobility across Cultural Boundaries*, ed. Ronald E. Krane. Leiden: E. J. Brill.

McDonald, G. W. 1980. "Family Power: The Assessment of a Decade of Theory and Research, 1970–1979." *Journal of Marriage and Family*, 841–854.

Messiri, Sawsan el-. 1978. "Self-Images of Urban Traditional Women in Cairo." In *Women in the Muslim World*, ed. Lois Beck and Nikki Keddie. Cambridge: Harvard University Press.

Muaty, Abdel A. 1984. "Some Social Aspects of Rural Labor Migration to Arab Oil Countries." In *Proceedings of the Conference on the Organization of Egyptian Labor Migration*, Cairo, January.

Myntti, Cynthia. 1984. "Yemeni Workers Abroad: The Impact on Women." *MERIP Reports* 124.

Nadim, Nawal al-Messiri. 1985. "Family Relationships in a Harah in Old Cairo." In *Arab Society: Social Science Perspectives*, ed. Saad E. Ibrahim and Nicholas S. Hopkins. Cairo: American University in Cairo Press.

Sanday, Peggy R. 1981. *Female Power and Male Dominance: On the Origins of Sexual Inequality*. Cambridge: Cambridge University Press.

El-Sayed Said, Mohamed. 1990. "The Political Economy of Migration in Egypt: 1974–1989." West Asia and North Africa Regional Papers, no. 36. Population Council, Cairo.

Sell, Ralph R. 1988. "Egyptian International Labor Migration and Social Processes: Towards Regional Integration." *International Migration Review* 22, no. 3: 87–108.

Shorter, Frederic. 1989. *Cairo's Leap Forward: People, Households, and Dwelling Space*. Cairo Papers in Social Science, no. 12, Monograph 1. Cairo: American University in Cairo Press.

Singerman, Diane. 1990. "Politics at the Household Level in a Popular Quarter of Cairo." *Journal of South Asian and Middle Eastern Studies* 23, no. 4: 3–21.

———. 1995. *Avenues of Participation: Family, Politics, and Networks in Urban Quarters of Cairo*. Princeton: Princeton University Press.

Taylor, Elizabeth. 1984. "Egyptian Migration and Peasant Wives." *MERIP Reports*, June.

Tucker, Judith. 1985. *Women in Nineteenth-Century Egypt*. London: Cambridge University Press.

Wikan, Unni. 1985. "Living Conditions among Cairo's Poor: A View From Below." *Middle East Journal* 39, no. 1: 7–26.

Yasa, I. 1979. *Yurda Donen Isciler Ve Toplumsal Degisme* [Returned Workers and Social Change]. Ankara: Todaie Yayini. Quoted in Keyder and Aksu-Koc 1988.

4

WHAT'S THE USE?

The Household, Low-Income Women, and Literacy

K. R. KAMPHOEFNER

EDUCATION CAN BE an empowering process; the eradication of ignorance improves the quality of life in essential ways. It can contribute to improved hygiene and health care and better child nutrition, for example. But while literacy and education may be essential to the improvement of living conditions, does it always have a positive impact? Does education necessarily result in the empowerment of women? Are there ways education makes women's lives more complicated, ways in which it may add to their burdens? Can education even be used to further exploit and oppress women? This chapter considers these issues in the context of Cairo.

The first part of this chapter provides historical background on the growth of education in Egypt, describes the role of the Egyptian state as the primary provider of education, and looks at obstacles in the school system which stand in the way of national literacy. The second part examines the views of illiterate women toward becoming educated. Their perspectives vary, depending largely on class position and practical circumstances within the household. Because women's educational goals often differ from those of the state, I suggest that this may help explain why few adult women attempt to become literate. As a society moves toward increased literacy, it undergoes a series of major economic, social, and cultural changes. The final part discusses the implications of the transition from orality to literacy in Egypt, in conjunction with changes in women's status and the national economy.

A Brief History of Education in Egypt

Among the central slogans of the 1952 Free Officers' Revolution that overthrew the monarchy in Egypt was a call for the eradication of illiteracy; adult education classes were subsequently established throughout the country. The formal educational system has since expanded, but illiteracy remains a serious obstacle to development in Egypt. Only 51 percent of the adult population is able to read and write; 37.8 percent of men and 62.2 percent of women are illiterate (CAPMAS and UNICEF 1993:113).

During the years 1952–1970, Egypt acquired a reputation throughout Africa and the Middle East as a leader in education. Indeed, the two major accomplishments associated with the Gamal Abdel Nasser era are the eradication of "feudalism" through its land reform program (Abdel-Fadil 1975), and the universalization of education. New schools were built throughout Egypt, with emphasis on bringing schools to rural areas and establishing free public schooling from the elementary to the university levels.

Under Anwar Sadat, universal education continued to be promoted as essential to Egypt's progress. However, one result of the shift in economic policy away from Arab socialism to Infitah (the Open Door Policy) and the reduction of the state role in providing welfare was the increased privatization of many sectors of the economy, which included the mushrooming of a new system of private schools. Many new foreign-language schools, teaching the full curriculum in English, French, or German, opened (Leila Kamel, personal communication, 1986).[1] These foreign-language schools did little to contribute to the economic and social development of Egypt; in fact, as educator Judith Cochran asserts,

> Foreign schools had not educated these [wealthy] Egyptians to have a concern for the poor with whom they shared neither common values, language nor social status. So while there were more Mercedes in Cairo than in Dallas, completed phone calls, sugar and potable water were luxuries for others. (1986:55)

Private schools met the needs of the wealthy population, while a combination of factors led to a decline in the quality of education in public schools. By the late 1970s, the quality of the public school system had so deteriorated that only the poorest of the poor were sending their children to government schools. Every family that could afford to do so sent its children to private schools (Leila Kamel, personal communication, 1986). Because the level of one's education has been the single most important determinant of one's class and social mobility since the Free Officers' Revolution, these new divisions between private and public schools have had significant social consequences for Egypt. Nasser's government did much to make education accessible to the poorer segments of society, making it, in turn, the most significant vehicle for social mobility for the Egyptian public. As Andrea Rugh has summed up,

To a considerable extent it [education] permits access to the opportunities that determine the level and distribution of individual incomes while qualifying people to reach valued social statuses. Prolonged education serves as the most significant division between the lower and middle social classes, more significant even than such economic factors as income levels. (1985:239)

Until the late 1970s, secondary school graduates could expect to find positions as government clerks, and college graduates were guaranteed government employment, which meant job security and middle-class status. Today, this has changed dramatically; as the state has ceased to expand, there are fewer employment opportunities for an ever-increasing number of university graduates. Furthermore, civil service salaries (ranging from the equivalent of U.S. $30 to $75 per month) have fallen significantly below private sector salaries for comparable jobs, making them less appealing to those in search of employment. At the same time, a shift has occurred; in the new economic situation, the *hirafiyiin* (tradesworkers: furniture makers, auto mechanics, carpenters, plumbers, painters, etc.), who have little or no formal education, are earning much higher incomes than educated government employees (Singerman 1995).

This has made formal education less attractive, especially for those who cannot afford the cost of private education. Hence there are high rates of school dropouts and a growing illiteracy problem. Despite efforts aimed toward universal education, the absolute number of illiterate people continues to grow, though percentages decline; the number of illiterate women increased from fifteen million in 1976 to seventeen million in 1986 (CAPMAS and UNICEF 1993); see table 1.

Given the importance of the role of literacy in contemporary developed societies, Egypt would have to first introduce corrective measures to curb the growth of illiteracy and then introduce effective adult literacy programs. Besides economic conditions, a myriad of problems within the school system contribute to the growing illiteracy problem; the most important of these are logistical and organizational problems, teacher-related problems, dropout and nonenrollment problems, problems with curriculum and pedagogy, and the hidden costs of education.

Logistical and Organizational Problems

Owing to a shortage of school buildings, in the 1980s, the majority of Cairo's schools held two or more daily shifts of classes (Swanson et al. 1981, 71), meaning some students had only three hours of instruction per day. By the early 1990s, only about 30 percent of students attended a full day's program of

Table 1. Adult Literacy Rates in Egypt, 1937–1986

Census Year	Illiterate Males Number	%	Illiterate Females Number	%	Total Number	% of Popultation
1937	4,468,422	76.6	5,416,858	93.8	9,885,280	85.2
1947	4,443,348	64.3	5,964,624	84.3	10,407,972	74.5
1960	5,048,662	56.2	7,539,024	83.1	12,587,686	69.7
1966	5,591,000	50.0	8,072,000	76.0	13,373,000	63.0
1976	5,726,187	42.0	9,367,828	71.0	15,094,015	56.0
1986	6,807,171	37.8	10,357,455	62.2	17,160,672	49.4

Source: CAPMAS and UNICEF 1993, 113.

classes, while 48 percent were attending two-shift schools and 1.1 percent were still in three-shift schools.[2] This situation deteriorated further because of damage caused by the October 1992 earthquake (CAPMAS and UNICEF 1993, 111). Classes with sixty to seventy-five pupils remain fairly common.[3]

A general lack of facilities and equipment has diminished the quality and relevance of education and contributed to students' reasons for dropping out. The lack of opportunity for hands-on experience with new technologies is problematic; in science classes, for example, students must memorize the formulae for experiments that they never actually see or perform. Manual and technical training classes also lack even the most basic equipment for providing important practical experience.

Teacher-Related Problems

The distribution of teachers is another serious problem. New teachers are assigned to the public schools where they are most needed, but fewer college graduates are becoming public school teachers, preferring lucrative and prestigious private sector jobs. The shortage of teachers is exacerbated by the fact that many teachers take leaves of absence to migrate to the Gulf states for higher salaries.

Overall, however, the problem lies primarily with the quality of teaching. Teacher training programs have been too few, too brief, and generally inadequate for effective training. In addition, many teachers themselves do not have a high level of basic education. Prior to the 1988–89 school year, teachers were not required to be highly educated, and the Ministry of Education employed a large number of uncertified teachers.[4] Today, 85 percent of Egypt's teachers who entered the system prior to the 1988 educational reforms are poorly trained graduates of the two-year Teaching Institutes, and there is a real need to update and extend their skills (World Bank 1992, 4).[5]

If the educational system in Egypt is to attract more educated teachers, there needs to be a drastic rise in teachers' salaries. In 1991–92, monthly salaries ranged from 70 to 240 Egyptian pounds (World Bank 1992, 5), which does not cover even the basic needs of a family. "A teacher's salary is only 80 pounds per month. My *sufragi* [servant] makes 250," observed Dr. Horeya Abdel Aziz, a college professor of education in Cairo (personal interview, 1994). With entry-level jobs in the private sector starting at 600 Egyptian pounds or more, the system stands to lose talented potential teachers because public school salaries are so pitiful in comparison.[6]

Dropout and Nonenrollment Problems

Nonenrollment and students dropping out are significant problems. No system exists to track students who have never enrolled in school or who are truant, and the dropout rate appears to be rising. While enrollments have climbed steadily, so has the school-age population. Primary school enrollments increased to 74 percent of all school-aged children in 1966–67 (CAPMAS 1989, 102), 81 percent in 1986, and 84 percent in 1994.[7] Historically, boys have had higher enrollment rates than girls, who are more likely to drop out before completing primary school. Ministry of Education figures for 1988 showed that 74.1 percent of eligible girls (age six to eleven) were enrolled in elementary school compared with 88.1 percent of eligible boys (CAPMAS 1989, 105). From 1981 to 1990, primary school enrollment increased by 41 percent, with female enrollment up by 57 percent. Though 80 percent of school-age girls were enrolled in primary school by 1991 (Prosterman and Hanstad 1992, 16), this number does not indicate how many actually attended.

A study by Swanson reported reasons students gave for dropping out: 55 percent gave reasons related to family welfare or family preference; of these, 25.5 percent left school to enter the labor market or work at home and 12 percent gave reasons of illness, death, divorce, or other family circumstances. Others reported pedagogical factors as influencing their decision to drop out, including 22 percent who cited a failed grade, inability to understand the lessons, or fear of exams and 15.7 percent who expressed a general antipathy for school and teachers (Swanson et al. 1981, 11–12). More recently, it seems that over half of those who drop out do so for economic and social reasons, while 10–15 percent attributed leaving school to the irrelevance of the curriculum (World Bank 1992, 6).

The rate of the population growth in Egypt has declined to 2.3 percent, which is not significantly greater than the European rate of population growth (Fargues 1994, 7), however, 40 percent of Egyptians are under age fifteen, creating huge demands on the schools. Rural migration to the cities also adds to the number of urban schoolchildren. Despite the construction of new schools, the demand exceeds the number of school places available and is not likely to decrease until well into the next century, even assuming that Egypt's efforts to control population continue to succeed.

Although, officially, education is compulsory and there is even some structure in place to follow up on truancy, many obstacles prevent their being enforced. There are children who have never been issued birth certificates; many families live at unregistered addresses; and, most significantly, the government cannot afford to enforce universal enrollment and attendance when it is already drastically behind in providing places for children already enrolled. Cairo's population is increasing by a thousand every day and by a million every nine months, and one consultant's report concluded that "if mandatory attendance laws were fully enforced, the resulting intake of students would overwhelm the system" (Swanson et al. 1981, 2).

The growing number of schoolchildren means that despite increased spending on education, real spending per pupil (on items other than teachers' salaries) dropped from £E 7.1 in 1980 to £E 2.4 in 1990 (World Bank 1992, 6). The population growth of the last twenty years has meant a focus on absorbing more and more students into the schools while curriculum development, school maintenance, and the quality of teaching have suffered and "the system experienced an overall reduction in educational quality and effectiveness during that period" (World Bank 1992, 6). The needs of families, coupled with problems within the school system, are primary factors influencing the dropout rate and obstructing the achievement of universal education. Clearly the needs of the whole household must be considered in addressing the dropout problem. A work-study cooperative program might be one option, tying on-the-job training or an apprenticeship program to school attendance. This would allow children to continue their studies while gaining both practical training and income.

Problems with Curriculum and Pedagogy

Textbooks, while often beautifully illustrated, are poorly developed, poorly organized, and not adequately tailored to children's age levels. Very difficult material is assigned to be memorized in lower grades, and vocabulary levels are particularly unsuited to grade levels. Lessons are not organized into manageable units and do not provide sufficient repetition of concepts. Each lesson briefly presents new material with definitions and descriptions to be memorized. There are few exercises which apply the concepts presented in the textbooks, although exam questions sometimes require such practical understanding. Corporal punishment is a common means of discipline, and end-of-the-year examinations place severe constraints on teaching methods.

Homework and classroom work in the last two months of the school year focus on exam preparation, which in effect requires private tutoring. This system places great strain on family finances as well as being highly stressful for students. Students who fail the May exams are allowed to retake them in August. Students who fail them again in August either repeat the year or drop out. After age fourteen, a student can no longer repeat a year of primary education. So important are the year-end exams that during the months preceeding them the entire country seems focused on exam preparation. The failure rate for the government examinations is 15 percent per grade (Cochran 1986, 56). A 1986–87 study found that nearly 30 percent of students had dropped out by the end of primary school (CAPMAS and UNICEF 1993, 112). The dropout rates are higher in levels five and eight, as students leave rather than face the exams at the end of the primary and preparatory levels (Rugh 1981, 48). These dropouts are likely to lose many of the skills acquired in school, and eventually they lose the degree of literacy they had achieved.

The Hidden Costs of Education

The hidden costs of "free" education are many despite provisions made by the government. These range from costs for uniforms, stationery, workbooks in addition to those provided by the government, and the increasing cost of registration for final exams.[8] In addition, though, there are two greater hidden costs of education for the poor. First, there are the losses of income from the the labor of children who are in school. Second, because of the overcrowded classes and unskilled teachers, all-but-mandatory private lessons are essential for success at school, and their rising costs burden poor families further. Because the poor are unable to pay the fees for private lessons, their chances of getting ahead in school and later in society are reduced. As Katz has argued,

> Children from poor families do not receive this intensive one-on-one preparation and are therefore clearly less likely to achieve high marks on the

exams—tests that will, to a large extent, determine the future courses of their lives. (Quoted in Cochran 1986, 64)

In 1986, private lessons cost from £E 2.20 monthly (U.S. $1.20) for group lessons at the primary level to £E 15 ($8) an hour for individual tutoring at the secondary level. As Ansaf Asis, a social worker in Bulaq, told me, even poor families are under pressure to spend as much as £E 200 per month in private lesson fees in the months preceding the end-of-the-year exams (personal communication, July 1994). Middle-class parents spend much more, typically £E 3–8 ($1.50–$3.50) per hour for lessons as their children approach end-of-the-year examinations, in addition to private school fees. By 1994, group lessons had risen to £E 20 per month per student for groups as large as fifteen students (Leila Kamel, personal interview, 1994).

The prevalence of private lessons has undermined one of the original purposes of the examination system, which was to loosen the rigidity of the class structure through education.[9] Children of the poor, unable to afford adequate private lessons if any, fail examinations and drop out or score lower and are tracked into technical institutes at the secondary level, making them eligible only for lower-status jobs. To cut their losses, many students from low-income families drop out of the school system and join the labor market long before they acquire sufficient literacy skills. Thus the examination structure and the system of private lessons help perpetuate a cycle of illiteracy and poverty—a cycle Egypt has to break out of as its developing economy and society increasingly require a written culture. One response has been a shift in the focus of education toward addressing adult illiteracy.

The State of Adult Literacy Programming

With the call for the eradication of illiteracy, an adult literacy program has been introduced through the local schools and the educational system. Every school is required to assign one teacher each year to conduct adult classes, usually in the afternoon. But the funding for such classes is inadequate and the motivation of already overworked teachers to implement adult education successfully is lacking. In effect, this area is mostly left to the private sector, development agencies, churches and mosques, and social service organizations. Mosques and churches offer literacy classes and encourage people to read the Qur'an or the Bible. On the whole, the literacy education efforts that exist are far too few and are implemented in a fragmented way, with no overall plan. No umbrella organization to coordinate nationwide literacy programs existed until 1989. The United Nations Development Program (UNDP) is currently coordinating adult literacy strategies with various international organizations, including UNICEF, GTZ, UNESCO, and the Ford Foundation (World Bank 1992, 7).

To sum up, the educational system expanded dramatically in the years following the 1952 revolution, achieving large gains for the nation. But with the shifting of priorities under Sadat's leadership, the school system fell into disarray to eventually arrive at its current inadequate state. The percentage of the gross national product allocated to education did not increase significantly between 1975 and 1985, while Egypt's population increased from 37 million in 1975 to 48.5 million by 1985 (United Nations 1992). The complexity of the problems I have outlined demonstrates the dramatic decrease in the quality of public school education. A 1993 report published jointly by UNICEF and Egypt's Central Agency for Public Mobilization and Statistics (CAPMAS) summarizes the school situation:

> Educational effectiveness is low as a result of poor teaching standards and morale, limited and often inadequate instructional materials and incomplete implementation of curricula changes. There is uneven access to education, particularly for girls and poor children. The result is poor quality of education and teaching standards, and high repeat and dropout rates. There is continual low access to primary education particularly for the girl child, resulting in relatively high illiteracy rates for women. (CAPMAS and UNICEF 1993, 108).

The Relevance of Education to Gender Role Expectations

A further reason for the high dropout rate and prevailing illiteracy is that Egyptian educational content has taken little account of gender roles, rendering much of the acquired education irrelevant to the lives of men and women. This is particularly true where it concerns low-income women, a point I shall come back to in light of the interviews I conducted among low-income women. Low-income women generally cannot envisage having jobs as white-collar workers or even anywhere within the formal sector, and for this reason they do not stay in school. I observed that because of the lack of opportunity to utilize literacy skills, many women had effectively lost them, even those who had completed as many as six years of education, and thus contributed to the swelling ranks of illiterates in Egypt. A successful literacy program, particularly for adults depends highly on making such efforts relevant to the lives of the people who are to benefit from these programs.

Gender Roles—Tradition and Change

The pervasive gender role ideology of lower-class Egyptian society designates the husband as the primary breadwinner for the family, responsible for paying the rent and household expenses. Traditional married women manage the household, care for the children, and budget the allowance that their husbands provide to meet all the household needs, including household supplies, food, clothing, and children's school supplies. Education for men is seen as a rational economic investment, improving their opportunities for success in the job market. This ideal of complementary gender roles is severely strained by the realities of the Egyptian economy. Supporting a family when prices are constantly on the rise often means that husbands work two or three jobs.[10] Even then, the income is often insufficient. Consequently, many lower-class women also work outside the home in factory jobs or low-level service occupations. These economically trying times have changed women's roles outside the home and attitudes toward women's employment. While traditionally men considered it shameful for their wives to work, this is less true today, with additional income becoming essential. Women who have an education are gaining respect and are considered desirable candidates for marriage, since they can work and help support their families (Ibrahim 1980).

Despite these socioeconomic shifts, the power base for lower-class women continues to be the household. Anthropologist Evelyn Early noted in her ethnographic account of poor women in Cairo that "rules for gender interaction establish women's priority over domestic space (indeed, the man is *excluded* from his home at times) but female society flourishes there and beyond" (1980, 7). The Egyptian house is not "a man's castle, it is the woman's" (Early 1993, 67). Women control the home, which is their primary locus of activity, the arena for their socioeconomic status, and the source of their respect within the community. A woman's reputation is based largely on how well she manages her home, its resources, and her children, often on a very meager budget.

The immediate relevance of education to women's role in the household may be obscure at best. Very poor women are generally exclusively housewives and mothers, out of necessity and because there are few other options. The amount of work required to care for the home and children is phenomenal. Even in situations where a woman works full time outside the home, she must still labor long, hard hours after work to keep her household members fed, clean and clothed.

Women's Views

The following discussion of illiterate women's views on education is based on a content analysis of interviews I conducted with twenty-five illiterate and semiliterate women in 1986.[11] The women in this sample can be divided into two groups, women who work outside the household and women whose work is primarily within the household. Of the ten women who work outside their homes, nine are maids and one is a physician's assistant. The fifteen women who work at home were initially contacted at a social service center to which they went for nutritional supplements and occasional financial help; they represent the poorest of the poor in Cairo, their incomes being generally less than 50 Egyptian pounds monthly.

Nine women were Muslims and sixteen were Christians, and their ages ranged from twenty-seven to forty-five. Fifteen were married, four were widows, two were separated, three were divorced, and one had never married. The average family size in Egypt ranges from 3.6 in Port Said to 8.2 in the Fayoum (Fargues 1994, 8). The average number of children per family for this sample (6.6) exceeded the early 1980s average family size of 5.5 (Cochran 1986, 58). This is despite the fact that a relatively high number (ten) of the women in my sample were female heads of households. Limiting family size tended to be practiced more by the middle and upper classes; the educated have opted for smaller families, while the poor continued to produce big families. Economically, the working women were better off than the housewives. Zuzu, who worked as a doctor's assistant in a medical clinic, drew a salary slightly better (£E 150 monthly) than the women who worked as maids, but she supported four other persons: her daughter, her parents, and a younger sister, who was in school. Mona and Umm Eyman, both maids in wealthy homes, had some disposable income because they worked six days a week and did not support dependents (Mona had no children, and Umm Eyman's children were grown and working). Umm Eyman was a careful saver and invested her savings in gold bracelets for her retirement. At the time of the interview, she had recently purchased two new bracelets (worth about £E 300 each) to add to the three she already owned.

The housewives' economic conditions were, in contrast, much worse. Hoda's husband gave her only 30 £E (worth about $15 at the time of the interview) per month for child support, which went to feed Hoda, her two children, and her ailing mother. Her mother required so much care that Hoda could not work outside her home. The least advantaged housewives in this sample were Sayeda and Farida. Sayeda's husband gave her very little for household expenses and food for five young children. A social worker remarked that Sayeda's husband was "not a good man." Sayeda had the gaunt, hollow-cheeked appearance of malnutrition. Farida was a widow who also had five children, one of whom was disabled, requiring that she too remain at home. After her husband died, her eldest son left school to go to work. Both Farida and Sayeda, in their extreme poverty, had sent their eldest sons out to work. Sayeda's eldest boy was nine years old.

The women of the study were all from lower-class backgrounds, both urban and rural (see table 2). While illiteracy existed among all strata in Egypt, it was, and is, most common among this class, the *awlad al-balad* (El-Messiri 1978), the "traditional" people of Egypt. My estimate is that 90 percent of women of this class were illiterate. A 1983 government estimate reported that illiteracy among women in two rural governorates, Assuit and Fayoum, ran as high as 90 percent (Cochran 1986, 58). The women I am discussing were for the most part born in rural areas or were the daughters of migrants from rural Egypt. My experience revealed that virtually none of them could read or write, those who could were born in Cairo after 1960, when mass education began to be implemented. Several who had attended school through level six had not used their skills since leaving school and had forgotten how to read and write.

Thirteen of the women in this sample were born outside of Cairo; nine were from Upper Egypt (the Saʿiid) and four were from Lower Egypt (the Delta). Only two of the women born outside Cairo went to school as girls: Maha continued through the sixth level, whereas Assia attended only one year before her family migrated to Cairo and took her out of school for good. When these women were young, few villages had schools and educating girls was a new idea. Mona moved to Cairo at age eight, after the death of her father, but there was (and still is) no way to enter school at a later age if a child is not enrolled at age six. Mona started working at age ten.

Farida, although born in Cairo, is from a Saʿiidi (Upper Egyptian) family, and neither she nor her six sisters and brother went to school, because, she explained, "my father was Saʿiidi and he didn't support the idea of school." The stereotype of the Saʿayda (pl.) is that they are backward, traditionally conservative, and resistant to change. Statistically, fewer Saʿayda than Lower Egyptians have had formal education. Enrollment figures for school-age children (ages six to twelve) have historically been lower in the Saʿiid. For example, a

Table 2. Demographic Information on
Twenty-Five Lower-Class Women from Cairo

Name	Age	Household Size	No. of Children*	Marital Status	Years of Schooling†
Born in the Saʿiid					
Omneyya	27	7	5	Married	0
Assia	35	7	5	Married	1
Umm Hashim	35	9	7	Married	0
Hosnia	35	4	3	Married	0
Gameela	40	6	5	Married	0
Maha	42	6	5	Widowed	6
Nabeyya	44	6	5	Married	0
Umm Mikhail	46	9	7	Married	0
Janine	50	8	6	Married	0
Born in the Delta					
Mona	32	5	0	Single	0
Karima	40	2	0	Divorced	0
Zeinab	43	2	0	Divorced	0
Leila	55	4	3	Married	0
Born in the Cairo Metropolitan area					
Ayten	29	7	5	Married	6
Nashwa	30	6	3	Married	0
Zuzu	32	5	1	Divorced	6
Lateefa	32	3	3	Widowed	0
Hoda	35	7	2	Separated	6
Sayeda	35	6	5	Separated	6
Nafissa	35	6	4	Married	1
Farida	37	4	5	Widowed	0
Umm Eyman	40	3	3	Widowed	4
Umm Saaber	42	10	8	Married	0
Safy	43	8	5	Married	0
Umm Amaad	45	5	4	Married	0

*Includes only children living in the household at the time of the survey.
† Figures do not include years of adult education.

1979 report showed that the average enrollment rate for rural Upper Egyptian governorates was 58.7 percent of school-age children, compared with 70.25 percent for rural governorates in Lower Egypt (Human Resources Management August 1979, 75). In my sample, seven of the nine Saʿayda were never enrolled in school, while six of the twelve Cairo-born women attended school as girls. Ayten, Zuzu, Hoda, and Sayeda went through six years of primary school but didn't pass the end-of-the-level exam to continue on into preparatory school. Nafissa attended school only briefly before her father decided to take her out. Umm Eyman went to school until the fourth grade but said she didn't understand anything and today cannot read or write anything except her name. She said that because she had difficulty learning in school, her teachers would often beat her, and then her mother would beat her again when she got home. So, at age ten, she convinced her mother to let her stay home and help with the housework. At age twelve she was married.

Of the women who attended primary school (the conventional definition of literacy), only Zuzu seemed to be literate. Zuzu learned to sew in a manual arts training program after her second divorce and worked on basic reading and writing skills. She used reading and, to a limited extent, writing in her job. Sayeda could write her name but said she never learned to read and write in school and had difficulty with simple math. Assia said she reads, but I suspected it was only to a limited extent, since she went to only one year of school as a child. Hoda said she had forgotten most of what she learned because she hadn't used it since she left school.

Two of the literate women in the sample, Hosnia and Mona, had no education as children. Hosnia attained the equivalent of a fifth-grade education through two summer courses. Mona pursued all of her education in government-sponsored adult literacy classes. She attended classes periodically, completed primary and preparatory level certificates, and at the time of interview was working toward the secondary examination, which she had failed in a previous attempt. In order to retake it, she tackled the review of difficult texts in history, geography, math, science, Arabic, English, and French on her own. She seemed to enjoy learning for its own sake. "What do you want to read?" I asked her. She replied, "I don't know. I just want to know, I just want to be educated. I don't have any special idea of something I'd like to read or write. I want to know many things, like highly educated people, everything about my country, about other countries, about good or bad people." I asked her, "What would you do differently if you were educated? Could you get a better job?" Mona didn't think her education would help her find a better job. She hoped to get married and be able to stay at home and not have to work so hard. She explained:

> An educated woman knows how to talk to people, knows how to do everything in the house, how to raise the children. When she reads a book she can know everything about children, about the man, about everything—about herself as well. That's better. When a woman's not educated, it's very difficult. If she has children, it's difficult to help them with their studying. That's very difficult for them.

Hoda agreed that education was somewhat useful, but she hadn't used her reading and writing skills since she left school and didn't find these skills to be of immediate practical use. Sayeda was ambivalent about making any effort to become literate. She said she wished she could read and that she would love to be able to read newspapers and magazines like "the respected people" do, but the "world isn't just." She felt it was an impossible task for her to take on, though she felt literacy would allow her to help her children with their lessons. Umm Eyman was completely uninterested in learning to read or write anything, claiming she could not learn, "*mukhy maqful*" ("my mind is closed"). Gameela, Farida, and Lateefa similarly stated that education was not important for them.

The women's assessment of the value of education for themselves ranged from completely unimportant to highly important. The perceived need to learn to read and write was based largely on the women's occupations. Their immediate circumstances played a direct role in determining their attitudes toward becoming educated. Those working outside the home felt it was from moderately to very important, while the housewives saw very little point in becoming literate. The women who worked outside their homes wanted more schooling in order to obtain a *shahada* (a primary school certificate) so that they could get better jobs. This certificate is often required for factory jobs. These women saw formal sector employment as a step up; they perceived such jobs as easier and more secure. Factory positions provided a steady income, with benefits (as opposed to domestic work, which is very unpredictable and provides no social insurance). The housewives saw no need to become literate, which suggested that literacy skills were of little relevance to their role in the household.

The Ideal—Education as Highly Valued

Education is clearly an important cultural ideal. All the women paid lip service, at least, to this with such statements as "girls should go to school," "educated girls can marry better," and "educated boys can marry easier." They believed that education improves one's status. However, when the women were asked if they personally wanted to learn to read and write, many said no, for reasons that will be discussed.

The very real pressures of daily life are obstacles to women's pursuit of education. Hosnia's comments succinctly pointed out the conflict between the desire for education and the ability to pursue it:

> Every time I want to do something, I don't have the chance. When I have time, there are no classes, and when there is a class, I don't have money and I have to work. . . . Life is like that. Every time I want something, there's something else standing in my way.

Lack of time was the most common reason given for not taking adult literacy classes. These women's responsibilities within the household made it difficult for them to take on anything new, particularly outside of the household: too many children, young children at home, too much work at home, health problems and sick relatives to care for.

Without home appliances, supermarkets, and the prepared foods that are taken for granted in the developed world, basic housework, laundry, and food purchase and preparation make for a full-time occupation. Many of the poor must carry water from a communal tap. Labor-saving devices, such as major household appliances, are rare in lower-class households. Cairo's winds blow in a new layer of dust every day, and cleaning it away places demands on women's time. Shopping is very time-consuming, as items must be purchased from many different small shops. Buying the cheapest staples means waiting in long lines in front of the *gamʿiyya* (the government cooperative). All cooking is done from scratch. Vegetables have to be scrubbed and rice has to be sifted through by hand to pick out dirt and small stones. Dishes are typically washed in cold water and hauled upstairs to the apartment from the common water faucet. Clothes are laboriously washed by hand in washtubs and hung off balcony clotheslines to dry. Basic housework is far more than an exhausting day's work. It's no wonder that one of the most common complaints is "*ana taʿabana*," "I'm tired."

Ironically, it is among the lowest-class families (which most desperately need a second adult's income) that women stay at home and work as housewives all their lives. It is the educated classes that have more disposable income to spend on labor-saving devices and on maids, allowing wives the option of outside employment. Leisure time, which for poor women is at a premium, is spent recuperating, relaxing, visiting, and watching television. The possibility of an economic payoff for pursuing adult education is remote, if not nonexistent. Thus there can be a large gap between the ideal valuation of education and the ability and willingness to actually attend adult education classes.

Belief in the value of education is most clearly reflected in the women's conversations about their hopes for their children. While many women won't invest in their own education, the children's education is a priority for most families. Umm Amaad, a forty-five-year-old mother of four, said, "It's very, very important for the children to be educated. I want them to become educated, not be ignorant like my husband and me." Lateefa said the children must be educated so that "they will achieve status, find their way in life, and live well." Farida wants her children to have schooling in order to "learn to change and improve their condition." Hosnia said she and her husband feel education is the best way for the children to get good jobs, and she added that she will encourage her daughter to pursue her education. Zuzu hoped her daughter would love learning and continue all the way through university. But not all the women shared this attitude toward education for girls. Umm Eyman put both her sons through high school, and they are now working; her daughter, on the other hand, completed primary school (sixth grade), which, according to Umm Eyman, was sufficient education for a girl who ideally should marry and stay at home.

With the traditionally defined gender-role expectations still prevalent in Egyptian society, it might be expected that the allocation of family resources for education might favor boys; nevertheless, support for education is not as clearly gender-biased as might be assumed. Most parents expressed the desire that both sons and daughters become educated. However, practical considerations sometimes lead parents to take their children out of school. For example, in the countryside, girls are sometimes kept home to do the chores that boys can't attend to because they are in school. In the city, economically hard-pressed families may send their sons out as apprentices or to work, as was the case for Sayeda's and Umm Amaad's sons. Apprenticing boys to a trade has become more common as trades become more lucrative than government clerical jobs. The preferred occupation for girls, though, remains *muwazzafa* (government employee), which requires a high school diploma.

Elder daughters who were past the school-enrollment age of six when mass education began in the mid-1950s often did not have the opportunity to go to school, particularly in rural areas, where expanded school programs took longer to be established. When mass education was first implemented, families tended to send sons to school and preferred that daughters remain modestly at home. This has changed considerably over time, and even rural families are much less resistant to sending their daughters to school.

In Cairo, where public schooling was accessible earlier than in the rural areas, during the 1950s many girls were kept at home to help with household chores. This is sometimes the case even today. Several of my informants said their older sisters never went to school, though younger siblings did. "The older ones only married," said Assia of her sisters. Madame Fatima, a seamstress in the Meet Okba neighborhood, is the oldest girl in her family and the only one not educated. Her two younger sisters both have college degrees. She said, "My mother was always pregnant so I stayed home to help her with the younger children" (personal communication, 1986).

With large families and limited budgets, families pick and choose which children to educate based on what they see as the most effective use of family resources. The education of children is viewed as an investment in the family's future. Anthropologist Andrea Rugh describes the process of deciding who gets educated in the poor Cairo neighborhoods where she did her fieldwork:

> It is not uncommon to find families with some children in school, some as apprentices to skilled laborers and some at home. Parents weigh in the balance the whole complex of family needs and use scarce resources to support in school those with academic talents and those upon whom rest their hopes for future financial security. Families are the lowest common denominator . . . it is their collective needs that are generally considered above those of individual members. (1981, 45).

Real Uses for Reading and Writing
Skills among Lower-Income Women

Did the women need basic reading or math skills to conduct their daily affairs? No. Most could read numbers and so were able to do marketing and ride the city buses. Those unable to read numbers simply asked others. The women knew food prices; the cost of living was a salient topic of discussion, since prices had been rising rapidly. The woman from whom I regularly bought vegetables could neither read nor write but could add up my bill accurately in her head every time and much faster than I could. When occasional government paperwork needed to be completed, literate relatives were called upon for assistance, or a scribe was hired.

Unless reading and writing skills are tied to income generation or to some concrete skill that will have some fairly immediate economic payoff, lower-class Egyptian women will continue to see little use for reading and writing.[12] Their immediate concerns, especially economic ones, take precedence over any ideal value for education. The women in my sample identified two main uses of education for themselves: to obtain the primary certificate required for factory work or related employment in the formal sector and to be able to help their children with homework. On the first point, however, the supply of workers for such jobs far exceeds the demand; the certificate requirement has been instituted by employers to narrow the pool of applicants. In fact, literacy may not actually be required on the job (Papanek 1985, 227). Furthermore, most lower-class women who engage in income-generating activities do so in the informal economy, either working for cash (as maids, for example), making things at home to sell (knitting, crocheting, sewing, fixing sandwiches or popcorn), or performing services, such as taking in washing. Such activities do not require literacy or numeracy skills. On the issue of helping children with homework, lower-income households often cannot afford the private lessons essential to the children's success in school. When there is no one at home with enough education to help children with schoolwork, the possibility that children will complete their schooling is diminished.

The Meaning of Socioeconomic Changes for Lower-Income Women of Cairo

As development continues in Egypt, major changes are occuring in terms of modes of communication (the shift from orality to literacy), economic relations, and gender relations. These three areas intersect, and each set of changes impacts the shape and content of daily life, affecting both macro and micro levels of cultural organization.

Changes in Communication from Orality to Literacy

Whereas historically in Egyptian society the predominant means of conveying messages has been oral, the push toward literacy has integrated written communication into daily transactions at every level. With this shift, bureaucracy has become more complex, with subsequent expansion and specialization. Replacing memory are log and account books, which keep business accounts, and daily calendars. Archives take the place of the local storyteller in preserving traditions, a pattern Ivan Illich (1983) notes is characteristic of literate culture. Knowledge becomes something that is separable from speech and can be accumulated in vast amounts.

The shift from orality to literacy also generates changes in the organization of cultural tradition. Where previously elaborate practices of alliteration, rhyming, and other mnemonic devices helped the teller remember lengthy traditional tales, written versions now preserve stories in faithful detail. But writing down stories changes their nature; they become formalized and crystallized. Books give stories a permanence they did not have in the oral tradition, where tales changed over time, reshaped by each teller, the audience, and the times. Written stories, especially ideologically charged stories such as those concerning religious traditions, are rendered unchangeable. Texts can thus culturally become ossified and resistant to change in the transition from oral tradition to literacy.

Thought patterns move from holistic, circular patterns into the linear, logical forms enabled by writing. The syllogism, for example, is a by-product of writing; its form is too complex to be carried solely through oral channels. Mathematics and the sciences are also dependent on writing. The process of simple addition is an oral one, but multiplication and division require writing, as do more complicated algebraic functions. So the shift from predominantly oral communication to literacy changes how people think, in the direction of greater complexity.

One significant impact of this shift in modes of communication is on the pattern of interpersonal relationships. Whereas in primarily oral cultures socialization occurs within community, within families, and among neighborhood groups or in church or mosque settings, reading is essentially an individual means to knowledge and a solitary activity. This may result in a weakening of community bonds. I am not suggesting that the shift from predominant orality to predominant literacy precipitates only negative consequences, I emphasize the losses because they represent the unanticipated human costs of the shift toward universal literacy and thus become obstacles to full literacy. I also draw attention to the negative aspects of change, as they are not inevitable, but probable. By discussing such costs, perhaps their more destructive ramifications may be prevented, or at least their impact lessened somewhat.

Change in Economic Patterns of Organization

As the economic system moves from traditional structures toward more complex industrial relations, this too generates significant social change. Living arrangements shift, increased urbanization occurs, and traditional communities weaken. The expansion of industry has created more employment and encouraged the growth of urban centers, as people seek better livelihoods for themselves and their children in the cities.

In the case of Cairo, increased urbanization has meant serious overcrowding. By 1981, the population of Cairo had been doubling every ten years (*New York Times*, March 21, 1981, p. 23); it is now estimated at sixteen million. While it is not the largest city in the world, it is the most densely populated. Forty-seven percent of Egypt's population lives in urban areas, primarily in the greater Cairo metropolitan region and in Alexandria. Egypt's level of urbanization is predicted to reach 60 percent by the year 2000 (World Bank 1992, 1). Overcrowding precipitates many side effects: increased air, water, and noise pollution, increased stress, acute housing shortages, overtaxed systems of transportation and public utilities, drastically overcrowded classrooms, insufficient school buildings and teaching materials, and a drastically overburdened health care delivery system.

Urbanization has also contributed to the breakdown of traditional neighborhood patterns. Where formerly families typically lived in the same quarter, young Cairene couples are relocating their nuclear families to newly urbanized areas such as Bulaq al-Dakrur, Mohandisiin, Zawiyya al-Hamra, the more distant parts of Shubra al-Khaima, and other neighborhoods that have sprung up on the periphery of the city since the 1960s. The population of these new neighborhoods is composed primarily of recent migrants from the rural areas and young nuclear families with extended families residing in the older neighborhoods of Cairo (see Hoodfar 1984 for an elaborate description of a Bulaq al-Dakrur neighborhood). These new neighborhoods lack the class diversity typical of the older, traditional neighborhoods, making things more difficult for low-income residents who were traditionally able to count on community ties with wealthier neighbors to get them through times of financial crisis. The relocation of families away from their extended families also represents a shift in family patterns and encourages the spread of nuclear families, which now account for 84 percent of all households (Nawar et al. 1994, 18). Moreover, the relocation often deprives women of the support they traditionally received from kin who lived in the same neighborhoods and makes it more difficult for women to take advantage of opportunities, such as attending literacy classes, which the changing social and economic system may offer them.

The new political economy and the changes in consumption patterns have emphasized the need for cash.[13] Yet as more children go to school, the decline in child labor means greater pressure on the household economy and increases in the cost of childrearing to the family. Ironically, the new economic and residential patterns have deprived many middle- and lower-income women of their cash-generating activities. Many, particularly poor women, who within the traditional social organization participated in family- or community-based businesses have lost their place in the labor market as many of these types of enterprises have become obsolete or moved outside the residential neighborhoods. On one hand, this has meant increased isolation for many women.[14] But, on the other, this shift has contributed to further solidify the sexual division of labor, since men emerge as the producers of goods and services for the labor market while women reproduce labor.[15]

As Egypt's economy becomes more industrialized, the need for a literate and time-oriented work force makes schooling of children essential for the economy. Gradually schools take over from the family and from community and religious institutions as the primary agent of socialization. Thus women and mothers experience an erosion of their roles within the family and the community.

Changes in the Organization of Gender

Women in Egypt have historically lived under conditions of patriarchy, predicated on the subjugation of women in most spheres of life. Traditionally, women have been confined to the domestic sphere. This contrasts with the current position of women in the industrialized West, who are characterized by Illich (1983) as living under conditions of "institutionalized sexism." This term refers to a context where women have been integrated to a large extent into the work force, while structural inequality and gender discrimination persist. Though women are not completely subjugated, their positions in society relative to men remain subordinate. The two oppressive systems are very different in form and effects, although they share similar patriarchal ideologies. They differ significantly with regard to women's place in society and especially in the economy. In traditional patriarchies, women's roles are segregated from the mainstream economy; their work is located primarily in the household and in the informal sector. In industrialized societies, women are more integrated into the formal economy.

Women's daily lives in a patriarchal society engender a particular experience of oppression. Patriarchy offers women a separate domain—the household—as well as status and respect for the role performed within that domain. The household is controlled primarily by women, who exert considerable influence on family matters. Men are designated as protectors, obligated to support women in their roles as wives and mothers. In the context of industrialization, under "institutional sexism," women lose this protected and influential status in the household. A rhetoric of gender equality supports the employment of women, ostensibly under the same conditions as men. Household labor becomes devalued, because it does not generate income—the measure of value within the structure of industrial economic organization. Rather than achieving equality with men in terms of respect and status, institutionalized sexism continues the oppression of women under the guise of equality. For example, working women's salaries in the United States continue to lag as far behind men's as they did twenty years ago; women receive significantly fewer promotions than men, and 80 percent of employed women still work in traditional "female" jobs (Faludi 1991, xiii).

The change in women's primary locus of activity from home to workplace means that the duties of wife, mother, cook, and household manager, once considered a full-time occupation, have now expanded to include employment outside the home. While a woman's domain has broadened considerably, so have her responsibilities, burdening her with a double workload. As Egypt becomes more industrialized, the definition of women's roles and responsibilites are also changing. These changes, as Homa Hoodfar and Arlene Elowe MacLeod have noted in their chapters in this volume, have meant a loss of power for Egyptian women within their traditional arena of influence, the household. As household managers, women reproduce the political connections and crucial social and economic alliances of the family. These are important resources for sustaining women's influence within the family and for the maintenance of the entire household's quality of life. For low-income families, these activities have been essential survival strategies.

While women's status in the outside world has been elevated to some degree, there has been a loss of respect and status in the private lives of many waged women. Work at the office is not regarded as socially important. MacLeod (1991) notes that traditional homemakers are valued by their households.

> They value this labor and praise the woman with the clean and peaceful home, the good cook, the thrifty shopper, the good mother. These tasks are not de-
> · graded or regarded as inconsequential, on the contrary they are highly esteemed and prestigious activities which can be performed only by women. (25)

Hence, at least some women have been receptive to one of the dominant themes of Islamist movements, which is the demand for the return to more traditional gender roles for women as a way of reasserting Islamic identity. However, some Islamist women activists in Egypt and in other Middle Eastern countries, notably the Islamic Republic of Iran, reject this call as "patriarchy in an Islamic costume." They point out that this perspective promotes patriarchy rather than providing an accurate reflection of Islamic values (Hoodfar 1994; Mahmood 1994).

The changes I have outlined in this chapter have significant ramifications. Various problems are embedded in the complexity of the economic, social, and cultural factors at play in Egyptian society. Two broad questions reveal key issues that lie at the heart of Egypt's educational, social, and economic policies. First, what is the value of schooling for women, in their traditional roles and in a changing society? Second, what does it cost women to enter the work force, in terms of alienation and loss of power? These two questions illuminate the dynamics of the literacy problem for women and suggest why women have lagged behind men in becoming literate.

For women in traditional roles, schooling is of little use. The two most common reasons housewives in my sample gave for wanting to read and write were to become eligible for formal sector employment and to help their children with their homework. Clearly their children's homework was a salient concern, as explained earlier. Although they frequently mentioned wanting to read their sacred texts, I suspect this was the correct, socially prescribed answer. I rarely saw literate women reading these texts. Most religious knowledge still seems to be derived orally. Generally speaking, the women in my sample did not need reading or math skills to conduct their daily affairs. Education, however, did become important in the context of women's entry into the formal economy. It is no coincidence that the women of my sample who worked outside their homes, in the formal economy, were interested in improving their reading and writing skills, while the housewives were not.

Modernization, in the form of the democratization of education, has effectively widened the economic gender gap. Beginning in the 1930s, education, previously the privilege of the elite, became increasingly accessible to the masses. As Fargues (1994, 9–10) has noted, as boys initially entered the schools in much larger numbers than girls, "the gender gap increased up to the generation born between 1950–60, the most unequal of all. . . . Inequality between the sexes created by educational institutions today affects the generation between 40 and 60 years old—the age of power."

Today, the costs to women who become literate in order to enter the work force are significant, in terms of both loss of status within the household and alienation from their socioeconomic networks. These costs are at the heart of the question as to why more women do not become literate. In my sample, the women's assessment of the value of education for themselves ranged from completely unimportant to highly important. Their immediate circumstances played a direct role in determining their attitudes toward becoming educated. Those working outside the home felt their education was of moderate to strong importance, while the housewives saw very little point in becoming literate.

Poor women draw on whatever resources they have for survival; time is one such resource. A significant number of hours of each day are spent managing household affairs. Housework for most lower-class women is a mammoth amount of work; in addition, the maintenance of the household's social and economic networks is crucial to the family's well-being and takes a great deal of time. Working outside of the household means women are unable to cultivate their networks as effectively. Hoodfar, in her discussion in this volume of survival strategies and the political economy of the household (chapter 1), points out the importance of networking for social reproduction and demonstrates how household consumption patterns, which are typically managed by women, work to ensure the long-term security of the household. She draws attention to the variety of activities women are engaged in to bring material benefits to their households, including the utilization of public goods and services. It is the skillful management of available resources, she points out, that is important to the satisfaction of both intermediate and long-term needs of the family, minimizing the need for cash. For low-income families, these diverse means of acquiring cash, goods, and services are essential. While the major source of cash income tends to be from the husband, women's real contributions in the form of channeling goods and services into the household and exploiting public resources are essential.

The household is the stage where the major changes occuring in Egyptian society are played out, with considerable impact on the daily lives of low-income women and their families. While these changes may broaden the scenes in which women's lives unfold, they also place new demands on the women. Changes in women's roles present serious costs in terms of the loss of services essential to the well-being of low-income households, but it is the less tangible costs, in terms of women's power and status, which may be the most salient reasons for resisting integration into the work force, particularly if their options remain low-status and low-paying jobs. When women enter into the formal work force, not only does their workload double, but they also lose prestige, respect, and power.

The question remains: is education necessarily equated with empowerment? Though the benefits of education can be significant, the motivation to learn must come from perceived social and economic gains and cultural validation. That requires an education and literacy system which is tied to the needs of women and a curriculum which empowers them in their present circumstances. The present literacy system is not geared toward empowering women within the spheres they view as important for them and their households. Rather, it is focused on providing them with the abilities minimally required for their entrance into the formal labor market, which rarely provides them with much opportunity owing to the severe unemployment problem in Egyptian society. While the benefits of literacy for women are linked only to participation in the labor market, lower-class women do not see significant and attainable advantages in becoming educated.

NOTES

1. Leila Kamel was Director of Development at the American Research Center of Egypt when I interviewed her in November 1986, and when I interviewed her again in 1994 she was an educational consultant.

2. This is despite government attempts in 1986 to limit school shifts to two, which resulted in a rise in the number of students per classroom in some areas from 75 to 150 (Kuttab 1986).

3. There is a severe shortage of school buildings in Egypt. A government report in 1980 concluded that out of 8,027 school buildings, only 4,453, or 56 percent, were suitable for educational purposes; 11 percent needed to be torn down, and the rest were in need of basic repair. In 1987, U.S. AID funded the construction of 1,850 new rural schools, and Egypt had a first-grade enrollment 18 percent higher than expected (Prosterman and Hanstad 1992, 16).

4. Only 1 percent of primary school teachers were university graduates; only 48.8 percent had teacher training, while the remaining 50 percent were not certified teachers (Cochran 1986, 66).

5. Teachers' training requirements were revised in 1993 to require a university degree. The two-year Teaching Institutes are being phased out or reorganized into four-year specialized colleges of education (World Bank 1992, 4).

6. The problem is compounded by the fact that teaching is considered to be a very low-status profession.

7. Official statistics, derived by tracking those who enroll at age six until they graduate from primary school estimated the dropout rate to be 20 percent for the 1979–80 school year (CAPMAS 1989, 107). From 1984 to 1992 the dropout rate increased nearly

15 percent, with a further 10–15 percent leaving school by the end of the preparatory level (World Bank 1992, 5).

8. Fabric for school uniforms is provided by the government, but someone must sew it, or a ready-made uniform must be purchased. Schools do not provide enough notebooks for all the required subjects, each of which demands separate ones for classwork, homework, and examinations.

9. Instead, wealthier families hire better tutors who help their children achieve higher exam scores, and that allows them to seek professional degrees.

10. There was some decline in urban and rural poverty in the 1970s and early 1980s. Since then, poverty has persisted. Approximately 4 percent of rural families and 51 percent of urban families (49 percent of all families) live at or below the poverty line (World Bank 1992, 1). The per capita income for 1993 was $640.

11. The first names used are not the informants' actual names.

12. Projects that combine literacy lessons with income generation, such as the Association for the Protection of the Environment (*Gamaʿat Himayat al-Bīʾya min al-Talawuth*) among Cairo's *zabbaleen* (garbage collectors), represent this kind of approach (Assaad and Garas 1993).

13. This need has been further exaggerated by the dissolution of extended families and close-knit communities. For example, major appliances are purchased for each separate housing unit (by those who can afford them).

14. Since the early part of this century, this shift has meant the decline of cottage industries, and women's participation in small and medium-sized enterprises has subsequently been drastically reduced. Tucker (1985) has documented women's participation in family business, characteristic of nineteenth-century Egypt. The roles of women in the economy have varied depending on class position; upper-class, educated women have moved into a variety of occupations and into political life (Sullivan 1986).

15. Even white-collar jobs are not necessarily more satisfying than the traditional roles of men and women in rural settings. For women, the shift into the workplace is not always empowering; the costs to their households often outweigh the benefits of employment. Mundane government jobs, generally more available to women, pay considerably less than comparable positions in the private sector.

WORKS CITED

Abdel-Fadil, Mahmoud. 1975. *Development in Income Distribution and Social Changes in Rural Egypt, 1952–1972.* Cambridge: Cambridge University Press.

Arab Republic of Egypt Ministry of Education. 1980. *Developing and Innovating Education in Egypt: Policy, Plans, and Implementation Programs.* Cairo: Ministry of Education.

———. 1981. *Basic Education in Egypt: Theory and Practice.* Cairo: Ministry of Education.

————. 1989. *Working Paper on Developing and Innovating Education in Egypt.* Cairo: National Council for Educational Research.

Assaad, M., and N. Garas. 1993. *Experiments in Community Development in a* Zabbaleen *Settlement.* Cairo Papers in Social Science, no. 16, Monograph 4. Cairo: American University in Cairo Press.

CAPMAS (Central Agency for Public Mobilization and Statistics) and UNICEF (United Nations Children's Fund). 1989 and 1993. *The State of Egyptian Children and Women.* Cairo: CAPMAS and UNICEF.

Cochran, Judith. 1986. *Education in Egypt.* London: Croon Helm.

Early, Evelyn. 1980. "Sociability and Health Care Practices among Baladi Women in Cairo, Egypt." Ph.D. diss., University of Chicago.

————. 1993. *Baladi Women of Cairo: Playing with an Egg and a Stone.* Cairo: American University Press.

Ethelson, S. 1994. "Gender, Population, Environment." *Middle East Report* 190: 2–5.

Faludi, Susan. 1991. *Backlash: The Undeclared War against American Women.* New York: Anchor Doubleday.

Fargues, P. 1994. "From Demographic Explosion to Social Rupture." *Middle East Report* 190: 6–10.

Hassouna, Wafik A. 1983. "Education of Women—for What?" In Cynthia Nelson, ed., *Women, Health, and Development.* Cairo Papers in Social Science, no. 1, Monograph 1. 2d ed. Cairo: American University in Cairo Press, 52–55.

Hoodfar, Homa. 1984. "Hygienic and Health Care Practices in a Poor Neighborhood of Cairo." Regional Papers. Population Council, Giza.

————. 1994. "Devices and Desires: Population Policy and Gender Roles in the Islamic Republic." *Middle East Report* 190: 11–12.

Hopwood, Derek. 1982. *Egypt: Politics and Society, 1945–1981.* London: George Allen & Unwin.

Human Resources Management. August 1979. *Basic Education in Egypt: Report of the Joint Egyptian-American Team.* Washington, D.C.: Human Resources Management.

Ibrahim, Barbara L. 1980. "Social Change and the Industrial Experience: Women as Production Workers in Urban Egypt." Ph.D. diss., Indiana University. Dissertation Abstracts International, DDJ81-12444.

Illich, Ivan. 1983. *Gender.* London and New York: Marion Boyars.

Islam, I., P. J. Bryan, and T. Pulley. May 1991. *Women, Economic Growth, and Demographic Change in Asia, the Near East, and Eastern Europe: Conference Proceedings.* Washington, D.C.: U.S. Agency for International Development.

Katz, Greg. 1983. "Education." *Cairo Today,* February.

LaTowsky, Robert J. 1984 "Egyptian Labor Abroad: Mass Participation and Modest Returns." *MERIP Reports,* May, 11–18.

Lerner, Daniel. 1959. *The Passing of Traditional Society*. Glencoe: Free Press.

MacLeod, Arlene Elowe. 1991. *Accommodating Protest: Working Women, the New Veiling, and Change in Cairo*. Cairo: American University Press.

Mahmood, Saba. 1994. "Islamism and Fundamentalism." *Middle East Report* 191 (November–December).

El-Messiri, Sawsan. 1978. *Ibn Al-Balad: A Concept of Egyptian Identity*. Leiden: E. J. Brill.

Nawar, Laila, Cynthia B. Lloyd, and Barbara Ibrahim. 1994. "Autonomy and Gender in Egyptian Families." *Middle East Report* 190: 18.

Papanek, Hanna. 1985. "Class and Gender in Education-Employment Linkages." *Comparative Education Review* 29, no. 3: 31–46.

Prosterman, R., and T. Hanstad. 1992. "Observations and Recommendations on the U.S. Economic Aid Program to Egypt." Rural Development Institute Reports on Foreign Aid and Development, Cairo.

Rugh, Andrea. 1981. "Participation and Relevance in Basic Education: Lower-Class Parents' Strategies in Educating Their Children." In *Basic Education in Egypt: Theory and Practice*, University of Helwan Conference on Basic Education, Sir il-Layyan, Egypt, 41–52.

———. 1985. *The Family in Egypt*. Cairo: American University in Cairo Press.

Saad, Samir L. 1980. *Dropouts from Primary Education: 1956-57–1978-79: A Statistical Study*. Cairo: National Center for Educational Research, in collaboration with the World Bank.

Singerman, Diane. 1987. "Avenues of Participation: Family and Politics in Popular Quarters of Cairo." Paper presented to the annual meeting of the Middle East Studies Association, Boston, November 23.

———. 1995. *Avenues of Participation: Family, Politics, and Networks in Urban Quarters of Cairo*. Princeton: Princeton University Press.

Sullivan, Earl L. 1986. *Women in Egyptian Public Life*. Syracuse: Syracuse University Press.

Swanson, E., S. Abdou Saleh, M. El-Hamshawy, and S. Soad. 1981. "The Retention of Literacy/Numeracy Skills: An Overview for Basic Education in Egypt." Discussion Paper no. 4, World Bank, International Study of Literacy and Numeracy Retention (RPO 61–55).

Tucker, Judith. 1985. *Women in Nineteenth-Century Egypt*. Cambridge: Cambridge University Press.

United Nations. 1992. *Statistical Yearbook 1988–89*. New York: United Nations.

U.S. AID. June 1992. "Egypt: Basic Education; Third Amendment, Project Paper (263-0139)." Washington, D.C.: Agency for International Development.

U.S. AID. August 1992. "Draft Final Executive Project Summary, Arab Republic of Egypt–Basic Education Project." Cairo.

World Bank. 1972. *Staff Appraisal Report, Arab Republic of Egypt, Basic Education Improvement Project.* Population and Human Resources Country Department III, Europe. Middle East and North Africa Region.

INTERVIEWS

Abdel Aziz, Horeya, Associate Professor of Education. 1994. Interview by author, June. Cairo.

Asis, Ansaf, Social Worker, Bulaq Social Services Center. 1994. Interview by author, July. Cairo.

Kamel, Leila, Director of Development, American Research Center in Egypt, and School of Education, Columbia University, 1986. Interview by author, November. New York.

———, Educational Consultant. 1994. Interview by author. Cairo.

Kuttab, Paul, Director of Literacy Programming, Caritas Catholic Charities. 1986. Interview by author, October. Cairo.

Saad, Samir, Ministry of Education, and Co-Director, Ecumenical Literacy Council. 1986. Interview by author, September. Cairo.

Salah, Said, Assistant Director, Bulaq Center. 1986. Interview by author, October. Cairo.

5

THE STATE, URBAN HOUSEHOLDS, AND MANAGEMENT OF DAILY LIFE
Food and Social Order in Cairo

NADIA KHOURI-DAGHER

> Serious conflicts over the food supply occurred not so much where
> men were hungry as where they believed others were unjustly
> depriving them of food to which they had a moral and political right.
> —CHARLES TILLY, "FOOD SUPPLY AND PUBLIC ORDER IN MODERN EUROPE"

> The time of empty talk and hypocrisy has passed, and you are heading
> to an epoch where nothing will divert you from your most urgent
> needs, such as obtaining additional rations of materials, of sugar,
> of kerosene, of oil, white bread, and the decrease of the meat price.
> —NAGUIB MAHFOUZ, *ZUQAQ AL MIDAQ*

"FOOD RIOTS" in Egypt, as in other Arab countries, have become a major means of political expression in the past two decades. In January 1977, the street demonstrations which followed announcements of price increases resulted in hundreds of deaths and more than one thousand arrests, "the worst massacre in the history of modern Egypt" (Shoukri 1979); Egyptian citizens also took to the streets to protest food price increases in 1981 and 1984. Food issues are highly politicized in Egypt, and, along with the Islamic movements, food riots are one of two main expressions of political protest in the 1990s.

Whereas considerable attention has been devoted to the study of Islamic movements, very little has been paid to the political weight of the food issue. Food riots are often interpreted as hunger riots—spontaneous popular reactions to economic change. In the past, such an analysis was also applied to food riots in European societies. Historians, however, have recently shown how the "automatic response of the belly" interpretation—"the image is hydraulic:

hardship increases, pressure builds up, the vessel bursts"—was shortsighted (Tilly 1975). Instead, some historians suggest political explanations: food riots are not the expression of an objective economic situation but rather the expression of people's expectations and perceptions of the state and its economic responsibilities.[1]

This chapter attempts to shed light on the political character of the food issue in Egypt today. Why is food of such political importance? Can food riots be described as simply "hunger riots"? How can we explain the outbursts of protest following food price changes, and, more important, how do we explain that there are not more food riots? What accounts for the apparent relative stability of a social system which is under so much economic pressure?

Some answers to these questions are proposed here. The fact that the Egyptian state presents itself to its citizen as a "provisioner of food" is significant. Most significant, the major portion of a household's budget goes to feed the family, and government price control policies and subsidies are not always effective; getting food has become the paramount problem of daily life for many Egyptian families, the symbol of their daily economic hardships—and of the state's weaknesses.

This study is based on fieldwork carried out from 1984 to 1986 in Mansheyet Nasser, a lower-income "unplanned" neighborhood of Cairo. The basic data were updated during additional research trips in 1991 and 1994.

At the time of the initial research, the analysis of peoples' perceptions of the state's responsibilities suggested a complex range of responses, from criticism to feelings of indebtedness. Egyptians at that time were evolving strategies to cope with their daily difficulties; these included seeking psychological support through recourse to "tradition" and relying on social networks for economic survival. With increasing economic problems over the last few years and declining access to food combined with the growing inability of the state to fulfill its commitments to a population increasing by 1.3 million annually, perceptions of the state's role may be changing. The absence of widespread reactions following food price increases in 1989 and 1991 and the growing number of Muslim women wearing the veil in Cairo may signal that Egyptians are turning to forms other than street demonstrations to voice their political protest.

Food: The Wages of the Urban Poor

Issues of food are critically important in contemporary Egyptian households. During the mid-1980s, expenditures on food represented more than 50 percent of an average family's budget and could be as high as 70 percent for the lowest economic quartile of the population (Alderman and Von Braun 1984, 24). In comparison, food represents only 16 percent of the family budget in France and 13 percent in the United States. In other words, to make a living in Egypt is almost literally "to earn one's bread and butter." Indeed, bread has always carried a high symbolic value: it is significant that in Egyptian Arabic the word for bread, ʿaish, is derived from the same root as the word for life, ʿaisha.

With such a large proportion of the family budget allocated for food, the first result of rising food prices is a notable decrease in real income. Moreover, since food is the most basic of needs, price increases and food shortages are perceived as a threat to one's survival or to the survival of one's children.[2] Consequently, food has come to symbolize economic security: it is significant that when Egyptians want to express the notion of poverty, they use the word hunger; al-shaʿb gaʿaan ("the people are hungry") is an expression often used to explain that people are poor.

The State as "Food Provisioner": Access to Food as a Political Right

One reason food issues are so politically sensitive in Egypt today arises from the state's explicitly stated mandate to provide food for its citizens. In fact, the Egyptian public considers access to inexpensive basic food items a right of citizenship. This is a legacy of the Nasser era (1952–1970), and part of the more general "welfare state" approach the government has taken since then. The Nasser regime stressed the rights of all citizens to employment and to basic needs such as housing, health, education, and inexpensive food. And despite the move towards Infitah—economic liberalization—since the Sadat era (1978–1981), the state's responsibility to its citizens, at least theoretically, has remained unchanged.[3]

The primacy of the state's role in providing food is evident from analyses of the president's political speeches, interviews with officials in the press, and the general coverage in the national media, which are principally controlled by the government.[4] But the government pays a high price to play this role of provider, notably through the subsidization of basic food items. Food subsidies represent the bulk of government subsidies on basic goods (such as kerosene, soap, and construction materials); these subsidies have varied since the mid-1970s, from 15 to 25 percent of all public expenditures (Issawy 1985, 8). Despite calls from Egyptian creditors to decrease subsidies, in 1993 they amounted to £E 3.6 billion pounds (with subsidies for wheat accounting for one billion pounds), up significantly from the two-billion-pound yearly average subsidies of the 1980s.[5]

Apart from subsidies, the state controls the prices of nonsubsidized food items; a complex system has been developed whereby the state controls the entire food sector, from production to retailing, regulating the import of basic goods at one end and market prices at the other.

The credibility and legitimacy of the state are closely linked to its success in fulfilling its role as "food provisioner." A failure of the state to guarantee access to food is likely to symbolize the failure of its larger welfare mandate. When the Egyptian people judge the general efficiency of the government, they first look at—and talk about—the food issue.

We will now turn to the concrete issues concerning the provision of food for Egypt's population. Where do the problems lie, and how successful is the state in providing all citizens access to inexpensive basic foodstuffs?

Food Issues in Daily Life: Price Increases, Shortages, Quality, and Black market

The Egyptian government has established a very complex system in the food sector which has three functions: first, to guarantee the availability of basic food items through control at the supply level; second, to make goods affordable to the consumer through price controls; and third, to ensure a "vital minimum" of food by subsidizing basic commodities.[6]

There are, however, deficiencies in the state-controlled food distribution system. Control over imports, production, and distribution channels—and thus over prices—cannot be comprehensively enforced, and a black market diverts an important portion of state-subsidized goods away from the intended beneficiaries. Since the mid-1970s, food prices have continued to rise and frequent shortages of basic goods have occurred, combining to make access to food a real problem of daily life for many families—and for the government. As an Egyptian journalist once put it, "nothing occupies the minds of the housewife, of the head of the household, and of the minister of the interior, as much as their concern about the problem of prices and markets."[7] We will briefly review here the basic problems related to food access.

Bread as a Basic Staple

Bread is the basic Egyptian staple: it represents on average half the caloric intake for persons in the lowest urban quartile and as much as 35 percent of the caloric intake for persons in the highest quartile.[8] An Egyptian consumes almost five hundred grams of bread daily, and the traditional peasant diet relied heavily on bread. It is sold at substantially subsidized prices—in 1991 the subsidy was eight piasters for a loaf which sold for five piasters (100 piasters equal one Egyptian pound).[9] But the vast number of bakeries makes quality control and price regulation impossible. In 1986, although the price of subsidized bread was officially two piasters per loaf, loaves were often less than regulation weight or slightly bigger and sold at five piasters.

Rationed Goods

Ration cards in 1986 entitled families to a monthly amount of rice, sugar, oil, and tea at heavily subsidized prices; tea has since been eliminated from ration cards. Allotted quantities do not cover monthly consumption but guarantee a "vital minimum" to the majority of citizens. Certain grocers in every neighborhood are designated by the Ministry of Supply to act as distributors of rationed goods. A survey conducted in 1982 indicated that 93 percent of urban households possessed a ration card and 92 percent of them received their rations regularly (Alderman and Von Braun 1984), which strongly suggests that ration cards are an effective way of guaranteeing a "vital minimum" of basic goods to the majority.

State Shops and Other Subsidized Goods

Additional quantities of rice, sugar, oil, and tea, at less heavily subsidized prices, as well as other subsidized goods (frozen meat, chicken, fish, beans, lentils, and cheese), are sold in government shops called cooperatives (*gam'iyyaat*). Only those with a ration card in hand can shop at cooperatives. Despite this policy, instituted in 1984 to direct the supply of food to those in need, access to subsidized goods remains problematic. In 1986, there were only 2,000 of these state shops for the entire Cairo metropolitan area (ten to eleven million inhabitants), and thus there were obvious problems of distribution.[10] People stand in line for hours, and the availability of goods is very irregular. The long lines that form in front of cooperatives every day are the visible manifestation of distribution bottlenecks.

Because of this situation, a sizable black market has developed. Some employees of cooperatives arrange to divert subsidized goods in order to resell them at higher prices. The problem is that most basic goods (rice, sugar, oil, flour, beans, and lentils) are not readily available on the open market because the Ministry of Supply controls the production and importation of these essential food items. Moreover, the government tends to distribute these scarce resources through its own channels, i.e., ration cards and cooperatives. Because food obtained with the ration card does not meet family consumption needs, shortages of such essential items at cooperatives mean that people must either find substitutes (which is possible for some goods, such as rice, and impossible for others, such as sugar), or they must turn to the open market or the black market and pay up to ten times the price.

The table shows the range of prices in 1986 for four rationed items.

Prices and Quantities per Person of Four Rationed Goods in Egypt, 1986

	Monthly Rationed Quantities[1]	Prices (Piasters/kg)			
		Ration Card[1]	Co-op[2]	Grocers[3]	Black Market[4]
Sugar	750 g	10	35	60	80–100
Oil	450 g	10	30	200	100
Rice	3kg/family (<5persons) 7kg/family (>5persons)	14	30		100
Tea	40 g	138	—	1,000	

1. There are two kinds of ration cards, the red and the green. Quantities given here are for the red card, which almost all people possess. The green card is held by families with the highest income, designated at under 3,000 Egyptian pounds per year. With the green card, quantities allotted are greater, and the prices of the rationed goods are equivalent to cooperative prices. In 1986 the market price of the Egyptian pound equaled approximately U.S. $1.50.
2. These goods were not always available in cooperatives.
3. Sugar was almost never available in grocery stores, although a special variety of sugar, called "touristic" sugar, was supposed to be available. Oil sold in grocery stores was imported, which explains the high price. Rice was never available in grocery stores.
4. There was an active black market for all four goods except tea, as it is widely available in every grocery.
Source: Personal fieldwork, 1986.

Street Food

Prepared food sold by street vendors from small carts is a very important part of the urban dweller's diet. Workers eat breakfast and lunch outside the home, and cafés play a vital social role in men's life. Subsidized wheat, rice, oil, beans, lentils, tea, and sugar are available to street food vendors, and cafés are registered with the Ministry of Supply. These establishments sell popular street dishes, such as *fuul* (baked broad beans), *taʿmiyya* (bean sandwiches), and *kushari* (a rice, macaroni, and lentil dish). Prices are fixed by the government based on the subsidized price of ingredients. But because many vendors are not registered with the Ministry of Supply and consequently do not receive subsidized goods, and because most of the registered vendors and cafés have to buy additional quantities on the black market, fixed prices are never applied.

Markets

Nonsubsidized foods such as vegetables, fruits, and meat are subject to strict price controls calculated weekly by the authorities. Inspectors from the Ministry of Supply are supposed to visit markets to control price levels, but again, the number of retail outlets and the often unrealistically low fixed prices make enforcement difficult.[11] The prices of goods sold in grocery stores are controlled by a law restricting profit margins of producers and grocers at the wholesale and retail level, but again the law is easy to circumvent.[12] All these factors, combined with increases in world food prices since 1973, have resulted in shortages and great consumer price hikes as illustrated in the graph.

Food, the Number One Problem of Daily Life

The aim of the food distribution system is to guarantee access to food for all citizens. But the shortcomings of the system explain why access to food has become one of the major problems for urban Egyptians; in daily life, food appears to be the main preoccupation and source of anxiety for many Egyptians, as evidenced by both conversational and media content.

In Cairo, like most other commercialized urban societies, the price of food constitutes a noticeable part of housewives' conversations. But what is remarkable is that often conversations among men and even youngsters also revolve around complaints about the cost of food. When men talk of the various problems of daily life, food is, if not the first, at least among the first topics to be mentioned. Hussein (forty-five years old) described the problems he and his neighbors had when they first came to live in Mansheyet Nasser:

> When we first settled in this area, we were all poor people. We could not afford to pay for bricks or build our houses, and we built our houses gradually. We had real bad times at the beginning: we had to go to fetch vegetables from Al-Azhar and water from beyond the railway, and we had to wait three or four years until we got a sewage system.

Note that the topic of food is brought up after the housing problem and before water and sewage. In another interview, Abu Walid, a father of three, said, "If

Evolution of Egypt's Consumer Price Index (1967–1968 = 100)

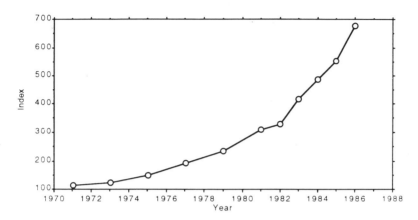

Sources: H. Alderman, J. Von Braun, and S. A. Sakr, *Egypt's Food Subsidy and Rationing System: A Description*. International Food Policy Research Institute, Washington, D.C., 1982, 20; and The Economist Intelligence Unit, Egypt 1987–1988, August 1987.

rice costs one [Egyptian] pound and meat six pounds, how can I possibly feed my children?"

Price is not the only concern. Lack of availability of goods is another common topic of conversation and source of complaints. Ahmed's comment on the worsening conditions of life is typical of many men and women who are trying to meet their families' daily needs. He said: "Before, you used to find everything in the shops; now, there is nothing to buy. You don't even find *halawa* [a common sweet]." Note that when he says "everything" Ahmed actually means food.

A clear sign that food has become an issue of primary importance is the extensive coverage given it in the press, an indicator of the preoccupations of newspaper readers. Almost daily, the semiofficial *Al-Ahram*, Egypt's largest circulation paper, publishes at least one article, if only a small one, dealing with markets, cooperatives, or bread. Other newspapers and magazines regularly devote entire series to the food question, sending reporters to markets and state shops for on-the-spot accounts of the "crazy" price increases or the long lines of weary people waiting for the distribution of subsidized goods. The newspapers are read predominantly by men in Egypt, indicating that the food problem concerns everyone. A citizen told *Al-Ahram*: "Running after food items has become one of our major problems and has become the main occupation of the people. It is as if we live only to be able to eat."[13]

Particularly in Cairo, food problems are not expressed only in terms of prices. Proximity to a market in an ever-expanding metropolis, difficulties in gaining access to subsidized goods, frequency of shortages, and the necessity of buying on the free market at higher prices all occupy a place at least as important in daily conversations as the problem of price increases. When people talk of the food problem, they do so in terms of money, time, and effort, and the latter factors are no less important than the first one. One woman said:

> My neighbor Umm Hassan is happy and rested because it is her husband who looks after everything. She doesn't have to make an effort, either to go to get the things or to think, "My God, what will I give my children today?" Because, you see, one day you can save on food, but the next day you have to think of buying nourishing things. (Amina, thirty years old, two children)

The fact that "looking after everything" is synonymous here with "looking after the food items" demonstrates the centrality of the food issue to all daily problems. The words "happy and rested" (*mabsuuta wa mirtaaha*), which Amina uses when speaking of the food issue, are highly significant; the opposite terms, "unhappy and tired," are thus implied to characterize a woman who has to take responsibility for her family's food. And the physical effort of obtaining food and the mental effort of composing a nourishing meal on a very limited budget are presented as two facets of the same problem. This is evidence that there is equal concern with inefficiency in the subsidized food distribution system and with price increases.

Daily Coping Strategies:
Social Networks and Reinterpreting Reality

In order to cope with their daily food provisioning problem, Egyptians have developed two sets of strategies. One is the creation of alternative, informal exchange networks for the supply of food; the other is a psychological device, through which constraints are transformed into deliberate choices.

Reliance on Social Networks

To fulfill their basic needs in a situation characterized by shortages, high price increases, and irregularity of supply, people must know which day the rice is due to arrive at the cooperative or where to get flour when it has disappeared from the market. Egyptians have developed networks of exchange, production, information, and assistance. People develop systems that are parallel to the market or to the state system when they are marginalized vis-à-vis both the market (by their income) and the state distribution system (because of defects in the system). The nuclear and extended family, the neighborhood, the village, and other social networks are mobilized to address the food problem.

Neighbors probably form the most significant network in an urban context where family members may live long distances from each other. The neighborhood networks are primarily networks of women, since men are generally absent from home during the day. Neighbors, especially those living in the same building, constantly exchange information about where to get this or that item, about the maximum quantity of oil or rice being distributed at the cooperative, and so on. Neighbors also borrow essential goods from each other in periods of shortage, send each other's children to buy small items, and help one another carry home the monthly supply of goods obtained with the ration card. Better-off families may help their neighbors by storing subsidized frozen meat in their refrigerator or by giving their kitchen waste to households who raise chickens or sheep.

Assistance from family is solicited when essential foods that cannot be substituted (sugar, for example) are needed. Among family members, however, goods will often be given as gifts rather than as loans to be repaid. These gifts are often from parents to daughter, but in some cases young couples may also help poor parents. Newly married couples also help out their parents by not establishing their own household ration cards; this way the number of shares allocated to their parent's household are not reduced.

Another common form of exchange is with the extended family living in the countryside. Our research has revealed the importance of village-to-city informal food flows where city dwellers exchange nonfood items such as clothes, materials, and soap for highly valued food items such as chicken, clarified butter (samna), dried fish (fisikh), and cheese. A growing resource, which was negligible when our original research was conducted, seems to be the Islamic associations working in low-income neighborhoods, which provide financial assistance to families in need.

If, however, these networks function partly as a response to deficiencies in the state system, they also feed these deficiencies: for example, to be able to exchange goods for chicken and samna from the countryside, subsidized detergent, sugar, or rice must somehow be obtained. Thus the very strategies which address the defects of the system at the same time promote them.

Since networks function on a give-and-take basis, it is not surprising that those who have the least to offer are also the ones who benefit the least from informal networks. Though we might expect that these networks help counter economic marginality, experience shows that integration in the formal economy and the informal exchange networks often reinforce each other; people with regular jobs may benefit from occupational networks, and people who have status in the neighborhood will gain access to more information than others. In other words, people who are the most socially and economically integrated are also the ones who benefit most from the informal economic food exchange networks.

Postrationalization: Turning Constraints into Choices

Facing a difficult situation, people have adopted several coping strategies which are worthy of close examination. Perhaps the most striking is the process of postrationalization, whereby people transform action by constraint into deliberate choices, thus justifying the situation to themselves. An example of this is found among people who are excluded from the cooperative distribution system. Studies have shown that the quantity of goods bought at the cooperative increases as income increases (Alderman and Von Braun 1984). This can be explained in part by the smaller number of cooperatives in the so-called spontaneous or informal low-income neighborhoods of Cairo, and underscores how poorer people are less likely to profit from the cooperative system.[14] However, lower-income households describe their exclusion from the cooperatives as a personal choice. One woman said, "I never buy any meat, fish, or poultry from the cooperative—they taste like soap." Abu Hussein, forty-three years old, put it this way: "I don't let my wife go to the cooperative. It is demeaning (*bahdala*) for her to be mixed with all these people." Amina said, "I don't go to the cooperative. It's dangerous. A woman died in front of the cooperative after having been beaten by a cooperative employee who was putting order in the line."

It becomes evident that these explanations are justifications after the fact when cooperative shopping becomes accessible and all these reasons for not shopping at the cooperative disappear. When they can, women stand in line for hours and then talk at length with their neighbors about their trip, the line, and what they purchased. This proves that they are not at all ashamed of going to the cooperative, and certainly don't fear they will be beaten to death! And when it comes to justifying a trip to the cooperative that made it possible to buy meat for three pounds per kilo instead of eight, the quality argument is reversed: "Who said the meat from the cooperative isn't good? Look, it's as clean as a flower, all red and juicy," said Umm Wala' while showing off her purchases.

Relying on Tradition

It is important to note that postrationalization is often framed in cultural or traditional logic, that is, based on values which cannot be debated. Thus one of the most common rationales for accommodating lack of access to the cooperative is that standing in lines for hours and fighting crowds is demeaning for a woman. The idea that the market is not a place for women, which has historically been reinforced by Arab urban culture, surfaces here.[15] Though the women of these neighborhoods go to the market almost every day, they still invoke this argument for tradition without being conscious that it is transparently contradictory.

By evoking tradition when postrationalizing situations of exclusion, people in Mansheyet Nasser are only using a device that they use extensively in all areas of their daily life. For example, most women in lower-income areas of Cairo justify not being employed by explaining that in their culture it is shameful for women to work: "In our society, women do not work"; "For us Saʿiidis, women do not work." Actually, most women in these neighborhoods are uneducated and thus represent a work force unsuited to the present labor market; moreover, they have children to take care of, and very few jobs are available. If by chance they do find a job, the traditional argument that "women do not work" is forgotten and replaced by another justification, also based on traditional values: women work in order to better feed their children and to be able to send them to school—in other words, to be better mothers. Similarly, the necessity of taking children out of school so that they can contribute income is justified by saying "the child was not gifted, so we took him out of school." Here again, the constraint—financial—becomes a deliberate choice of what is best for one's children.

Postrationalization turns imposed situations into choices. When it is framed in traditional values, it also has the advantage of making people feel that they are living the right way, in accordance with their culture's precepts. Thus this form of rationalizing a situation decreases the degree of frustration people feel. This should be no surprise; reformulating a negative situation as a positive one in order to make it more bearable is a tactic we all use, probably as unconsciously as people in Cairo do.

Hunger Riots?

The interpretation of food riots as hunger riots stems from a view of urban populations in developing countries such as Egypt which implies that persons protesting price increases are so deprived that they will be hungry as a consequence of these price increases. But two factors militate against the simplistic view of food riots as hunger riots: the importance that families put on quality—and not only quantity—in making dietary choices, and the relatively sophisticated knowledge Egyptians have about the working of the economy and the long-term effect of sectoral price increases, most notably for bread and meat.

Poor People, Not Miserable People

In 1977 and 1984, when the most important "food riots" burst out in Egypt, the country was in a period of economic prosperity. Egyptians were experiencing a rise in their overall standard of life—including nutritional status—as can be seen from the analysis of family consumption and investment patterns. Despite the ideological polemics about the effects of Infitah on Egyptian families, it is now clear that the impacts of migration, tourism, and a rise in salaries engendered a kind of "golden age" for Egyptians from the mid-1970s until the mid-1980s, far from the brink of starvation.[16] In 1986 I noticed that many families were buying the better-quality five-piaster bread loaf instead of the two-piaster one. This led me to question the explanation of food riots resulting from fear of starvation due to bread price increases. More generally, people paid close attention to quality when selecting the food they purchased. This suggests a capacity for choice, even among lower-income families. And the concept of choice, as opposed to constraint, means that we are not faced with totally deprived, helpless, miserable people, reacting only with their bellies.

Any visitor can notice how people select food in an Egyptian market. Shoppers spend time carefully choosing vegetables and fruits, and will handle half a dozen tomatoes or loaves of bread before selecting one. People make comparisons between the meat sold at the cooperative and that sold by the butcher, between brand-name pasta and generic pasta sold in large sacks. At home, women spend hours cleaning rice or lentils, removing the small stones and the bad seeds, even going so far as cleaning pasta because they want everything "as clean as a flower."

An example will show the importance of quality. Umm Sherif lent some rice to her neighbor, Shameyya, in a period of rice shortage. After a couple of weeks, Shameyya managed to get some rice and returned to Umm Sherif the quantity borrowed. Umm Sherif protested energetically; she had lent Shameyya "good" rice, of the Egyptian type, and Shameyya was giving her back Philippine rice, "of much lower quality and lesser taste." Shameyya had to wait until she could get Egyptian rice to pay back her debt.

When women consider what to feed their children, they make a distinction between "nourishing things" and other items. Generally, people have a relatively sophisticated knowledge of the nutritional value of the various food items. Proteins (meat, fish, eggs, cheese) are considered the most nourishing, followed by fresh vegetables, dried vegetables (lentils, beans), and cereals (rice, pasta); bread is at the bottom of the nutritional scale. Even in a lower-income neighborhood like Mansheyet Nasser, families do not eat only to ease their hunger but also to have a balanced and quality diet.

Popular Knowledge of Economics

Urban Egyptians have probably a greater knowledge of economics than simplistic analyses might suggest. What distinguished economists call "the inflationary spiral of prices" is a familiar phenomenon Egyptians express by saying: "If the price of bread is raised to five piasters, how much do you expect the other items to cost?" In other words, they are aware of the interrelationships of all price increases and of the longer-term effect, on other goods, of sectoral price increases.

Bread and Meat: Two Ends of the Scale

When analyzing people's conversations it becomes clear that two food items play a specific role: bread and meat. As noted earlier, these two items constitute the two extremes of a socially constructed food scale, in terms of both nutritive value and price. These two foods are symbolically significant; historically, bread constituted the major part of the Egyptian peasant's diet, and meat was typically food of the rich, reserved for special occasions among the poor.[17] This means that while the price of bread is expected to be low, the price of meat is expected to mark the upper limit of all prices, since meat is the most highly valued food item. People become alarmed if the price of ordinary food approaches the price of the more valued foods; if items are at the lower end of the food "status" scale, they should also be at the lower end of the price scale.

I would argue that in Egypt the price of bread plays the role of a gold standard, a kind of monetary unit in the food price scale. People expect that if the price of bread rises, all other prices will rise proportionally. The price of meat represents the maximum tolerable price for food items, and an excessive increase in the prices of ordinary food items is unbearable because it upsets the traditional hierarchical scale of food. A cartoon in *Al-Ahram* showed a poor man eating a plate of *fuul* on a Cairo street. The line underneath read: "They have been telling us that beans had as much protein as meat, until the price of beans (*fuul*) reached the price of the meat. . . . "

The characterization of food riots in urban Egypt as hunger riots thus seems inappropriate. It is doubtful that people will literally starve if bread or other food prices increase. One explanation of the public protests following changes in food prices may be found in the psychological and symbolic impact of these changes. People protest against price increases in anticipation of general inflation to follow and subsequent hardship and general decline in the quality of life. But people are not moved by economic motives alone. We will now turn to an examination of Egyptians' perceptions of the state and its relation to social order.

People and the State: Between Criticism and Indebtedness

We have seen that access to affordable basic foodstuffs has become the paramount focus of daily life, and the level of complaint regarding this issue is high. What are the perceptions that Egyptians have regarding the state's inability to fulfill its mandate as the guarantor of a "vital minimum" of food for its citizens?

People's Awareness of Their Rights

As Diane Singerman points out in this volume (chapter 7), ignorance of one's rights can hardly be considered a problem in lower-income neighborhoods of Cairo. I found that families know exactly how the state-controlled system should ideally work, and how it actually functions. First, they have widespread knowledge of the eligibility requirements for rationing and the legal prices of subsidized goods. Women know the quantities they are allowed to buy with the ration card and know current food prices by heart. Though most women in these areas are illiterate (and thus unable to access information through the newspaper), and though most rarely leave their neighborhood (and some their own street), they know of any changes in price or ration allot-

قعدوا يقولوا الفول المدمس فيه بروتين زى اللحمة
بالضبط لغاية ما الفول سعره ارتفع زى اللحمة ... !!

"They have been telling us that beans had as much protein as meat, until the price of beans (*fuul*) reached the price of the meat. . . ." Cartoon by Nagi Kamel. Reprinted with permission from *Al-Ahram* (February 9, 1985).

ment almost as soon as they are announced. Children, particularly girls, help out with household chores, especially shopping and waiting in line for subsidized goods, and they understand at a very young age all the details of a system that may appear rather complex to an outside observer. Abir, a fourteen-year-old, explained to me: "My sister has not yet arranged to have a ration card for her family. So she is still registered on my parents' card, and mother gives her ration to her every month. But if she had her own family card, with her husband and two children, they would be allowed four rations."

In a context where most essential goods are not available in grocery stores, the ration card is an important asset. This is clearly evidenced by the bargaining that takes place around the ration card, for example between co-wives who are allotted only one family ration card between them. We have also seen that some couples deliberately remain registered on their parents' ration card as a means of support. Clearly, for poorer families a ration card is a financial asset.

People's Awareness of Inefficiencies in the System

If all the details of the ideal workings of the food distribution system are known to everyone, so are all its failings. The black market is not a taboo subject at all; newspapers write about it at great length, and people make no secret of the fact that they buy some items from the *dallalaat*, the female black market dealers. Most people clearly understand the intricacies of the black market. Umm Suʿad (and many others) provided me with examples of the workings of the black market: "I am allowed three kilos of sugar every month. When I go to the cooperative, the man gives me only two kilos, tells me there is no more sugar left, and resells the third kilo to the dallalaat to make a profit for himself." Dallalaat in turn sell goods to the people in their neighborhoods at higher prices.

The prevalence of black marketeering has resulted in the normalization of illegal trading. This is not to suggest that people are happy with this state of affairs. Buying from the black market is too expensive, and most people wish that the black market would be curtailed. Everyone wants to use ration cards; as in other areas of daily life, the predominant desire is to escape marginality by participating in the state-directed system. This is simply a matter of good sense, since participating in the informal economy in Egypt is often much more costly than officially sanctioned market exchanges.[18]

Self-representation as Excluded People

When lower-income Egyptians discuss their daily food provisioning problem, they present themselves as being completely overlooked by the government and disadvantaged relative to higher-income groups. Hussein, a forty-five-year-old man, put it in the following words:

At our [public sector] company there is a cooperative. But important people come first, they take everything, and when we, the small people, arrive there is nothing left. The important people not only come first, but they take home whole packs, and they do not even have to make the effort of carrying things since they just put their backsides in their cars.

Umm Sherif expressed the problem this way: "Nobody cares about us. People in the government are sitting behind their desks, and they know nothing of reality." Another man said, "Here the strong eat the weak." It is notable that the domain of food is only one of numerous areas where lower-income groups feel marginalized. Abu Marwa, age thirty-seven, stated:

> Subsidies are not for us. They are for the employees of the public sector. We have to buy everything from the black market. It is just like our houses—we don't have a building permit, so we can't get any subsidized building materials. In Heliopolis [a higher-income neighborhood], however, rich people have permits for their buildings, and they can get subsidized materials.

However, behind all these representations of themselves as excluded people and of the state as inefficient, at the time this research was carried out people were in fact taking advantage of the system. Their actions and the implicit meaning behind their words reflected a recognition of the state's efforts to guarantee their daily subsistence.

Rhetoric vs. Reality: Indebtedness behind the Criticism
Taking Advantage of the System

Without exception, everyone complains about the black market, illegal dealings, and the dallalaat. Yet many are quick to admit that they share part of the responsibility for the defects in the system. Abu Sharbat, fifty-six years old, explained to me:

> If I could buy the whole cooperative, I would buy it, and I would work as an illegal grocer [taagir min dakhil, or grocer from within]. The problem is that everybody is trying to take more than what he is allowed. If everyone took only what is due to him, everything would be fine.

Similarly, Abu Wala', forty-three years old, expressed this view: "We all trade among ourselves. This is what makes prices increase."

Remarkably, these sentiments are not expressed as a counterargument to complaints about illegal dealings. Perception of oneself as the victim of a flawed system does not preclude the recognition of oneself as an actor perpetuating the dysfunctioning of the system. During the course of my fieldwork I discovered, for example, that the same women who complained that the cooperative employees sold only to dallalaat were actually dealers themselves! If they often view themselves as victims of a corrupt system, people admit that given the opportunity to benefit from illegal market activity they would do so.

This means that people are constantly changing roles: "victim" today (buyer on the black market, for example), and "actor" tomorrow (dallaala, for example). Most probably, people in low-income neighborhoods like Mansheyet Nasser are victims nine days out of ten. This is why they speak of themselves as marginalized people. But what is important is that they know that tomorrow they might become an illegal grocer, and even if that tomorrow is far off, it remains a possibility. Coping with daily life is like a game at the casino: the player loses often but wins sometimes, and he continues playing because he knows he has a chance of winning again.[19]

More generally, the idea of shifting from one role to another functions in other areas of daily life. The mere possibility that one's present circumstances, however bad, may someday improve is the difference between a poor and a desperate situation, between poverty and misery, between frustration and resignation. The case can be made that one of the effects of Egypt's Open Door Policy (Infitah) since the 1970s has been to allow anyone to dream of some day running his own business or flying to a Gulf country—and, in fact, social mobility has been real for millions of Egyptian families. The frequent denunciations in the press of the corrupt *manfatihaan* may have served to encourage these dreams, and thus to decrease frustration among less fortunate people.

Feeling Grateful to the State

Egyptians continually criticize the government, denounce the deficiencies of the state system of food distribution, and characterize themselves as marginalized. But the nature of this rhetoric is superficial, and people's recognition of the beneficial aspects of the state is revealed by their actions. Despite their critical words, great efforts are made to obtain ration cards, ration cards are employed as monetary instruments, and people stand in lines for hours to buy subsidized goods. This behavior suggests that citizens are seeking protection from the same system they apparently denounce as inefficient and discriminatory.

A study conducted in the 1980s in the urban areas of Egypt showed that the source of more than half the daily caloric intake for the urban population was subsidized goods. For the lower half of the urban population, as much as 70 percent of the daily caloric intake was from subsidized goods (45 percent from subsidized bread and 25 percent from goods obtained with the ration card or at the cooperatives). For the lowest quartile of the urban population, 26 percent of the food budget was spent on subsidized goods (Alderman and Von Braun 1984). All nutrition studies on Egypt indicate that the daily caloric intake is sufficient. The severe malnutrition that exists in urban centers in other countries at a similar level of development, for example in many Latin American cities, is not present in urban Egypt.

Even when Egyptians criticize the state, recognition of the government's efforts is implied. The following apparently critical observations illustrate this awareness of the state's mandate to help city dwellers:

> Before, the bread was better. But ever since they decided to feed everybody the bread is terrible.

> Cooperatives exist in cities. In villages, they do not have them. It is because they have everything in the countryside: they have poultry, they grow things, they have *samna*.

> In the countryside there are no cooperatives, and prices in the market are the double that in cities. Sugar, for example, costs eighty piasters; here it costs fifty piasters.

Based on our analysis, we understand that despite the critical rhetoric of citizens, Egyptians grudgingly recognize their indebtedness to the state for providing them with enough food.

Food Security and Political Protest

I suggest that protests which occurred in the late 1970s and in the 1980s following changes in subsidized food prices were in fact protests against a diminishing of the state's role as food provisioner. Despite all the criticisms, people knew their daily subsistence was tied to government intervention and that a reduction in the level of subsidy might endanger this security.

Since the mid-1970s, the Egyptian state has formally adopted economic liberalization policies, which imply a retreat from its role as welfare state. The World Bank, the International Monetary Fund, and the United States (through its Agency for International Development in Cairo) are pressing for fewer subsidies, particularly for food. The street demonstrations expressed people's demand for continued state intervention in the food distribution system—symbolic of a continuity of the welfare state structure inherited from the Nasser era. The political nature of the slogans shouted during the demonstrations was clear as well: a general rejection of the Infitah policy and the subsequent growth of the private sector, increasing consumerism and ties with the United States.

I have mentioned how the state's role in ensuring access to inexpensive basic foodstuffs is part of its broader role as welfare state. It may not be a coincidence that the food debate in Egypt parallels debates over other issues, such as the privatization of the educational system and public enterprises. If the debate over food is of political importance today, it is because it has come to symbolize the debate over the political choices Egypt faces with the advent of the Infitah—choices between the Nasserist, welfarist ideology and a market-oriented ideology.

The political nature of the food issue may be changing in the 1990s. With Egypt's population increasing at 1.3 million annually, the state is less and less able to practice welfare paternalism. Over recent years, food subsidies have represented a declining portion of total public expenditures. And it is very likely that today subsidized food constitutes less of the average Egyptian diet than it did in the 1980s. Moreover, in 1994 more than half of the Egyptian population was under twenty-five years of age, born after Nasser's death. The newer generations grew up in an era that saw a decline in the state's paternal role and diminishment of the government's ability to provide jobs and other opportunities: graduates must now wait eight years for a state-guaranteed job which will provide a salary that is hardly more than symbolic; education is theoretically free but teachers supplement their meager salaries by providing private lessons, which are practically essential for any student wishing to succeed; the free health care system is of such poor quality that many people prefer to go to private doctors.

The younger generations grew up learning to count on themselves; emigration abroad and state policies encouraging private enterprise have impressed upon them that private initiative is more rewarding than dependence on the state. Moreover, younger adults have seen that small civic associations, such as the ones active around mosques in the lower-income neighborhoods, may prove to be more efficient than the state in providing such basic services as education, health, and unemployment pensions. Because they may have lower expectations of the state in terms of social welfare, they may be less sensitive to a reduction in state paternalism and the diminution of subsidies. Because Islamic ideology is not opposed to market-oriented economic policies, opposition to economic liberalization policies may also be diminishing with the increasingly Islamic social movement. These factors may explain the absence of popular protests during the price increases in 1989 and 1991. Egyptians' millennial reliance on the state may be diminishing at this juncture of economic change and Islamic revival.

NOTES

This chapter is based on fieldwork carried out from 1984 to 1986 in Mansheyet Nasser, a low-income, "spontaneous" neighborhood of Cairo, in preparation for a Ph.D. degree in the socioeconomics of development at the Ecole des Hautes Etudes en Sciences Sociales (Paris). Additional stays in Egypt were made in 1991 and 1994. Research was made possible through a Young Researcher Award from the Ecole des Hautes Etudes en Sciences Sociales, a grant from the Urban Department of the Institut Français de Recherche Scientifique pour le Développement en Coopération (ORSTOM), a Middle East Award from the Population Council in Cairo, and a grant from the Centre d'Etudes et de Documentation Economiques et Juridiques (CEDEJ) in Cairo. This research was also integrated into a research program on Access to Food and Energy in developing countries, carried out by the United Nations University, which has published part of it (Khouri-Dagher 1987). Some results have also been published in *Etre Marginal au Maghreb*, ed. F. Colonna and Z. Daoud, Paris: CNRS, 1993. I am most indebted to Professor Ignacy Sachs, of the Ecole des Hautes Etudes en Sciences Sociales, who has provided continuous intellectual support for this research, and who taught me that "the best tool for an economist is more probably a good pair of shoes for the field than a computer."

1. Thompson (1971) sees the interpretation of food riots as hunger riots as "an abbreviated view of economic man." See also Tilly (1971); Kaplan (1984).

2. Research on food perceptions in history has shown that the effects of shortages and rising prices are similar. According to Kaplan (1981), "Le peuple ne fait guère de cherté entre la cherté et la famine (People make no difference between high prices and hunger)."

3. In fact, political analysts have all stressed that liberalization policies have not so much replaced the previous Nasserist, centralized, socialist ideology but have rather been added to it. See Waterbury (1983); Roussillon (1982).

4. A typical example comes every year when state budgets have been approved: headlines in the newspapers always stress the budget devoted to subsidies—which are mainly food subsidies—along with the budget devoted to salaries (of public sector employees) and pensions.

5. Figures from *The Middle East and North Africa* (London: Europa Publication, 1994).

6. For a more detailed description of the state-controlled system of subsidies and food distribution in Cairo, see Khouri-Dagher (1987, 1988).

7. *Al-Ahram*, August 13, 1978.

8. Alderman and Von Braun (1984, 28 and 31, tables 13 and 14).

9. *Al-Akhbar*, April 24, 1991.

10. At the time of the research, no official data were available on the number of cooperatives or their geographical distribution. The figure of 2,000 was given by the newspaper *Al-Siyasa* (January 12, 1986). *Al-Ahram* (August 20, 1986) gave the figure of 11,000 for the whole country.

11. Prices of agricultural products are calculated on the basis of prices of subsidized inputs (fertilizers, for example) to which many peasants do not have access, and on labor costs that far from correspond to reality.

12. A system of false sales bills is widely used by grocers to bypass the law (cases are often related in the newspapers).

13. *Al-Ahram*, August 20, 1986.

14. If we take the minimum figure of 2,000 for all of Cairo, we have an average of one cooperative for 5,000 people. In the area I studied, which housed 75,000 people in 1984, there were only two cooperatives.

15. See, for example, in Naguib Mahfouz's novel *Bayn al Qasrayn* the description of the only visit that the wife of the hero, Abd el Gawwad, makes—it is described as a secret act of incredible boldness, and she feels very guilty about it.

16. See Khouri-Dagher (1985) and Martin (1987).

17. Bread traditionally represented the basis of the Eyptian peasant's diet. As for meat, Egyptian literature provides illustrations of its social status. In his famous novel *Zuqaq al Midaq*, Naguib Mahfouz writes about the poor girl Hamida: "Actually, she did not detest lentils, but she knew they were the food of the poor people, and what they used to have at their table. She did not know anything about the food of the rich, except that it was meat, meat, and more meat."

18. For example, building without a permit obliges people to buy construction materials on the free market because they cannot get subsidized materials. To have an illegal hookup to the water or electricity network is more costly, since one must pay the neighbor who has the official connection the price he asks. For more details about the cost of illegality in Cairo, see Khouri-Dagher (1987).

19. For a conceptualization of urban dwellers as "gamblers," see Sachs 1988.

WORKS CITED

Alderman, Harold, and Joachim Von Braun. 1984. "The Effects of the Egyptian Food Ration and Subsidy System on Income Distribution and Consumption." Research Report, no. 45. International Food Policy Research Institute, Washington, D.C., 24.

Alderman, Harold, Joachim Von Braun, and Sakr Ahmed Sakr. 1982. *Egypt's Food Subsidy and Rationing System: A Description.* Washington, D.C.: International Food Policy Research Institute.

El-Issawy, Ibrahim. 1985. *Subsidization of Food Products in Egypt.* Food Energy Nexus Program, United Nations University, Paris.

Kaplan, Steven Laurence. 1981. "Les subsitances et l'ancien régime." *Annales* 36, no. 2: 294–300.

———. 1984. *Provisioning Paris—Merchants and Millers in the Grain and Flour Trade in the Eighteenth Century.* Ithaca: Cornell University Press.

Khouri-Dagher, Nadia. 1985. "La survie quotidienne au Caire: Discours et réalités." *Maghreb-Machrek*, no. 110: 56–71.

———. 1987. *Food and Energy in Cairo: Provisioning the Poor.* Food Energy Nexus Program, United Nations University, Paris.

———. 1988. "La 'faillite' de l'Etat dans l'approvisionnement alimentaire des citadins: Mythe ou réalité?" *Peuples Méditerranéens*, no. 41/42: 193–209.

Lapidus, Ira. 1967. *Muslim Cities in the Later Middle Ages.* Cambridge: Cambridge University Press.

Mahfouz, Naguib. 1970. "Passage des miracles, Sindbad," *Zuqaq al Midaq.* Paris.

———. 1983. "Impasse des deux palais, Lattès," *Bayn al Qasrayn.* Paris.

Martin, Maurice P. 1987. "Les années de vaches maigres." *Etudes*, 366, no. 1: 19–28.

Raymond, André. 1984. *The Great Arab Cities in the Sixteenth–Seventeenth Centuries.* New York: New York University Press.

Roussillon, Alain. 1982. "Continuités et ruptures dans l'Egypte de l'Intifâh: Le secteur public en question." *Annuaire de l'Afrique du Nord* 21: 413–453.

Sachs, Ignacy. 1988. "Vulnerability of Giant Cities and the Life Lottery." In *A World of Giant Cities*, ed. Mattei Dogan and John D. Kasada. Beverly Hills: Sage.

Shoshan, Boaz. 1980. "Grain Riots and the Moral Economy: Cairo 1350–1517." *Journal of Interdisciplinary History* 10, no. 3: 459–478.

Shoukri, Ghali. 1979. *Egypte Contre-Révolution.* Paris: Le Sycomore.

Thompson, Edward Palmer. 1971. "The Moral Economy of the English Crowd in the Eighteenth Century." *Past and Present* 50: 76–136.

Tilly, Charles, 1975. "Food Supply and Public Order in Modern Europe." In *The Formation of National States in Western Europe*, ed. Charles Tilly. Princeton: Princeton University Press.

Tilly, Louise. 1971. "The Food Riot as a Form of Political Conflict in France." *Journal of Interdisciplinary History* 2, no. 1: 23–57.

Waterbury, John. 1983. *The Egypt of Nasser and Sadat: The Political Economy of Two Regimes.* Princeton: Princeton University Press.

❖ 6 ❖

BEYOND PARADIGMS OF DEVELOPMENT

A Pragmatic Response to Housing
Needs in Cairo's Inner City

NAWAL MAHMOUD HASSAN

THIS STUDY EXAMINES the ways in which social and economic pressures affected the housing problems of lower-income households, the urban fabric of life, and traditional craft occupations in Gamaliyya during the late 1970s and early 1980s.

This topic was of natural and immediate concern to the Center for Egyptian Civilization Studies, which I established in 1971 to research and support the cultural, architectural, and craft heritage of Egypt. Progressively, the center became involved with the problems of the community within the urban context of the historic city center. The center decided to turn toward research in order to determine the problems affecting the community, and in 1979 it established the Association for the Urban Development of Islamic Cairo, which, through its affiliation with the Ministry of Social Affairs, could legally act on behalf of the community, while the center undertook the Survey on Families in Gamaliyya Living in Historic Monuments in 1978, on which this chapter is largely based. The association, with its official status, could help write petitions to the ministry for retirement pensions and special aid, or letters of recommendation to doctors and hospitals for treatment, as well as concern itself with the historic monuments of the area. At a later point we founded an aid committee, or *lagnat al-zakah*, under the auspices of the Nasser Social Bank to aid families evicted from the historic monuments in December 1979 and the same aid committee later came to the aid of earthquake victims in October 1992.

As this study progressed, the center/association became increasingly aware of the problems facing literally hundreds of families who were being evicted from old-stock housing when unscrupulous outside speculators would try to purchase increasingly valuable real estate. In addition, old-stock housing was collapsing either through negligence or willful demolition by new landlords. Those families that were left homeless had been directed to local mosques and other historical monuments that served as "temporary" housing. Many of these historic mosques, homes, and commercial buildings dated back to the medieval period and were not in very good shape to begin with. They lacked basic facilities, particularly for the needs of large families. Temporary housing was often set up in the courtyards of these monuments, and some residents had remained there for years on end. In short, the situation for these families worsened as property values rose and landlords had greater financial incentives to rid their buildings of tenants who paid low rents frozen by rent control laws.[1] It became clear that something had to be done.

Beyond economic pressures on densely populated neighborhoods and the unsuitability of these monuments as "temporary" housing, a third factor contributed to the government's desire to quickly relocate these families: international tourism. President Anwar Sadat instituted the Infitah or Open Door Policy in 1974 and encouraged investment in tourism. Egyptian officials were very concerned about the conditions of historic monuments, and they were embarrassed to have tourists meet up with poor families washing their clothes and cooking food during their visits to these monuments.[2] The decision to place people in "temporary" housing had taken its toll on the monuments, and plans to renovate or refurbish these buildings were also more difficult to execute if the residents remained.

The local newspapers and television media stated that these monuments were inhabited by squatters from rural areas and that this was disgraceful, since the monuments were a part of Egypt's national heritage. However, it quickly became evident by talking to these families that they were from the district itself. At this point, we at the center/association decided to survey these families to find out about their backgrounds, their lifestyles, and their housing needs.[3] The purpose of the Survey on Families in Gamaliyya Residing in Historic Monuments was to be able to approach the local governing bodies with the pertinent information needed to better identify housing needs of the families. The survey was conducted in cooperation with students from the High Institute of Social Work during the summer of 1978 and encompassed 268 families living in historic monuments in the Gamaliyya district.

We began in-depth interviews of the families which brought out their perceptions of their housing problems and their ideas for possible solutions. Their concerns were not limited to housing, and we gained some insight into their thoughts about occupation and health as well. Once the information had been gathered, we immediately began to lobby the governorate for a new housing construction program for these people. We had determined that they had all resided in Gamaliyya. To our dismay we discovered that the law offered these families no protection from speculators buying up old-stock housing and tearing it down regardless of its condition. Buildings which were structurally sound were at risk because owners pursued their economic interests and tried to demolish sound but unprofitable housing. It remained relatively easy for speculators to obtain the necessary permits for demolition. Generally, people living in Gamaliyya who owned buildings did not have the heart to tear down the buildings themselves but would sell the rent-controlled building inexpensively to someone from outside the area who would be less inhibited about getting a permit.

In fact, the law actually encouraged this arrangement. The engineers of the Municipality of Cairo were personally liable and could be imprisoned if a building collapsed. In 1978, three engineers were imprisoned when a building which they had certified as being safe collapsed. As a result, when anyone applied for a permit to tear down part of an "unsafe" building, government engineers would protect themselves by saying either that the entire building should be torn down or that the upper stories of the structure would have to go. Some engineers were so afraid of lawsuits that they would issue a permit for demolition without even inspecting the building. It was left up to the people living in the building to contest the decision in court. The buildings' inhabitants were often at a loss as to how to go about trying to delay the demolition of their homes. The center/association approached the Ford Foundation and it supplemented the research grant with a legal aid program to advise people how to go about applying for a "stay of execution."

Our experience in assisting the residents of temporary housing in Gamaliyya revealed a common and pervasive problem which lower-income communities faced during this era. We found repeatedly that economic forces were even more powerful than the influence of top decision makers or other persons in positions of authority. At the very beginning of our interest in this issue, the Governor of Cairo, who was an engineer with a real interest in the historic city, was approached by the center about a special case of a historic Arab house dating from the eighteenth century which was inhabited at the time by 110 persons. It had a traditional courtyard, *mashrabiyya* or latticed windows, a loggia on an upper floor, and a column engraved with Turkish and Arabic script and floral designs. We felt that the building and its grounds should have been on the official register of historic monuments. It was our intent to interest the governor in the problem in order to save the building from its likely fate of being torn down.

It so happened that the governor was interested in the building and agreed that historic buildings were indeed a part of the Egyptian heritage and should be protected. He was also concerned about the fate of those living in the monuments, for whom he would have to find alternate housing in mosques. The governor contacted the engineer in charge of the quarter and asked him to report on this particular building. The engineer responded that there was little need for concern since the building's occupants had a case in court and no decision to tear down the building would be taken until a structural engineer inspected the building for the court. For the time being, according to the engineer, the building's occupants were safe. As far as he was concerned there was no problem whatsoever because these court cases were always deferred and it would take at least three or four years until a decision on the matter was rendered.

In the meantime we assured the people living in the building about their safety. We also told them that we were going to contact the Committee for the Preservation of Monuments in the Ministry of Culture so that it would classify the building as a historic monument to prevent it from being torn down. In the interim, the new owner, who had bought an empty lot next to the building in question, wanted the extra space in order to build a new high-rise apartment building. He was doing a number of things to actually cause structural faults to appear in the building such as hosing the brick walls with water at night so that cracks would appear in the plaster and eventually in the mortar. We had reached the point, however, where the governor had written on the application for demolition that the building was awaiting classification as a historic monument and that everything should be done to save it. Furthermore, the administrative head of the quarter was well aware of the ongoing efforts to classify the building as a historic, and therefore untouchable, building and thus the residents felt the building was protected by several powerful interests.

As it so happened, when I was traveling in Iraq for two weeks, the governor was transferred to become head of the Egyptian Hotels Association. When I returned I discovered that as soon as the governor was transferred, the new owner had approached the municipality again and immediately received his permit to demolish the building. The municipality immediately sent the *shurtat al murafiq*, or utilities police, to surround the building and evict everyone within twenty-four hours, which they had the authority to do if the building had been found to be in imminent danger of collapse. This is just one example which shows that even at the highest levels of government—at the level of the governor himself—it is extremely difficult, if not impossible, to prevent the needless destruction of existing housing stock due to economic pressures.

Despite this the center/association tried lobbying in various ways and publishing articles in the press to publicize the real story of the quarter and the fate of the persons living there. We soon became involved with the quarter's local politicians and discovered that the member of Parliament from the Gamaliyya district, Ulfat Kamel, was very concerned about this problem. She had been involved in social work before being elected, and her husband had been a politician representing the district before the Nasser period. When he was forbidden to run for election during the 1950s because of his perceived loyalty to the political parties of the ancien régime, people in the community asked him to consent to permit his wife to run for political office. They told him that they had great confidence in her because of her work in the quarter and felt that she would serve the community well. Indeed, it was a widely held view that she filled the role excellently even though she married young and did not go to university. Her strong personal character and responsiveness to the needs of her constituency was supplemented by a very good grasp of the salient issues concerning the neighborhood and the nation.

The center/association joined forces with Ulfat Kamel in order to pressure the government to do something about the housing shortage. We determined the best way to do this would be to bring hundreds of applications to government officials from people seeking housing following the collapse of their old homes. Our efforts were piecemeal because we had to focus on those families which demonstrated the most urgent need. Unfortunately, only some of the people were successful in securing public sector apartments. In a sudden reversal of policy in 1980, however, the government launched a massive construction program for low-income housing.

What was the strategy employed that resulted in the government's launching into a housing program? I cannot say that it was the result of our long-term lobbying efforts. In fact, the support for this program came from an unanticipated source. Certain well-connected persons, interested in the preservation of monuments, had approached Mrs. Sadat, the wife of the president, and were able to convince her of the value of maintaining the monuments as part of Egypt's heritage. They argued that the monuments should not be inhabited by squatters because of the fragile condition of the buildings and that some sort of accommodations for the people had to be provided by the government. There was also a hope that monuments in better condition would draw more tourists and their foreign exchange. Mrs. Sadat then told the governor that he would have to find the squatters alternative housing, preferably by January 1, 1980, of the coming year (six months away). In effect the government took the decision to relocate these families.

The people who had been living in the monuments and mosques were relocated to an area which seemed to them far away from central Cairo, on the Muqattam hills, to the north of Manshiyyat Nasser, in Doueka. Not surprisingly, the construction program was left to the last minute because the governorate's committee was trying to decide what type of housing, temporary or permanent, would be appropriate, and where the housing should be located. When the deadline approached and there was still no housing, the government enlisted the army to construct makeshift bungalows. The army built 1,000 units in sixty days, which was quite a record, but without water connections or sewerage. Army personnel also were able to build one health care unit (also without water connections), one kindergarten, and a mosque.

We continued to play a role in helping the new residents adapt to the new housing development and to try to procure housing for those not originally included on the governorate's list. The governorate's survey of the families living in the mosques included only those families who were present on the exact day of the survey (probably because it could not provide housing for all the families). Although many families had at least one member present on the day of the survey, others were out working or shopping. Because they were not on the list they did not have the critical receipt stating they were eligible for government housing. On December 20, the people who had been officially registered on the government's list were told that they had to find their own way of transporting their belongings to the camp in Doueka. All had to vacate the monuments whether they had been allocated housing or not.

At that point, the governor issued statements to the press saying that everyone in Cairo had now been housed and there was no one left in the mosques, in tents, or on the street. However, many families had not received housing and many problems still existed. We contacted professional groups to let people know that there was still a housing problem. The media responded. Journals, including *Sabah al-Khair* and women's journals, carried articles (one entitled "The Day of the Census") with photographs showing people living in tents beside the monuments. When asked if the people had been housed or not, the minister of housing, who was a reputable engineer, would only say that the governor had stated that no one was still in the mosques. He knew the situation had not been completely resolved.

Our committee had many things to do. We had to help the families immediately because it was a very cold December. We had to provide tents, blankets, and provisions. We had originally tried to raise contributions through our Association for the Urban Development of Islamic Cairo, but the Ministry of Social Affairs, which has close supervision and control of voluntary associations, claimed that there was no provision in the statute of our association to provide financial or other aid. The ministry itself had no special category of programs for nongovernmental organizations to organize emergency relief. Determined to respond to the urgent needs of the residents of Doueka, the center/association finally organized the aid committee attached to the Nasser Social Bank, similar to those charitable associations usually affiliated with mosques or schools. Fortunately, through the Red Crescent Association (the Muslim version of the Red Cross) we were also able to acquire what we needed immediately. The Red Crescent Association was for many years an effective private voluntary association whose secretary general was Dr. Yehya Darwish, dean of the High Institute for Social Work and former undersecretary in the Ministry of Social Affairs. He was able to respond immediately to aid disaster victims without bureaucratic red tape.

In the new housing "development" in Doueka, there were other problems, most notably the lack of services that needed to be addressed as well. The two buses ran daily too late for residents to get to work or to school on time. And, as mentioned, water and sewerage had yet to be installed. There were no markets and only one cooperative, which sold only canned goods. The residents were so frustrated with their new homes and the lack of services that when they saw delivery trucks coming in, they stoned them. Occasionally, we were able to improve their situation. For example, we were able to convince the deputy governor of North Cairo to request extra buses to service the camp and to regularize the bus schedule. But there were other things which we were not able to change at all.

One of the main problems for these people was that they were not allowed to work or to build kiosks or workshops in the new residential area. The governorate reasoned that if the people were allowed to set up shops, they would turn officially "temporary" housing into "permanent" housing. To avoid this transformation of a new housing development, people had to travel back and forth to their workplaces in other areas. The only person who managed to get a permit for his workshop was the local representative of the ruling National Democratic party.

According to our estimates, the residents of the historic monuments in Gamaliyya included sixteen carpenters, six candy vendors, two builders, five tin-

smiths, thirteen merchants, two contractors, two scaffolding carpenters, three
construction laborers, seventeen (mobile) vendors, two policemen, thirteen
employees (generally low-level white-collar positions), twenty-two government employees, nine carters, and at least one representative of the following
professions: varnisher, weaver, baker, printer, butcher, bicycle maker, broom
maker, embroiderer, and moneylender. This list provides some insight into the
variety of occupations and the need of the people for space in which to work.
For example, when the carters moved into this new area there was absolutely
no space for them to put their carts or their animals. They had no choice but
to stay in the open air, and since it was December and January their animals
would probably have died without shelter.

The government never approved our association's request to set up a branch
office to help the people in the camp on the grounds that it was not needed
since the government itself could handle the situation. It was not able to handle
all the problems, however, but some of the representatives to the Gamaliyya
area came to receive provisions of the Red Crescent Association which we were
distributing. They were probably afraid of a group outside the government
working with people who might protest their living conditions.

Eventually the government built permanent housing on the outskirts of
Cairo in Ain Shams and Medinat Salam for the people who had been moved
to Doueka. These two sites now have low- and middle-income housing developments built by the government after 1980 in the style of residential apartment buildings. Later, private construction surrounded these developments,
and these areas of the city became heavily populated by a range of Cairenes in
search of affordable housing, particularly newlyweds from older areas of central Cairo who could no longer find affordable housing in the neighborhoods
of their birth, Egyptians returning from working abroad who invested their
hard-earned savings in housing, and rural migrants to Cairo.

Many of the problems which plagued those who were forced to move to
Doueka followed them to their permanent residences in Ain Shams and Medinat Salam. Again, the government did not build markets or small-scale workshops for the inhabitants. Most of these inhabitants were self-employed artisans, (mobile) vendors, carters, skilled and unskilled laborers.

When we approached the governor about the need for affordable working
space, the government now argued that they had built these magnificent modern apartments and it would spoil the appearance of the city they were building
if they built small markets and workshops for the people. In these new areas
the governorate had actually built large shops and workshops which were

rented by the public sector or sold by auction for prices ranging from £E8,000 to 12,000, clearly out of reach of people who were relocated to these areas. These shops and workshops were largely bought by outside investors who did not even use the space but typically waited approximately two years until they could be sold to others at higher prices or until the population increased and their businesses could be run profitably. We again tried to intervene on the people's behalf, telling government officials that we had located space for the construction of small shops and workshops which could be rented out. We argued that there was simply no need to separate residential and commercial areas. They had only to look at the old city of Cairo, where industry, residences, and shops co-existed, to see that it provided a successful model of urban living. Yet, many officials and planners are so impressed with European models that they want Cairo to be a copy of New York, Paris, and London. For example, they had issued a decree that all shops must close at seven, although most of the people survive by holding two or three jobs and working until eleven at night. But the people in government ignore the financial realities of lower-income communities and say, "Ah—but in London, Paris, and New York, shops close at such and such a time." These sentiments were expressed by the top officials, by the heads of the quarter, the local council, and the governor himself.

Despite the fact that many of the people in government originated in these quarters themselves, they have somehow "risen above it" and sit in their air-conditioned offices and plan what they believe to be the ideal community based upon a Western model. In the office of one of the top officials, a huge picture of New York City skyscrapers covers an entire wall. This is what Hassan Fathy, the renowned architect, has called "autocolonization," or the process by which Egyptians themselves copy Western models and dismiss indigenous practices (Fathy 1973). These policies penalize the traditional artisan, small entrepreneur, and petty tradesman and ignore the needs and requirements of self-employed people, artisans, and small-scale industrial and other informal sector enterprises.

It should be kept in mind that many persons living in these areas are poor and earn very low incomes. They are used to walking to work, not driving off to work in their cars like an American or European. Mixed residential and commercial neighborhoods have historically been predominant in Cairo. Placing areas for employment near residences would seem to be the logical thing to plan, as Ronald Lewcock has shown in his research on urbanism in the Arab world and street activities in the historic inner city of Cairo (1983a and b, 1986).

In the end, the government did provide the new areas of Ain Shams and

Madinet Salam with some services, such as department stores and cooperatives. However, these services do not meet the needs of poorer residents. Rather
than a large cooperative, the people need a small grocery where they can buy a
few olives or some cheese on a daily basis. They cannot afford to buy a quarter
kilo of cheese, which is sold at the government food cooperative. We told the
governor that voluntary organizations were willing to foot the bill of building
small shops to rent to these people. To redress some of these problems we had
identified unused land and provided government officials with the name of one
of Egypt's greatest architects, Hassan Fathy, a recipient of an Aga Khan Award
for Architecture, who would volunteer his time to design the shops. But the
governor declined our offer, saying that his designs were too old-fashioned and
that traditional architecture models would conflict with the modern designs.

We continued our efforts to change the prevailing attitude of successive gov-
ernors and those responsible for urban planning. The government had constructed wide boulevards in these new residential areas as if people were
wealthy enough to have cars and needed space for them. It had provided no
markets for the people to get their daily produce. Those who went back to work
in the inner city had to take two different transports, taking, for some, an hour
and a half. Their transportation costs increased fivefold. Housing costs in these
new areas were prohibitive as well. A new two-room apartment in the new area
of Doueka rented for £E22.5 per month, whereas residents had paid from
£E0.5–5 previously.

In conclusion, it is clear that we must change the attitude of the policy
makers, since many of the problems of the poor in Cairo and of urban development can be solved by them. On the other hand, we know that the people from
those neighborhoods use every *wasta* (intermediary or connection) and every
link they have in order to meet their needs. We tell them to go to their representatives, to take their requests and petitions, because this is the only way the
policy-makers' attitudes will change. Of course, they will change, but it will
take years before the government gives up its desire to control all policy, nongovernmental organizations, and planning.

NOTES

1. Typical monthly rents for rooms in the rent-controlled inner city during the late
1970s ranged from £E (Egyptian pounds) 0.5–5 (Hassan 1985). Rent control laws were
first instituted in 1941, when World War II and Cairo's role as a center for supplying the
allied armies increased both the demand and the price of housing. In 1947, Bill 121 was
passed by Parliament, freezing rents at their 1941 prices and including all leases signed

before 1944 under this new stipulation. A few days after the Free Officers came to power in July 1952 they issued a new law, 199/52, and subjected leases signed during the intervening years to the same conditions and decreed rent reductions of 15 percent on these leases as well. In 1958, in celebration of the formation of the United Arab Republic which united Egypt and Syria, the government reduced the rents by another 20 percent on leases signed between 1952 and 1958. Rent reductions on certain properties occurred again in 1961 and 1965, 1969, 1976, and 1977 (see Hanna 1985 and Feiler 1992). For a discussion of the ways in which population pressures have increased the demand for housing in Cairo, see Shorter 1989 and Feiler 1992.

2. Tourism has become one of the most important industries in Egypt. According to one source, by 1993, it had become the nation's primary hard currency earner and the largest employer in the country (Mattoon 1993).

3. The survey was partially funded by the Ford Foundation. The nature of the subject we were interested in required that the interviewing be purposive based on geographic location in Gamaliyya rather than relying on a random sample of squatters in all areas. As such, however, the limitations inherent with this approach are all too evident from a purely scientific standpoint. It is simply not possible to make generalizations about homeless families in other areas.

WORKS CITED

Fathy, Hassan. 1973. *Architecture for the Poor: An Experiment in Rural Egypt.* Chicago: University of Chicago Press.

Feiler, Gil. 1992. "Housing Policy in Egypt." *Middle Eastern Studies* 2 (April): 295–312.

Hanna, Milad M. 1985. "Real Estate Rights in Urban Egypt: The Changing Sociopolitical Winds." In *Property, Social Structure, and Law in the Modern Middle East,* ed. Ann Elizabeth Mayer, 189–211. Albany: State University of New York Press.

Hassan, Nawal Mahmoud. 1985. "Social Aspects of Urban Housing in Cairo." *Miramar,* 59–61.

Lewcock, Ronald. 1983a. "The Old City of Sanaa in Development and Urban Metamorphosis." *Aga Khan Award for Architecture,* Geneva.

———. 1983b. "The Technical Problems of Urban Rehabilitation and Upgrading." *Designing in Islamic Cultures* 3, MIT Aga Khan Seminar.

———. 1986. "Preservation versus Modernization." In *The Challenge to Our Cultural Heritage,* ed. Raj Isar. Paris: UNESCO.

Mattoon, Scott. 1993. "Terror Makes Its Mark." *Middle East Journal,* June, 4–10.

Shorter, Frederic. 1989. *Cairo's Leap Forward: People, Households, and Dwelling Space.* Cairo Papers in Social Science, no. 12. Cairo: American University Press.

THE FAMILY AND COMMUNITY AS POLITICS
The Popular Sector in Cairo

DIANE SINGERMAN

IN A DENSELY populated neighborhood of Cairo, a young woman sat before a hot mud oven baking a special bread eaten during the Islamic month of Ramadan. For the past four years she had returned to the same spot in a vacant lot, over an abandoned air raid shelter, and her customers would welcome her back. After I chatted with her about her work, she explained to me that she had invested her earnings to purchase land from her husband's family for a new home. They had finally bought a parcel of land, and this year her husband would use her earnings to buy the materials he needed to construct the house. Actually, she doubted whether he really had invested her earnings in this construction project, since he was only occasionally employed as a construction worker and wasted money on various pursuits. During the course of the conversation she explained that her difficulties in life began at an early age and stemmed from her unusual family history. She never knew her mother and had been raised by her father, who, she explained, married and divorced according to his business fortunes. When he remarried for the third time, her new stepmother treated her very poorly and she tried to escape her situation by marrying the first reasonable suitor at a fairly early age. Unfortunately, her husband also proved to be abusive at times and because she had no relatives to protect her and intercede on her behalf with her husband and his family, her life continued to be difficult. She explained: "I don't have a back [support]. And without a back, one gets beaten on the stomach." People empathize immediately with the meaning behind this popular saying: without the support of a strong, secure, respected family, one can expect problems throughout life. Her family was unwilling and uninterested in protecting her or mediating her marital conflicts.

Families, to be sure, are important throughout the world, for obvious rea-

sons. In Cairo, however, the family serves as an economic and political institution, as much as a social or affective one, and individuals maintain very close
ties to their relatives throughout their lives. Individuals both compete for family resources and cooperate to use the family to further collective interests. The
family has a pervasive role in allocating and distributing resources, in regulating morality and arbitrating conflict. This judicial, allocative, and distributive
role of the family furthers the interests of the community, since it provides
people with an institutionalized means of reaching decisions and solving
everyday problems. I will argue that the family is a political institution which
serves the needs and fulfills the objectives of its individual members. It is a
structure which moderates an individual's actions and behavior within the
larger environment of the community and the nation. The role of the family
is particularly important in communities which because of their economic or
social position do not have access to resources which wealthier or more politically powerful interest groups enjoy.

The political meaning and implications of relationships and activities in
particular communities can be teased out from the details of everyday life. This
study focuses upon the *sha'b*, or popular sector, in Cairo during the mid-1980s.
The *sha'b* literally refers to a collective mass, people, or Egyptian nation, but
is used in its adjectival form to identify lifestyles, neighborhoods, tastes, and
cultural practices which are identified with more indigenous phenomena. Upper-class or more Westernized Egyptians would use the term *sha'bi* to distinguish the more populist mainstream from themselves. The sha'b in Egypt share
collective identities that stand above class cleavages. There is some class het-
erogeneity within sha'bi neighborhoods, since families with incomes ranging
from very poor to middle and even upper middle class may live side by side
owing to their ties to neighborhoods or their preference for a "traditional" lifestyle. For the most part, however, these communities are composed of working-class or lower-middle-class families.

Methodologically, one has to invest time to understand the concerns of individuals and households before one can identify shared concerns and community dilemmas. Publicly and privately recounted stories, experiences, practices, disagreements, and debates gradually sensitize an observer to the politics
of the community. Through a methodology of participant observation, one
can eventually discern the ways in which a community is organized around
achieving certain goals, and the processes and institutions which people use to
achieve them. Individual strategies to accumulate savings, provide an education for a child, or migrate abroad are resolved in certain ways, and over time

the community develops institutions, largely informal, to fulfill these needs. The term *informal* is used here, in the tradition of research on the informal economic sector, to refer to "activities which largely escape recognition, enumeration and regulation by the government" (Abdel-Fadil 1980, 15; see also Hart 1973; Singerman 1995; Portes et al. 1989; and De Soto 1989). Within sha'bi communities, informal institutions are both political and economic in nature. Everyday decisions within these communities add up incrementally and evolve into a set of political and economic interests.

This study is rooted in an argument about the boundaries of the political and how to explain the political activities of the sha'b, both men and women, who do not participate in formal political activities. These boundaries have constantly changed as theorists, politicians, and dominant interest groups debate the proper relationship between individuals, groups, and the increasingly powerful state of the twentieth century. My suggestion that the family, informal networks, and other informal institutions be considered in an explicitly political light can only be proposed after rejecting two dominant conceptions of politics.

First, I am unwilling to accept the construction of politics which authoritarian regimes define and perpetuate. Doing so in Egypt would limit research on politics to Parliament, fettered political parties, bureaucratic elites, professional associations, etc. It would ignore the politics, the interests, and the preferences of the vast majority of citizens who are not *visibly* participating in legal, registered, and state-sanctioned collective institutions or state institutions *and* are not visibly engaged in opposition to the regime, which quickly attracts the repression of the authorities. While the government, following the Free Officers Revolution in 1952, instituted redistributive policies such as land reform, rent controls, free public education, subsidies of basic goods, etc., the real and perceived threats from opposition forces pushed President Gamal Abdel Nasser to deny freedoms of association and expression to Egyptian citizens. Mass political participation and inclusion in the political process was soon sacrificed to the competing desire for regime maintenance. The record of "politics without participation" has been extensively documented by many foreign and Egyptian scholars and it will not be reiterated in any detail here (see Waterbury 1983; Springborg 1982, 1989; and Hinnebusch 1985). Accepting elite-defined descriptions of politics in Egypt not only ignores collective life and political participation among the sha'b, it does not even suggest investigating the possibility of such activity. As James Scott argues, "So long as we confine our conception of the political to activity that is openly declared we are driven to con-

clude that subordinate groups essentially lack a political life or that what political life they do have is restricted to those exceptional moments of popular
explosion" (Scott 1990, 199).

Second, regardless of the nature of authoritarian rule in any nation or the
efficiency of its repressive apparatus, dominant notions of politics within the
discipline of political science have also served to deny whole groups a political
nature. The family is not normally viewed as a political unit representing collective interests. Rather, political scientists typically classify the family as a social institution within the private sphere. In classical political theory, the domain of the household, blood relations, women and children constituted the
private realm. Political debate, policy making and elite competition took place
in the public (male) realm of the *polis*, as defined by Plato and elaborated upon
by Aristotle (see Elshtain 1981). This taxonomy was accepted by political scientists who sought to understand the workings of government, the public arena,
the dilemmas of public policy, and leadership contestation. In more contemporary times, political participation thus referred only to "those activities by
private citizens that are more or less directly aimed at influencing the selection
of government personnel and/or the actions they take" (Verba and Nie 1972, 2).
If women of any class and lower-class men were not visible and active participants in this public world of politics and government, they were not seen as
politically significant or politically empowered (see Pateman 1980 for a critique
of the socioeconomic and gender biases of definitions of political participation). The family was primarily a regressive institution which limited the formation of class consciousness and "modern" political loyalties to the state.[1]
Most recently, feminist scholarship, class analysis, and African-American
scholarship, among other endeavors, have been engaged in rewriting history
and discovering new sources which can represent the voices of the excluded—
whether workers, peasants, women, African-Americans, or the sha'b in Egypt.
While we know that these groups have not been historically "successful" in
achieving elite power, we are more aware of their struggles of resistance and
the ways in which their interests have transformed and influenced elite interests. Situating my own work in this tradition, I utilize Scott's notion of infra-
politics, "or the circumspect struggle waged daily by subordinate groups," to
examine the political universe of the sha'b in Egypt. While infra-politics remains hidden and "beyond the visible end of the spectrum," in order to escape
the attention and retribution of dominant interests in society, people remain
engaged in political and economic struggles (Scott 1990, 183).

Among the sha'b in Egypt, individuals and families coordinate their interests through informal networks which weave in and out of households, markets, workplaces, government bureaucracies, private and public services, and the upper echelons of legislative and consultative bodies of the Egyptian state. Bound by loyal ties of kin and mutual interest, families utilize networks to secure housing, employment, and education for younger generations, arrange marriages that will ensure the reproduction of the family, save money in informal savings associations, and establish family-owned businesses and workshops. Informal networks are designed to coordinate and execute the demands and preferences of their constituents. Informal networks are penetrative, efficient, and responsive, filling a political need in the community by representing and furthering the interests of the shaᶜb. For optimal utility, networks incorporate diverse members of the community to maximize their effectiveness and enhance the network's access to people who can secure services or scarce goods for its members. They go beyond the limiting bounds of kin, occupation, region, gender, neighborhood, and class, since a range of members in networks means that they can be more effective and efficient.

Informal networks permeate daily life and are a critical, though concealed, facet of politics in Egypt. They have remained obscure because they lack formal, juridical recognition and legitimacy, but they enjoy popular legitimacy, which is crucial to their survival (March and Taqqu 1986, 5). From their obscurity and invisibility they derive their strength, since they are not encumbered by the controls of the state, the attention of political authorities, or associational rules. It is not that they are autonomous from the state or society, since they prosper in the gray area of mixed economies and uncertain elite political agendas, but that they move between the pervasive Egyptian bureaucracy, the community, the neighborhood, and family structures.

As they aggregate interests and connect individuals to each other, they allow for access to goods and services, inform their constituents about opportunities, and serve as forums to exchange ideas. Networks embody political organization and participation within shaᶜbi communities. Because they connect the private realm of the home to the public realm, they challenge the analytic distinction between the "political" public realm and the "social" private realm which many assume to be exaggerated in Egypt due to sexual segregation. Informal networks move imperceptibly through households, to businesses, local schools, tax offices, markets, mosques, police stations, and army units. Egypt's economy grew far more integrated into the international economy after the onset of the Open Door Policy (*al-Infitah*) in 1974, and informal networks now extend their reach throughout Egypt and the Middle East, particularly into the

Persian Gulf nations which have been the recipients of so much Egyptian migrant labor.

Though informal networks organize the demands and preferences of the sha῾b, their power is obviously mitigated by the control and resources of the state and its elite. In Egypt, despite some recent political liberalization, the state continues to control political expression and organization through a variety of mechanisms. Large segments of the population are excluded from the formal political arena and few of these people have the economic resources to influence elite politics. Broadening the locus of politics to various arenas of cooperation and competition within the community is not meant to deny the power of the Egyptian state, the resources it controls, nor the role of political elites, public or clandestine political parties, and interest groups. Because political scientists have directed their studies toward elite politics, however, they have often discounted or ignored the ability of informal groups to empower their communities or challenge the elite's political and economic controls. Arguing that politics extends beyond elite policy making and selection and interest group representation will, it is hoped, bring back into consideration the power of the supposedly powerless without minimizing the record of political repression and exclusion in Egypt. As Chazan argues, "politics, power and control are not of necessity coterminous with the state" (1988, 123).

The argument that the family is a crucial resource in the Middle East is not new. I am suggesting, however, that we take this piece of common knowledge and endow it with political meaning, recognizing the political implications of these relationships, as the community does. The family sees to the material and social needs of a community and fills a political vacuum. The family and informal networks are an important avenue of participation that complements or parallels the formal political sphere. While the power of the Egyptian state was felt daily by this community and men and women sought assistance from elites, state bureaucrats, and institutions, people also focused their energy, efforts, and resources toward strengthening their web of networks and familial ties.

The sha῾b, who through their daily experiences with bureaucracies understand the limits of state largesse, do not depend entirely on the state for their collective welfare, even as they keep up informal and formal demands on the state to maintain such redistributive policies as subsidies, free education, and public employment. At times people design networks to escape the regulatory, fiscal, or political power of the state. They also create certain networks to exploit the resources and services which the state distributes. This dexterity is necessary in a society where people must master both the informal and the formal face of any problem in order to overcome it. Knowing how to "deal" in both worlds is a valued and respected skill in these communities, and skilled mediators exchange their informal knowledge for various goods and services, whether in cash or in kind.

This chapter details the ways in which the family serves the material and social needs of members of households, arbitrates conflict, and shapes the ideological and communal norms of the community. A "familial ethos" pervades the community and is constructed by men and women to ensure and promote behavior which ensures the power and position of the family itself. This ethos will be described in more detail below. With intra-household politics accounted for, it is then possible to understand the interaction of familial and informal networks in fulfilling the common needs of the community, particularly the goal of reproducing the family, through the institution of marriage. This marital imperative dominates the local political economy and encourages the growth of informal political networks. In order to meet the economic requisites of marriage, for example, the sha'b have developed an informal savings mechanism, which I argue should be considered a public good. It is not only the government which influences the allocation and distribution of public goods, but sha'bi communities create and maintain public goods if their needs are ignored or misunderstood. Informal savings institutions are but one representative example of this type of activity. The politics of excluded constituencies, it will be demonstrated, influence the ways in which the state designs and implements certain policies.

The legacy of political exclusion in Egypt also helps to explain why people who are dissatisfied with the government often adopt more confrontational or violent forms of political participation. Since there is very little sanctioned and legal ground for participation, people are often forced to wage their political protest outside the system. The current violent struggle between Islamic activists and the Egyptian government is a tragic case in point. With little ground for legal politics, freedom of expression, and association, opposition forces with different visions of "the good" and the nature of the state gradually adopt the tactics of insurgents, as the government continues its campaign of repression and intimidation. The intensity of this conflict and its escalating violence may seem surprising to outside observers, but if we recognize the politics and the institutional life of sha'bi communities, we can understand not only common sources for dissatisfaction in Egypt today among lower-income communities but the ways in which informal political and economic institutions can serve the organizational needs of Islamic activists. Islamist groups have seized upon and reacted to the economic, political, and social problems which face the shaᶜb today in order to build support for their alternative agenda, and their agenda clearly resonates within these communities.

The Familial Ethos

The structure of the household and family dominates shaᶜbi communities and deeply affects the lives of men, women, and children. However, the household is not an undifferentiated "black box" which maximizes "familial" interests in a consistent and cooperative spirit (see Folbre 1986). Members of households maintain their individuality and protect personal interests. In these communities, where scarcity prevails, family members compete for resources and defend their interests within the boundaries of authority in a particular household. While gender roles set the parameters of acceptable behavior, both sexes are active participants in contributing, controlling, and distributing household resources.

Scholars typically analyze the family in the Middle East as a patriarchal structure. The patriarchal family structure accounts for the dominant position of men in society and the subordinate position of women. However, when one ventures inside of Egyptian homes, stereotypical images of the patriarchal family fade. Within the home women are active, demanding participants. They do not sit submissively by while husbands or fathers control the resources of the family. On the contrary, women are by far the more active and significant actors within the home. While power is not equally shared by all parties at all times, family members are deeply aware of their rights and their obligations to the family, and they protect those rights, demanding their due share of resources. Parents are not obeyed unquestioningly by children, nor husbands by wives. The presence of conflict within families is not due to an "Egyptian" personality of any sort; it is rather an indication that strict kinship, gender, or age hierarchies are often challenged.

In this chapter, I recount many conflicts and disputes within households, among colleagues and relatives. While fighting was common in some families, in others a calm, cooperative spirit prevailed. In both cases men and women were also very supportive and protective of family members. My emphasis on conflict is not intended to distort or deny the extreme closeness and affection that is so prevalent in family life in shaᶜbi communities. In Egypt, ties to family are strong and enduring. Relatives visit each other frequently and include each other in their economic, social, and political networks. Many of the conflicts that I refer to in this chapter reflect a process of renegotiation and redefinition of familial roles and responsibilities, when personal circumstances or external forces change. As the introduction to this volume explained, since recent socioeconomic phenomena have transformed many aspects of Egyptian society, the household has been the site of increased bargaining and the renegotiation of gendered roles and responsibilities. The resolution of conflicts attests to the resiliency and legitimacy of the familial ethos in these communities, and the presence of conflict suggests not that patriarchy rules but that challenges to power and authority are common.

Single incidents of conflict reveal a pattern of shared ideals and values. It is these ideals and values, defended and promoted within shaᶜbi communities and reflecting a general world view, which I refer to as the familial ethos. The values and traditions which people promote in this community are designed to strengthen family solidarities and power. Even if reality falls short of ideal notions, respected members of the community hold up these ideals to influence the actions and behavior of others. The "familial ethos" fashioned by the shaᶜb supports channels of arbitration, conflict resolution, economic assistance, cooperation in the community, and the reproduction of the family (or marriage and children). Clifford Geertz describes an ethos as "the moral (and aesthetic) aspects of a given culture, the evaluative elements . . . ." A people's ethos is the tone, character, and quality of their life, its moral and aesthetic style and mood; it is the underlying attitude toward themselves and their world that life reflects" (Geertz 1973, 126–27). Geertz sets an ethos in a distinctly cultural context but, while I would not diminish its cultural meaning, an ethos is also a product of economic and political dynamics and my arguments about the significance of the familial ethos have to be placed within a context of financial insecurity, considerable government intervention in the economy, and a tradition of political exclusion in Egypt. An ethos of cooperation, arbitration, and association with trusted individuals, which promotes a certain code of morality and propriety, is situated within the realities of everyday life among the shaᶜb. The Egyptian government, through its legal system, its executive power, and its intervention in the economy, also promotes its own vision of justice, development, "the good," and propriety. The state, through such vehicles as the educational system and the government-controlled media, attempts to influence values and norms in Egypt as well, so that a certain tension between communal norms and "official" norms and priorities pervades daily life within shaᶜbi communities.

A community's understanding of "the good," of justice, and of fairness, based on a widely shared consensus of values and norms, can obviously serve as the foundation of a wider-reaching political and philosophical outlook. Certainly, the principles of the familial ethos influence the ways in which the shaᶜb judge national events and politics and envision a better Egypt. A communal philosophy can set the parameters for theory construction and praxis. Sheldon Wolin explains how creating alternative norms and visions has an implicit political dimension to it which ultimately sets the ground for challenges to the prevailing order.

> The politics of founding or theory destruction, refers to the critical activity of defeating rival theoretical claims. Theoretical founding has both a *political* dimension and *politics*. The former is the constitute activity of laying down basic and general principles, which, when legitimated, become the presuppositions of practices, the ethos of practitioners. The point of engaging in the politics of theory is to demonstrate the superiority of one set of constitutive principles over another so that in the future these will be recognized as the basis of theoretical inquiry. Thus the founder's *action* prepares the *way* for *inquiry*, that is, for activity which can proceed uninterruptedly because its presuppositions are not in dispute. (Wolin 1981, 402–403)

The familial ethos in shaᶜbi communities, then, is quite powerful. It orders individual lives, sets parameters of behavior in the community, and shapes the political vision of many Egyptian citizens. Like all structures, the family is not wholly benevolent or harmless and the familial ethos is deeply contested within the community. It is an ideal which is shaped by an ever-changing variety of new material, social, and political forces. But men, women, and children understand the power and authority of the family and the meaning of the familial ethos as well as they understand the power and authority of the state and its underlying principles.

Expressing conflict in public involves a much wider community in regulating and perhaps resolving the source of tension. In densely populated communities many neighbors can hear family arguments quite easily. At times, people consciously advertise their disputes to make their positions known or inform the community of transgressions or the inappropriate behavior of others. Public involvement in disputes can be either positive or negative, depending on particular circumstances. While violence is not uncommon, it is not publicly condoned, even when communal norms have been violated. Regardless of whether people believe the use of physical force is legitimate, they fight back and protect themselves. Children, young girls, boys, wives, and husbands do not meekly accept physical abuse from others, but defend themselves. The youngest daughter of a particularly combative family takes on all attackers, claiming that she is not afraid of anyone, which is not proper "girlish" behavior by local standards.

The sometime combative interaction of family members calls into question images of the authoritarian family in Egypt and throughout the Middle East, where younger people and women are assumed to be passive and subordinate. These images and stereotypes are used by social scientists to suggest that Egyptians and other Middle Easterners are socialized through their families to accept authoritarian structures and that they then recreate them in both personal and public spheres and accept authoritarian leaders.[2] This authoritarian predisposition, scholars suggest, can then explain the difficulties that Middle Eastern regimes have had in instituting or adopting democratic principles of government.[3]

Households in sha'bi communities in Egypt were anything but authoritarian: men and women actively participate in the decision-making process and the political economy of the household. While the propensity to resort to violence in solving disputes varied from household to household, supposed authority figures were no more immune to attack than others. Contestants in these battles would perhaps be publicly chided for striking a pregnant woman or hitting an elderly person or small child, but the actions of men and women often contradicted the ideals of respect and consideration in the neighborhood. If the empirical reality does not fit the stereotypical image of patriarchal and authoritarian households in Egypt, then it logically follows that political theories and political analyses based on these stereotypes need to be revised. Furthermore, if women are active participants within the household and in the process of maintaining familial networks, then analyses and political accounts of the subordinated position of women in sha'bi communities also need to be revised.

Public homage to the strength of one's family as a means of support and power for individuals within the household differs from how those individuals achieve their ends within the community. While I have argued that patriarchal relationships do not typify the internal workings of households, women may publicly appeal to the role of powerful men in their families to provide for and protect the womenfolk and children. For example, after a major rift between a groom's family and the bride's over the payment of the dower and the date of the marriage's consummation, a local political leader (an associate of the bride's family, but not a relative) attempted to mediate the dispute. (A dower, *mahr*, is the gift due from a groom to a bride as part of the financial arrangements of marriage. A dowry, *gihaaz*, comprises the items which the bride's family provides for the couple.) The groom's male relatives paid a formal call to the mother of the bride. Despite the best intentioned efforts of this publicly respected and honored arbitrator, the widowed mother of the bride refused to compromise, saying she must first consult with the men in her family before coming to any decision. "Don't you realize that I have over 100 men to support me within my family that has lived in this neighborhood for centuries? I must also honor the strength and reputation of my husband's family when negotiating the marriage of one of his daughters." This woman had received some support from male members of her family, but she had also taken her husband's family to court for their failure to support the family after his death. In the end, it was clearly this woman, in consultation with her older married children, who decided her daughter's fate, not the male elders of the extended family. In this case, she turned the ideals of the patriarchal family against the prospective groom and his male relatives, successfully frustrating their plans.

A feuding family, however, is an inefficient institution that may lose opportunities to provide for its members, thereby diminishing its position in the community. Constant fighting not only absorbs the emotions and energies of the disputants but also can tarnish the reputation of the family in the community. Regardless, family disputes can be unavoidable when relatives are forced into taking sides. On the other hand, feuding factions of extended families reconcile when members of the family are threatened by outsiders, a group which includes spouses who marry into the family.

In one instance, two older married sisters had not spoken to each other for six months, despite the fact that one worked in the same building where the other sister lived. The daughter of one sister suffered a stroke while giving birth, and her husband's reaction to this crisis was to divorce her. In secret, he changed the lock on their apartment, thereby denying the daughter her right to reside in the apartment during her illness.[4] Immediately, the two sisters buried their differences, and they not only assumed the care of this young woman and her newborn daughter but also protected her rights and the husband's duty to support her through informal means (pressure on the husband's relatives, who condemned his reprehensible behavior) and formal means (registering a complaint through the office of the public prosecutor that forbade the husband to change locks and forced him to pay his wife's support and the child's). As the aunt of the partially paralyzed young woman said, "I have to stand by my sister in times of need (*laazim wa'if ma'ha*)." The sick woman's mother also started carrying a switchblade in her bodice to protect her daughter and her material possessions. It is this type of familial support which is so crucial within this community. Without this support, the daughter would have been homeless and unable to provide for either her newborn child's needs or her own critical health needs.

Disputes at other times are specifically staged in public to appeal to communal notions of justice and propriety.[5] A merchant stood in the street, in front of an associate's apartment, demanding that the friend repay a loan of 100 Egyptian pounds (approximately U.S. $70 in market prices in 1985).[6] He yelled that he was denouncing him "in front of the entire street," hoping to shame the man publicly. The merchant knew that ignoring debts contradicted communal principles and that a public attack would damage his friend's reputation and perhaps make it more difficult for him to find credit within the community in the future. In another instance a woman sat in a window directly overlooking the alleyway, crying and shouting that she did not deserve the abuse of her husband, who had beaten her. Rather than retreat into her home and internalize her anger and rage, she denounced her husband publicly.[7] This strategy protected her from her husband's further abuse by publicizing his violent attacks, thereby forcing the community to adopt the role of protector.

While powerful and resourceful individuals can dominate the household, selfish needs cannot hinder the ability of the household and family to act in a collective and collaborative manner when necessary. Once wives, husbands, children, or grandparents interact with the outside world to fulfill social, political, or economic goals, the smooth functioning of the household and extended family as a collaborative effort is critical. It is within this milieu that the importance of the household in the political community is most noticeable. While a few self-sufficient individuals can ignore their families, most individuals cannot and are forced to coordinate their needs with the families' larger needs.

In one large family in this community, for example, the elder son had supported his family since the death of his father twenty years earlier. The eldest brother had spent many years in various successful and unsuccessful businesses, providing for the needs of his mother, younger brother, and sisters and his own family of three children. This man, now in his early forties, had opened a machinists' workshop with his two younger married brothers. One of the brothers had spent four years in Saudi Arabia, accumulating enough capital to marry his fiancée and help his older brother purchase the machinery needed to start the family workshop. Each of his siblings had specific goals and needs they wanted to fulfill, whether that involved marriage, a business venture, or education. But each of these goals was also set within the context of family needs and priorities.

At one point, a major disagreement erupted between the brothers regarding their contributions to the family business and their respective profits. The married siblings of the family lived and worked in the same building, which the eldest brother had built at considerable personal expense. After the workshop had been open for more than a year, the two younger brothers became dissatisfied with their share of the profits and implied that the eldest brother was cheating them. The eldest brother was incensed by their impudent criticism, insisting that he had only opened the workshop to help them. He reminded them that he could have easily established far more lucrative ventures with other business colleagues.

An elderly uncle was called in by the eldest sister in the family to arbitrate this extremely sensitive conflict. In his admonishment, the uncle reminded the men that they were brothers, that blood ties were more binding than anything else, and that the older had to help out younger, even if the younger ones were critical and disrespectful. Interspersed throughout the uncle's argument were many references to the Prophet Muhammad and Islam, but the elder brother was so infuriated that he retorted that the Prophet and religion had nothing to do with this conflict. He even offered to give his brothers the money and machinery to open their own workshops, but the uncle said that this would not do, that a few words should not be allowed to destroy the family. Was he a *kaafir* (unbeliever) to say such blasphemous things about the Prophet and religion? It was unthinkable that each family member would go his own way.

The implications of the argument were so potentially destructive that the eldest sister in the family consulted a local woman, who visited the home to rid it of the evil spirits causing the bad blood between the brothers.[8] Eventually the disagreement was resolved and the brothers went back to work, but lingering resentments remained and the youngest brother quietly began exploring the possibility of emigrating temporarily in order to accumulate enough capital to open an independent workshop.

This example demonstrates the interplay between personal objectives, familial obligations, and the familial ethos. No one in the family denied that these brothers could easily dissolve their partnership and still succeed as individual businessmen. However, the preferred and socially proscribed path was to work together as a family, sharing responsibilities and profits. In this example, conflict was characteristically open and direct. Their relatives quickly recognized the severity of the dispute and sought out a respected elder of the family, who successfully averted a serious rift in the family. The arbitrative role of family elders and an appeal to the familial ethos convinced the brothers to resolve their differences.

In another example, when the shouting match between a mother and her eldest son spilled out of a ground floor workshop into the street, the boy's uncle chided them both, bringing them inside to avoid *kalaam al-naas* (gossip). The degree of antagonism between mother and son imputed not only their reputations but also the entire family's, and therefore it was the family's responsibility (in a collective sense) to resolve such disputes before they reached the public arena.[9] The consequences of failure to resolve conflict within the family can be extreme. In one incident in the neighborhood, residents were awakened by the curses of a woman who accused her son of stealing her money in order to marry a second wife, leaving his first wife, a cousin, with a newborn child. This dispute had broken out into a fight and part of the family had gone to the local police station to bring back an officer to arrest the son. When families voluntarily opt for the intervention of state authorities, familial institutions have already failed, and the family loses control over the resolution of the conflict.

This desire to resolve and arbitrate conflict through informal or extragovernmental means is very strong within this community. Prominent members of the community will hide their neighbors and relatives from the police, and if these strategies fail, they will support them with financial and legal assistance. In one incident, a tough young man came to the defense of the younger of two boys involved in a neighborhood brawl and stabbed the older boy after he was threatened with a knife. He immediately fled and the police were called to arrest him. The police searched for the young man's older brother to find out where he might be hiding. A prominent local woman in the community alerted the older brother of the police search in the area and hid this man in her apartment. The police let it be known that they would arrest the younger man's crippled mother if he did not turn himself in to the authorities. He then gave himself up. In this case the police used the familial ethos to compel the young man to surrender to the police.

In another case, a local politician had helped the niece of one of her constituents find a job in a charitable organization. The young woman and the administrator of the organization argued continually. Eventually the administrator fired her. Later, the politician learned that the young woman had filed a case in the labor relations court against the administrator. This suit angered the politician because she had not been informed of this disagreement before it was placed before the court, enabling it to intervene in "her" community's affairs. She was confident that she could have easily resolved the disagreement through informal means, if only she had been informed. Informal means are preferred by the majority of the community, since official decisions are generally more binding and coercive.

Economic Provision and Family Enterprises

Throughout this community the structure of the household and family is supported by common economic interest. Within central Cairo, shaᶜbi communities lie within mixed residential, commercial, and industrial areas. Large- and small-scale manufacturing workshops, wholesale and retail food markets, shops and markets are located under and next to residences and apartment buildings. Many of these establishments are owned or operated by families. Workers in these establishments may or may not be related to the owners, but the control and profits of the enterprise remain within family hands. Extended families commonly operate interdependent enterprises, where, for example, one relative markets lemons in a retail market, another tends to the wholesale market, another transports produce from rural areas to the wholesale market, and others cultivate lemons in family-cultivated orchards. Other relatives provide labor at critical times, staff the store, or keep the accounts. Men, women, and children in the family commonly contribute their labor, skills, education, and surplus savings to these family enterprises. They are similar to public sector enterprises in that both are organized to meet market and nonmarket objectives. Familial enterprises are designed to provide employment for family members, to increase and maintain control over the family's financial resources, and to enhance the economic and political prestige and power of a family in its community. Market pressures and rapid economic changes are cushioned among the shaᶜb if they can rely on family enterprises. It is often more socially acceptable for women to work with relatives rather than strangers and they are owners, partners, and workers in these diverse businesses. The mixed residential and commercial character of these neighborhoods reinforces economic interdependence among relatives, who often live and work together or nearby each other.

In order to capture the industrious character of this community, I recorded the primary, secondary, and tertiary sources of income.[10] In the community under study, family enterprises accounted for 19 percent of the primary sources of income of the economically active sample and 14 percent of secondary in-

comes.[11] Within private sector employment (private enterprises, family enterprises, and self-employment), family enterprises accounted for 45 percent of
primary and 32 percent of secondary income.[12] In order to earn additional income as consumer expectations rise and inflation grows, many people in these
communities take on second jobs (and, more rarely, third jobs). For the smaller
number of men and women who held two or three jobs, 14 percent worked in
family-based enterprises.

The locus of this study in households and workplaces revealed many economic activities of women (and men) which are not typically captured by labor force statistics. According to the 1986 Egyptian Population Census, female
participation in overall urban employment is only 16 percent and rural employment is 4 percent (Handoussa 1988, 49–50, 79). The World Fertility Survey
reports that 75 percent of "ever-married women" in Egypt between the ages of
fifteen and forty-nine had never worked (CAPMAS 1983, 9). Yet, in my own
study, women participated in the labor force in far greater percentages. Fifty-
six percent of the women in the economically active sample were engaged in a
primary economic activity, 27 percent were engaged in a secondary economic
activity, and *71 percent* earned income (in cash or kind) from either a primary,
secondary, or tertiary economic activity.[13]

The much higher rates of participation in the labor force in this sample can
be explained by my familiarity with the economic activities of women in the
community, repeated visits to many of their households, knowledge of their
financial affairs, and a methodology of participant observation. Many of the
women in the sample who were, for example, seamstresses, leaders of savings
associations, or involved in the black market would not describe their activity
as an occupation/profession (*mihna*), job (*waziifa*), or work (*shughl*) to an unknown government official, such as a census enumerator. To administer the
Egyptian Fertility Survey, census enumerators were instructed to ask women
whether they sold things, held jobs, worked on a family farm, or were self-employed (CAPMAS 1983, 92–93). From my experience in Cairo, many women
(and perhaps men)[14] who were economically active would respond negatively
to these questions, despite the fact that their activities fell under the definition
of work used in the survey.[15] Some people do not trust any government official
and would not reveal information about their finances which could possibly
be used against them by the tax authorities or other governmental agencies.
Others, particularly women in the presence of their husbands or male relatives,
might be embarrassed by their contribution to the family's income, since that
is customarily and legally the responsibility of the male head of the household.

In still other cases, both men and women might not reveal their financial resources to an outsider, not in fear of the government but as a strategy to maintain the secrecy of their financial resources from other family members. However, the higher percentage of economically active women and men in this
sample is most likely not a reflection of an unrepresentative or particularly industrious sample, but a methodology which more accurately captures primary,
secondary, and tertiary economic activities.

In order to understand the great significance of the family in the political
economy of these communities, we must also add the contribution of housework to our calculations. Married and unmarried women contribute indispensable labor, skills, and caretaking to families and communities. Lower-income families could not afford the replacement value of women's contributions
to the household economy. As Hoodfar argues in this volume (chapters 1 and
3), women are primarily responsible for many nonmarket economic activities
which are an indispensable component of survival strategies and the household economy. I therefore include the occupation of housewife under a larger
category of family-related economic activities.

The accompanying graph includes self-employed men and women under a
calculation of family-related economic activities as well. The men and women
in this category provide skills and services to the community but are usually
too poor to own enterprises or physical capital. They prepare food in their
homes, sew clothes for neighbors, give private lessons to neighborhood children, or serve tea to workers in nearby industrial workshops. Many of these
men and women are assisted in the organization, preparation, or marketing of
their skills by their families and are therefore included in this general category.
For example, one very poor, young widowed woman with several small children sold tea and hot drinks to the many industrial workers and merchants
whose shops surrounded her makeshift home in a vacant lot. The children assisted their mother in preparing and delivering the drinks.

The graph clearly demonstrates the importance of family-related economic
activities in these neighborhoods. Forty-two percent of the sample population
gained its primary income from familial sources. These figures serve to explain
the continued resiliency of family authority and power in shaʿbi communities.
It is interesting to note that an even higher percentage of those with secondary
occupations worked in family-related enterprises.[16] While men and women
may struggle to secure an education and training to gain employment in the
government bureaucracy or modern industrial factories, they resort to familial
networks to secure that extremely crucial secondary source of income. Men

Family-Related Economic Activities in Lower-Income Cairo Neighborhoods

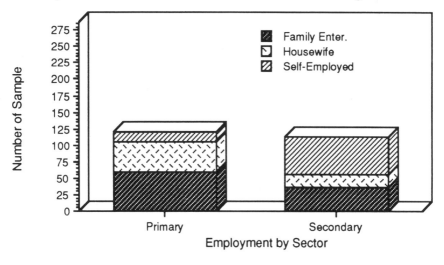

and women also use family connections to obtain positions in the private and public sectors. Some private enterprises in the community and, to a lesser extent, public sector offices were staffed and administered by members of the same family. An administrator of a public or private firm can hire relatives and also direct the routine activities of the organization to benefit family members.

Some family enterprises are quite large businesses and operate throughout Egypt and internationally as well. The most sophisticated and geographically extended family business in the neighborhood operated out of a "supermarket" in the area.[17] The family drew upon four generations for its labor supply. One brother cultivated land in Upper Egypt which produced sugar, honey, milk, butter, and *samna* (clarified butter, an expensive but vastly preferred cooking ingredient); the goods were then transported to Cairo and distributed wholesale to various grocers and markets. These same products were also exported to various Arab countries. Another brother, who had traveled extensively and spoke German and English, arranged the export of the products to Arab countries, assisted by his relatives, who worked in the Persian Gulf. At the same time, he traveled to Europe to import butter and other dairy products to Egypt, despite constant complaints about government trade regulations. The family then entered into negotiations with a British firm to buy a sophisticated industrial plant to produce and package dairy products on a plot of land they had bought for a mere £E30,000 ($20,979 in 1985 market prices) in one of the new satellite cities (aside from very low rates for commercial property, the government offers a ten-year tax holiday for businessmen who buy land in these cities). Their partner in this deal was another very large, wealthy, family-based contracting firm from the same village in Upper Egypt.

Younger members of the family continue to be drawn into the family business. Many young men and women in these neighborhoods, whose parents are either barely literate or illiterate, now attend the lower levels of the higher education system in Egypt.[18] Although they are training to be teachers, businessmen, lawyers, or skilled technicians, most of them realize that they will join their father's or mother's family business after completing their military or public service. Throughout their education, many of the young men, in particular, have learned the family craft or trade during school vacations and the long summer break. Discontented, underutilized, or overskilled family members cannot, however, exercise the "exit" option lightly and ignore their family enterprises. Men and women, despite their best intentions, are often forced to accept major responsibility in family enterprises, despite their formal university education, because younger siblings or elderly parents are supported by the business. They do not have the luxury of establishing financially risky business ventures, because of familial obligations. The family need for economic security outweighs personal occupational choices or entrepreneurial dreams. Furthermore, young adults from these communities have few opportunities to attain prestigious, professional positions in the private sector, unlike their counterparts from upper class or professional families, and it is therefore extremely rational to join the family business. In the past few years, as the government has reduced its financial commitment to public employment, it has even become difficult to attain low-paying positions in the public sector, as an alternative to family employment (see Handoussa 1991).

The bonds between family members who work together are obviously more interdependent. Business failure not only produces unemployment but threatens the economic security of the family. Several young men in this community had invested savings from their employment abroad to buy either a taxi or a small pickup truck. These young men held jobs in the public sector but saw the vehicles as a way of supplementing their incomes. In one case, members of the immediate and extended family loaned a young man money for a down payment on a taxi (£E3,000 or U.S. $2,098). His friends rented the car from him when he was at his government job. One week the taxi broke down, was not bringing in any revenue, and needed very expensive repair work. At the same time, the young owner of the taxi was desperately trying to save money for his marriage expenses so that his wedding would not have to be post-poned. Yet relatives who had lent him considerable sums of money for the taxi (£E500–600) demanded repayment. Three of his brothers-in-law, who had lent him money, began abusing their wives (his sisters) to force repayment. Conflict erupted at every family gathering over this issue. In the end, because he could not afford the repair bill and the car sat idle, he could not meet the monthly loan payments on the car (£E230) and the agency repossessed the car. The family suffered a huge financial disaster by losing their £E3,000 down payment on the taxi.

The family in shaᶜbi communities has been able to maintain itself as an important, if understudied, productive unit in Egypt's mixed economy. Family enterprises remain an important source of employment, income, and security for many men and women, particularly in shaᶜbi communities. The economic dimension of the family supports and strengthens its position in the community as those in control of these economic resources can exploit them to promote their social and political preferences. Among the range of interests supported is clearly the continued prominence of the family itself.

Informal Financial Networks in the Community

While families have extraordinary capacities to save money and furnish start-up costs for small business enterprises, they do not have the daily resources to meet unexpected maintenance or repair costs. Many individuals and businessmen who keep their money in banks and are knowledgeable about the banking system also use informal savings and credit networks to fulfill expected and unexpected financial needs. One's ability to obtain credit is a direct reflection of one's standing in the community, and the reputation of the family is a crucial component of that reputation. At the same time, certain individuals, despite the standing and position of their families, may be denied credit from relatives or colleagues because of their poor personal reputation and lack of integrity.

Within this community a parallel banking realm, organized by reputable and trusted women and men in the community, provides crucial financial services. *Gamᶜiyyaat*, or informal savings cooperatives, offer credit without interest to individuals who lack the collateral to obtain bank loans, cannot afford interest payments, or prefer to save their money with relatives, trusted friends or colleagues in order to keep their financial activities hidden from governmental institutions (or, in some cases, other relatives). In these associations a small group of friends, relatives, neighbors, or colleagues contribute a fixed sum to the leader of an association at regular intervals. Some associations are daily or weekly; more commonly they are monthly. The leader collects the money at the end of each interval and immediately gives the total sum to one participant. The payment schedule is agreed upon ahead of time by the members, according to their needs. In a sudden financial emergency, a friend or relative will organize an association and arrange to give the person in need the first lump sum payment. For the duration of the association, they continue to contribute each month, in a sense repaying a loan. For example, the eldest sister in one family had first begun organizing gamᶜiyyaat more than thirty years ago when a teacher's money was stolen. She found ten friends and relatives who were willing to save £E30 per month for a period of ten months. As is customary, the participants in the group decide ahead of time when each of them will receive their lump sum payment, and the leader of this group gave the teacher the first payment of £E300. This woman has organized these associations for years, incorporating colleagues, family, and neighbors into her financial networks. Informal savings associations are also popular because they do not offer interest, a practice which is forbidden by Islamic law but common in the conventional banking sector.

Typically, young men and women joined a gamᶜiyya to save for their wedding expenses which would include the dower, marriage apartment, the *shabka* or gift of jewelry for the engagement, household furnishings and household appliances. The entire expense of the marriage process from beginning to end amounted to approximately £E15,000 or $10,350, in this community. Mothers and fathers of affianced children also saved for the costs of the wedding in gamᶜiyyaat. Businessmen in industries that cater to the tourist industry organized gamᶜiyyaat to which they contributed daily (£E30 each business day for ten months). In industrial areas businessmen saved for capital investments in their workshops. A favorite goal of many women who saved in these associations was to purchase gold jewelry which could always be sold whenever they, or their families, were in need of cash. While wearing jewelry was a display of wealth and status, many women had far more gold stashed away in their homes, as insurance against future economic misfortune.

The leader of the gamᶜiyya is an indispensable member of the community whom people respect and honor. It can be argued that women are really the bankers of Egypt, since most of the leaders of informal savings associations are trusted and respected women in the community. Several women in the community ran three or four associations simultaneously. (Men tend to lead associations based on traditionally male occupational networks such as craftsmen or construction workers). These leaders have access to large amounts of cash and because of their vast network of relatives, friends, and neighbors, they can organize new associations as needs arise in the community or provide short-term loans. People also try to enhance their credit rating by contributing fractions of one membership in several associations, rather than a full membership in only one association.

This network of trust and informal financial services in the community informs relations in the local business community as well. Many of the small industrial and commercial enterprises, although licensed, regulated, and taxed by the state, do not keep organized (*munazzama*) accounts. Tax regulations differ according to the size, nature, and accounting system of industrial enterprises. The smaller establishments, which are more likely to keep "unorganized" accounts, are also more likely to prefer the informal banking system, to minimize government (tax authority) knowledge of their profits and net worth.

Although many of these enterprises can and do receive private and public sector bank loans and have collateral to obtain loans, at times they prefer to raise money informally, or join gamᶜiyyaat run by trusted businessmen. They loan and borrow money within the community. When they encounter financial difficulties, word spreads among their associates, who visit them to repay old debts or offer immediate loans. In one case, after investing £E75,000 in machinery alone, a businessman's project failed, and in a desperate moment he sold his workshop in an expensive commercial area for £E14,000. Coming to his senses, he unsuccessfully tried to buy back his property and machinery from the shrewd purchaser. News of his financial ruin spread through the business community, and all those to whom he had lent money in the past voluntarily came to repay their debts and brought attaché cases filled with cash. Because of his good reputation in the community ("my word is final") he was quickly able to collect enough money to begin another business venture.

Gamᶜiyyaat could exist only in a close, cooperative community infused with a strong sense of communal norms. People do not join these associations indiscriminately. The gamᶜiyya that they join frequently reflects their networks in the community and although they might not know all the participants, they trust the leader and the other participants enough to risk their savings. The pervasiveness of these savings societies among the shaᶜb and other segments of Egyptian society offers strong confirmation of the continued resilience of community and the familial ethos in Cairo.

Reproducing the Family: An Economic Imperative

Political preferences and demands evolve from people's most urgent needs and problems. Reproducing the family is one of the most basic goals of individuals and families within shaʿbi communities as well as throughout Egyptian society. Individual and collective behavior reinforces this goal and the community's actions are devoted to its realization. In a society where premarital sexual relationships are condemned on religious grounds (both among Muslims and Christians), marriage is the socially sanctioned route to emotional and sexual gratification. Marriage and establishing one's own household signify adulthood, and bearing children completes the regeneration of the family. By establishing a separate household a young man and woman create, for the first time, a measure of independence from their immediate family. For young women, whose movements in this community are restricted and controlled, the household offers an escape from the surveillance of parents and male siblings.

The goal of marriage and procreation vexes young men and women between the ages of sixteen and thirty-five, their parents, and the legions of relatives, friends, colleagues, and neighbors who are involved in the process. Marriage affects the career choices, education, workload, investments, migration, savings, and consumption patterns of men and women in shaʿbi communities. Parents organize their savings and consumption strategies around the marriage of their children, sacrificing their material comfort for the future of the family.[19] This goal can only be met through elaborate collective processes which the community supports. Typically, families are intricately involved in the political, social, and economic aspects of marriage. In this community many marriages are arranged by family members who are constantly on the lookout for prospective spouses for members of the family and community.

The economic costs of creating and maintaining new households place enormous pressure on shaʿbi communities. While most of the costs of marriage are born by families, the government contributes a modest share by distributing bonuses to dependent children when they marry if their parents are on government pensions, by constructing cooperative and public sector housing exclusively for newlyweds (some of which is available only in foreign currency to attract the labor remittances of Egyptian expatriates), and by offering "social loans" without interest through public sector banks to engaged couples. Yet these programs benefit only the small fraction of engaged couples who meet specific eligibility requirements. For the most part, the government does not contribute to the most capital-intensive need of every Egyptian family.[20]

The words *diligence, ingenuity, discipline,* and *sacrifice* aptly describe the characteristics needed to reproduce the family in Cairo today. Throughout sha‘bi communities, men and women utilize a variety of strategies to accumulate the capital to marry. They exploit their own labor power by working two or three jobs and long hours of overtime. Young men (and fewer young women) work abroad for many years in search of more lucrative wage rates and increased savings. Since the family contributes significant material resources to a marriage, it is important that men and women protect their power and position within the family as a means of securing scarce family resources for their marriages.

People in sha‘bi communities must have an extremely strong savings ethic in order to finance weddings, regardless of the personal and familial resources at their disposal. Earning a high salary, working sixty hours a week, or migrating abroad does not necessarily mean a person will save money. But the sha‘b have created an effective, legitimate, and flexible system of informal savings which assists that process of accumulation. Almost every wedding is largely financed by a gam‘iyya. The bride, the groom, and their families participate in them over the course of their engagement to finance major marriage expenses such as housing, key money, appliances and household furnishings, the dower, and the *shabka*, a gift of expensive gold jewelry for the bride. While people from middle-class and upper-middle-class backgrounds also use gam‘iyyaat, they are particularly pervasive in sha‘bi communities, since families of more limited means spend years accumulating the sums needed to marry and have less access to other credit sources. Some leaders of these associations claim that they are responsible for all the marriages among their neighbors and relatives.

The average cost of a marriage within the sha‘bi community I studied approximated £E15,000, or U.S. $10,490, in the mid-1980s. This sum includes costs which the groom or his family assumes, such as the dower, jewelry for the bride, the marital apartment, furniture, appliances, clothing, and the costs of the wedding itself. It also includes costs which the bride or her family assumes, such as furniture, a trousseau, carpets, household and kitchen furnishings, the cost of the engagement party, and a wedding band for the groom. The groom and his family generally bear two-thirds of the cost of marriage and the bride and her family a third.[21] Salaries in this community range from £E15 to £E1,200 per month, but most young men and women earn between £E75 and £E300 per month.

❖ Diane Singerman ❖

Accumulation on this scale within a low-income community suggests an impressive capacity to save. In fact, the pervasive savings ethic within sha'bi communities is far stronger than domestic savings rates estimate. Yet this disciplined behavior is rarely mentioned in standard economic analyses. To determine the sums that might be circulating in savings associations throughout Egypt, I used three different estimates of the cost of marriage and multiplied each one by the estimated number of marriage contracts in 1986.[22] (See the accompanying table.) The first estimate (A) in the table uses the figure of £E15,000, which is the average total cost of a marriage within the sha'bi community under study. The second estimate (B) of £E7,500 is lower because some marriage expenses are not a result of savings in gam'iyyaat, particularly if housing is inherited. The third estimate (C) of £E4,000 purposefully reduces the average cost of marriage to reflect the lower demand for consumer goods by rural or very poor urban families in Egypt, and a significant proportion of marriages obviously occurs in rural areas. However, using the cost of marriage among sha'bi communities as an upper estimate in this exercise severely underestimates the sums circulating in informal savings associations because marriages of the large middle and smaller upper classes of Egyptian society are far more expensive and elaborate.

The possibility that 131 percent of Egyptian gross domestic savings is circulating in informal savings associations suggests that the savings ethic in Egypt is far stronger than officials estimate. More important, this degree of activity suggests that informal savings associations are a public good fashioned by the sha'b to fulfill its needs. Even if the assets of informal savings associations approach the lowest estimate (C), they represent 35 percent of gross domestic savings (see World Bank 1989, 234–235). Because individuals, particularly businessmen, use savings associations for financial needs other than marriage, the assets of informal savings associations are much greater than the above exercise suggests.[23] The table confirms the value of informal savings associations to the community and the nation.

Informal savings associations contribute to solving some of the financial dilemmas surrounding marriage in Egypt. These economic issues represent only one kind of concern which families must address; they are also deeply involved in choosing appropriate spouses in the time-honored tradition of matchmaking. While it is certainly more common these days for young people to meet independently, arranged marriages still predominate. Well-connected members of the community are often approached by acquaintances inquiring about the supply of unmarried children in their families, with the intent of arranging

Three Estimates of Assets of Informal Savings Associations in Egypt, 1986

	Estimate A*	Estimate B†	Estimate C‡
Total assets	£E6,962,790,000	£E3,481,395,000	£E1,856,744,000
Percent of gross domestic savings (£E5.31 billion in 1986)	131	65	35
Percent of gross national savings (£E3.831 billion in 1986)	164	91	48
Percent of gross domestic product (£E38.356 billion in 1986)	18	9	4.8

*Based on average cost of marriage in community under study (£E15,000).
†Based on cost of marriage minus inherited housing (£E7,500).
‡Based on cost of marriage in rural areas (£E4,000).

a match. Within Cairo, consanguineous marriages are still common. In a representative sample survey of Metropolitan Cairo, 32 percent of the marriages reported were to kin, including 58 percent to first cousins. These figures have not varied much at all between women in older and younger generations (see Zurayk and Shorter 1988, 44–45). As one woman with two unmarried older sons told a particularly influential local figure, "we want to become related because everyone in the neighborhood loves you." The reputation of a family is taken into consideration because the negotiations and requisites of marriage are complex and if the other party to a match is frivolous or unreliable a son or daughter may be left devastated and a family will have wasted a great deal of time and money.

In arranging marriages and other alliances between families, one party will refer to their family's origins or ancestry as an indication of honor and prestige. This term implies that a family's lineage can be traced back to the time of the Prophet Muhammad and the birth of Islam, thereby implying a tradition of family piety and faith. But more generally it identifies one as coming from a "good family," which implies honesty, integrity, and position in the community rather than material wealth. Impolite men will be condemned by comments such as *huwa ma'andush asl* (meaning he has no lineage, manners, morals, or sense of propriety). Again, the familial ethos can be used to enhance one's reputation or condemn behavior and actions.

At the same time, however, the assumption that a family's reputation and standing in the community is crucial to a successful match falls short of reality. Despite the gravity of choosing a suitable spouse, many families announced engagements to people they barely knew.[24] A family on vacation met the young son of another vacationing family on a beach and hurried back to Cairo to suggest a match between an unmarried niece and the young man. In another incident, an elderly woman entered a local charitable association and complimented the manners and character of a young woman. She asked if the woman was married. The young woman responded that she was and had two small children, but that she also had an unmarried sister at home. Within a month the son of the elderly woman and the younger sister were formally engaged. Although engagements are formally announced when the two families jointly read the *faatiha* (or opening verse of the Qur'an) shortly after meeting, either party can withdraw from the agreement before the marriage is consummated. At this point, both parties will agree that *makansh fi nasib*, which translates as it wasn't fated (by God), and therefore no harm was done. This understanding of marriage minimizes personal blame and responsibility for the dissolution of the proposed marriage but does not erase antagonisms created by the failed engagement.

The financial arrangements of the marriage are publicly discussed and agreed upon before any commitment to marriage is made. Custom dictates that the groom is responsible for providing the dower, which is paid to the bride's family at a time agreed upon by both families. The groom must buy the marital apartment and appliances for the apartment (stove, washing machine, tape recorder, television, iron, blender, lamps, modern bathroom, kitchen and electrical fixtures, and a video cassette recorder if finances allow). In addition he purchases carpets and drapes and absorbs the costs of completely "finishing" the apartment, which can be high in a renovated or newly constructed apartment. The groom also purchases a number of heavy gold bracelets for the bride, wedding bands for each of them, and other less valuable jewelry throughout the period of courtship.[25] Finally, he pays for the wedding party and reception and the complete set of clothes that the bride wears during the final celebration before the consummation of the marriage. It is also customary for the groom to buy a new wardrobe for himself before his marriage and provide fabric and some items in the bride's trousseau as well. The mother of the bride usually keeps a document (the ʿ*ima* or *lista*) which lists the value of the possessions that both the bride and groom have contributed to the new household. In case of divorce, these possessions remain the personal property of the person who purchased them.

The parents of the bride accept the groom's dower and must spend at least as much as the dower, and more commonly twice its sum, to purchase a specific number of room furnishings, specified at the time of the public engagement. The cost, quality, and fashion of home furnishings is a popular topic of debate and discussion within the community. In the community where I conducted field research, the family of the bride typically bought three rooms of furniture that were purchased as sets: the bedroom, living room or salon, and dining room. These expensive, ornate, formal replicas of heavy French furniture completely dominate the small apartments that are now common in newer residential areas of Cairo (from £E500 for an entrée set, 2,000 for a bedroom set, and 3,000 for a dining room set, in 1985 prices). Wealthier families may demand an entrée, which is usually a less expensive and more casual living room set. However, there are other families in this community who cannot afford even one set of new furniture and marry with very basic furnishings and without elaborate ceremonies.

The bride's trousseau includes a complete new wardrobe, linen, kitchenware, and other minor household furnishings. Every item of the trousseau must be provided before the wedding takes place. The bride, following the example of her numerous female relatives, demands that her dowry include pieces of china, cutlery, and cookware similar to the ones that her relatives received. Families typically begin accumulating a girl's trousseau long before she is ready to marry. One family had accumulated a virtual storehouse of kitchenware and household furnishings throughout the course of marrying off four daughters. Every gift that came into the household for thirty years had been stored in the attic, to be used for one of the four daughter's trousseaus. For the youngest daughter, the trousseau was still incomplete but included 102 glasses of various shapes, 30 tea cups and saucers, 18 plastic trays, assorted sets of cookware, 45 bowls of various shapes, 8 ashtrays, cheap plastic dishes for daily use, miscellaneous serving dishes and plastic ornaments, linens, towels and a large suitcase filled with nightgowns and fabric.

These material demands have delayed marriage for both men and women, and it is not atypical for men to wait until their early thirties to marry. The average age of marriage for women has also risen in the past decade. In a 1980 sample of the Cairo metropolitan area, the mean age of first marriage for women was 23.4 and 28.9 for men (Zurayk and Shorter 1988, 15). The financial

requisites of marriage affect the career paths of both men and women. If men
want to marry before the age of thirty they must finish their education, serve
one to three years in the army, then accumulate £E5,000–10,000 in order to
marry. They have approximately five years, in the beginning of their careers,
to accumulate their largest single investment of capital in their lives.

This financial pressure explains the appeal of migration, during which
young men deprive themselves materially and psychologically in order to accumulate enough money to marry and perhaps start a small workshop when
they return. Often they will need to make several trips to the Gulf before they
can marry, and then they return to the Gulf directly after marrying to begin
saving capital for a business venture. The demands of marriage also mean that
one cannot afford to experiment with new business projects. The immediate
returns of any job, at this age, must be substantial. For those who are unskilled
and can find only low-paying jobs, the task is even more difficult. Despite the
fact that wedding expenses decrease among the poorest communities, in relation to their incomes they are still overwhelming. Even the poorest families will
sacrifice good health, housing, and material comfort in order to marry their
children at a much higher standard of living than their own. Interestingly, most
families succeed in this goal, and the material comfort of their children's
homes is visibly greater than their own. At the same time there are many tragic
cases of broken engagements due to unrealistic material demands from a family or the inability of young men to find and finance affordable housing.

Within this community, family after family decided to invest limited financial resources in engagements and marriage. Despite differences in familial and
individual resources, expectations, and marriage protocol, people struggled to
marry off their sons and daughters. Through marriage, the family transferred
wealth and status to the younger generation of the family. As a whole, these
individual and family decisions influence the political economy of this community, the national political economy, and the national allocation and distribution of scarce resources. If the political economy of shaᶜbi communities is
organized, in large part, around the goal of reproducing the family, then this
issue deserves far more systematic and sophisticated attention from economists
and policy makers.

To a certain extent, the demands which reproducing the family place upon
families and the political economy of Egypt is reflected in debates in the media
about problems surrounding marriage. In a long article, an opposition newspaper, *Al-Shaᶜb*, investigated two troubling phenomena related to the rising

cost of marriage: poor Egyptian girls who marry wealthy foreigners (largely older Arab men from wealthy Gulf countries) and poor or lower-middle-class Egyptian men who marry foreign women (largely Europeans). The article condemns "tourist" marriages, which have flourished within the last ten years, "because its sole objective is gratification and pleasure or to be more precise, a fixation with pleasure, which Egyptian families have resorted to because of poverty, and pressure on a girl." In Giza province, a fifty-year-old foreign man married a seventeen-year-old girl for a dower of £E 700 and two gold bracelets. "The girl was from a poor family in a difficult social position and she concluded that marriage to a poor young man would only increase her poverty. She wanted to live better and went to a woman who worked as a broker (*simsaar*) for this type of marriage." After she was married, her husband divorced her two weeks later and she returned to her family (al-ʿAshmaawy 1986, 9). The article describes another case where a fifty-five-year-old man from Dubai married an eleven-year-old bride (which is illegal). This man was already married and had grandchildren the bride's age; like many of these marriages, this one lasted only six months.

Social critics blame the poor economy for the increasing trend of marriages between Egyptian men and foreign women. A young man who was interviewed explained: "In Germany the costs of marriage are a great deal easier than here. . . . In Egypt, the dower and the *shabka* and the like, are so expensive. I am a young man from a modest background and if I waited the marriage train would pass me by." Another young man married an Italian woman whom he had met in Egypt. "I don't regret this step because my salary here was not more than £E80 and how could I live and think about an apartment or marriage?" (al-ʿAshmaawy 1986, 9). At the end of the article, "experts" argued that many of these marriages ended in divorce, were contrary to Islamic law, and produced troubled children. The subtext of this article, in an opposition newspaper, blamed the government for this phenomenon, since it associated such marriages with the rise of consumerism, the Open Door Policy, and the government's policy of promoting foreign tourism. As the economic costs of marriage escalate, social frustration can become a source of increasing dissatisfaction toward the government. Many analysts of Islamic activism in Egypt suggest that one of the primary sources of support for this movement comes from frustrated young men who are caught between the escalating economic demands of marriage, poor employment prospects, and a socially conservative familial ethos which condemns sex outside of marriage (though these critics fail to note that these same problems also affect women). It is clear that the goal of reproducing the family among the sha⁣ᶜb is shaping Egypt's political discourse and political sensibilities.

To this point, I have tried to make an argument concerning the importance of the family and informal institutions to the political universe of the sha⁣ᶜb. The organization of this community and its interests, however, have an impact on elite politics as well. In conclusion, I will present evidence which suggests that the Egyptian government does at times recognize the influence of the familial ethos and the presence of these institutions and that it designs state policies with them in mind. In the case of a black market for subsidized goods the government certainly recognizes (and is plagued by) the sha⁣ᶜb's ability to expropriate or redirect state resources to meet their ends. In the areas of education, health, housing, subsidy policies, and personal status laws, the state's sensitivity to sha⁣ᶜbi communities will be briefly described, although each one of these issues deserves far more extensive attention than can be provided here. Further complicating this analysis is the nature of infra-politics itself: the influence of informal networks, informal political and economic institutions and the familial ethos is indirect and somewhat invisible.

The government wrote in a Five-Year Plan (1978–82) that one of its primary duties is to "make available to the public both necessary and other foodstuffs, at prices much lower than their actual cost to the government" (Ikram 1981, as cited by Khouri-Dagher 1986, 9). The sha⁣ᶜb hold the government to this obligation by purchasing their legal share of subsidized foodstuffs and using informal distribution channels to purchase illegal shares of public goods. The sha⁣ᶜb are so skilled at this that the burden of financing subsidies had grown tremendously since the 1960s. Since the government fears that demonstrations will break out if prices rise (as they did in 1977), it employs indirect methods to decrease the subsidy bill, such as reducing entitlements to food, decreasing supplies, or distributing lower quality and cheaper goods. Between 1981–82 and 1986–87, in fact, food subsidies declined by approximately 50 percent (Zaytoun 1991, 248). Subsidized foods are a scarce commodity in sha⁣ᶜbi communities, where market prices are double or triple the government sales prices (see Alderman and Von Braun 1984 and Sokkari 1984). While food is distributed to over 95 percent of the population at subsidized prices, there remain serious inequities in the access to food and its availability, which Khouri-Dagher describes in more detail in this volume (chapter 5; also see Alderman and Von Braun 1984 and Khouri-Dagher 1986).

People cultivate networks of information and distribution in order to purchase needed, inexpensive food and constantly hover around government food cooperatives in the chance that scarce goods will be available. Those that are working or are too tired to confront chaotic and, at times, aggressive crowds become the clients of *dallalaat* (female peddlers), who have created an informal system of food distribution, deeply rooted in these communities.[26] Dallalaat are the backbone of the elaborate black market system that works in cooperation with the employees of food cooperatives. In shaᶜbi neighborhoods, dallalaat distribute food and other commodities (oil, soap, tea) to their clients. Sometimes they procure ration books, for a price, from local families in order to obtain greater quantities of subsidized commodities, and occasionally they are prosecuted and jailed. Exploiting the weaknesses of government distribution programs and the strengths of informal networks, the organizers of these distribution networks fulfill a need within the community and make a profit as well. These organizers become well known and occasionally notorious but always are in a strong position to trade their expertise, information, and supply of goods for other scarce goods and services. At times, these networks are so well organized that they are far more dependable than government cooperatives, even though some of the same employees staff both systems. Like many other manifestations of informality, the informal food distribution system works on the strengths and weaknesses of the formal. And when the informal system is deemed too threatening to the state, there is a severe crackdown on internal corruption and autonomous black marketeers. Within a short time, however, the networks are reorganized and are again distributing goods.

In July 1986, in an attempt to regain control over the distribution system and weaken black market food distribution networks, the government initiated a new two-tiered distribution system. Certain commodities had been available only in limited, rationed quantities through government food cooperatives and special grocery stores—or through the extensive black market that had grown up as a consequence of this policy. The government decided to offer more of these goods to customers but at unsubsidized prices. Many of these "expensive" items were sold in middle-class and wealthier neighborhoods. While there was still a problem of availability, the government was trying to regain customers and profits from the black market. When it initiated the new policy, the government intensified the regulation and surveillance of its distribution system, primarily to deprive the black market of its supply of commodities. Interestingly, the prices of the unsubsidized goods were higher at the government stores than they had been on the black market. The government would not need to design such new policies in order to destroy the black market and police its own employees if the black market was not so deeply embedded in sha‘bi communities.

The sensitivity of the government to one of the sha‘b's main concerns, food security, is obvious from the attention that food shortages and the subsidy system receive in the media. Shortages in various commodities, produced either by speculation, corruption, international market conditions, government ineptitude, or design, become the focus of exposés and screaming headlines in newspapers. In the summer of 1986, for example, three crises filled the headlines of newspapers (particularly the pages of opposition newspapers, which publicized these scandals to encourage opposition to the government): a tea shortage, a *kushari* shortage (the famous Egyptian fast food which consists of macaroni, lentils, onions, and spices), and a flour shortage. All three items are especially important to the sha‘b because they are very inexpensive and essential parts of almost every Egyptian's diet (kushari is even referred to in newspaper articles as a sha‘bi meal). One newspaper reported that the price of kushari had risen 500 percent during the previous three years as the government repealed its mandatory price controls. The headline asked whether a plate of kushari would turn into a tourist dish available only at highly inflated prices at five-star hotels (Abu Liwaayah 1986; see also Muhammed 1986). The headline of an article about the tea crisis was even more interesting: "The *Sha‘b* Warns the Government: Stay Away from [Our] Cup of Tea." When a reporter interviewed people around Cairo about their reaction to the price increase in tea, people responded by arguing that it was a national outrage, almost treasonous, since tea, as is well known, is the life-blood of Egyptians and the government's plea for people to reduce their consumption of tea was ridiculous (*Al-Sha‘b*, August 19, 1986). The official government newspaper, *Al-Ahram*, quickly published a long interview with the minister of food supply, who is ultimately responsible for food shortages and price increases. He attempted to explain the intricacies of the subsidy system and reported that he was forced to decrease the monthly ration of tea (for all those who are eligible to receive rationed, *tamwiin* goods) by 50 percent because the government did not receive a scheduled shipment of 7,000 tons of tea due to a strike by dock workers in India (Shihbun 1986). While there are many similar stories on food prices in newspapers throughout the year, what is important to remember is that the government is intricately involved in distributing basic goods and supervising the prices of a wide range of commodities in the market. Ministers in the government are interviewed constantly about these issues, and they promise personal supervision of distribution networks and retribution for those who break the law. The failure of the government to control prices is a frequent complaint, even though many people wish government intervention would decrease so that supplies of certain items might increase. One article, for example, argued that government price regulations no longer mean anything: "They have gone from being something enforceable, to wishful thinking, to nothing but numbers on paper. The price of fruit and vegetables has risen 300 percent, red meat and poultry 100 percent, fish 150 percent—all this for foods whose prices are government regulated! Is this greed on the part of some food sellers or is this impotence on the part of government price regulation?" While the shaᶜb may be unable to change the policies of the government, due to their political exclusion, the government is still extremely sensitive to their concerns about subsidies and opposition forces often seize upon this issue to express their disgust with the government.

In another important policy area, one can argue that the government maintains its support of public health care while tolerating a rapidly expanding system of private medical facilities and clinics in Egypt (many of which are unregulated and unlicensed). People who can afford relatively expensive private doctors avoid the crowds at public facilities and believe they are receiving better care. Those who cannot afford private doctors or do not allocate part of the household budget to health costs receive care in public facilities. For example, one well-established hospital was known by shaᶜbi women for its maternity care. Women would visit this hospital at specific times in the morning for sophisticated tests and pay less than a pound. Yet in the same hospital, in the afternoon, the hospital administered identical tests to women who had made appointments and would be charged more than £E30 for the tests.

In a similar fashion, education is compulsory and free to the age of fifteen in Egypt, though economic problems force many children of the poor to enter the illegal work force long before they turn fifteen (Abdalla 1988). The resources of the educational system in Egypt far outstrip the demand from a population which values education. While every administration since 1952 has attempted to extend the reach of the public educational system, the state has not, and perhaps cannot, invest sufficient resources for a high-quality education (see K. R. Kamphoefner in this volume, chapter 4).[27] The shaᶜb's answer to a deteriorating public educational system has been to "informalize" education through a system of private lessons. In communities throughout Egypt, teachers and other educated members of the community are paid to provide afternoon and evening lessons to augment public instruction. In families with several school-age children, routine monthly expenditures of £E30–50 for private lessons are not rare. The costs of private lessons increase as one moves through the educational system and can reach £E1,500 for a single chemistry course at the university level. Investing in education represents a financial sacrifice for many people in this community, but an education still offers hopes of upward mobility. Private lessons were always available to students who needed remedial help, but they are now almost required in order to succeed on competitive national year-end exams, which determine placement in university faculties and two-year vocational or commercial training institutes.

Teachers in the educational system support this informal system of education because their salaries are very low and they are eager to earn additional income. Since teachers represent such a large proportion of public sector employment, the government has resisted raising their salaries. It is technically illegal for teachers to give private lessons, but the government turns a blind eye, since it prefers this situation to raising teachers' salaries or investing more in education. To crack down on the practice of private lessons is untenable for the government, since it is obviously not willing to invest the resources in restoring a truly public, free educational system. At the same time it recognizes the importance of education to the shaᶜb and tacitly allows a well-established parallel educational system.

In another arena of concern to the shaᶜb, a publicly acknowledged housing crisis, particularly the lack of affordable housing, has forced families either to finance housing construction privately, rent expensive apartments, pay exorbitant key money, or use connections with politicians and bureaucrats to obtain subsidized public or cooperative housing. The demand for housing by newlyweds, rural migrants to urban areas, and prosperous returning migrants has been met, in part, by a surge of informal, unregulated, unlicensed, and illegal housing construction in what was previously agricultural or marginal land surrounding Cairo. One study estimated that over 80 percent of the housing constructed since 1960 has been built without permits (Abt Associates et al. 1981, as cited by Oldham et al. 1987, xvii), while another estimates the figure at 50 percent (Ikram 1981, 152). This informal construction is theoretically illegal, but people are rarely prosecuted, since the cost of enforcement would be prohibitive and the state indirectly benefits from the private investment. Many of these communities are populated by lower-income groups, but not the poorest strata of society, since people must have the resources to purchase land, build a home, or afford the increasingly high rent and key money.

In a very informative study, Oldham et al. (1987) describe one of the newer informal residential areas near Imbaba as a magnet for newlyweds from Cairo and immigrants from the countryside. Because these communities are built on agricultural land or state-owned property without authorization from the government, many are not serviced by government utilities, sewerage, transport grids, or public educational, health, and welfare institutions. Either a community begins the process of negotiating with government authorities to provide these services and resolves issues of property ownership and taxation or it pays for these services from private entrepreneurs.

Collectively, these communities place greater and greater demands on the state's infrastructure. Eventually, leaders within a community begin the process of articulating these demands by trying to incorporate the community into the state's delivery system through political negotiations. Although it has selectively reasserted its authority in some areas by evicting residents and bulldozing housing, the state has not been able or willing to control this massive growth in informal housing. If the state is unable to control the physical growth of the Cairo metropolitan area and the very visible settlement of large numbers of its population, it may not be able to control the political and economic activities in these new areas either. Businesses are not regulated, taxes are not collected, and the community develops its own mechanisms of law enforcement and arbitration. The growth of illegal settlements and communities, due in part to the seemingly innocuous "social" goal of reproducing the family, presents a political and economic predicament, if not challenge, to the Egyptian state.

A classic example of the "dangers" which relatively new communities can pose to the state can be seen in the confrontation which occurred in December 1992 between government security forces and radical Islamic activists in Imbaba. This area is extremely densely populated and while it was the beneficiary of subsidized housing during the Nasser era and had a relatively lower-middle-class constituency, since it is relatively close to downtown Cairo, it has become an attractive area for newly married couples from older areas of the city who could not afford housing in their parents' neighborhoods. It is the scene of increasingly violent disputes between Coptic and Muslim residents. The leader of the Gamaa al-Islamiyya (a radical politicized Islamic organization) had boasted that his organization had created a "state within a state" where its version of Islamic law ruled. The media reported that the organization had demanded that Christians pay taxes to it; had destroyed several churches, video stores, and stores which sold alcohol; had forced women to wear Islamic dress; and generally had harassed Christians in this district. Provoked by the growing power and aggressiveness of this organization, 14,000 members of assorted branches of Egyptian security forces swept through the area in a five-day raid in December, arresting hundreds (Murphy 1992, A12). While the government's response to this case of informal organizing within shaᶜbi communities is perhaps atypical, it exemplifies the ways in which alternative moral and political preferences can, under certain circumstances, lead to the formation of strong, organized, visible political movements which the Egyptian state is then forced to consider.

State recognition of the familial ethos and the strength of the family in shaᶜbi communities is most obvious in the government's extremely sensitive policies concerning personal status legislation. These laws regulate marriage, divorce, custody, and inheritance which influence the very structure of the family. In 1979, the personal status laws were slightly amended to allow a woman the option of divorce if her husband took a second wife and to give women the right to reside in the marital apartment until remarriage. Mothers were also given more significant custody rights over minor children. However, in July 1985 the Supreme Court declared that the legislation was unconstitutional because it had been signed into law by President Anwar Sadat under executive powers of Emergency Law provisions.

As a result, an alliance of women's organizations in Egypt established the Committee for the Defense of the Rights of Women and the Family in order to pressure the government to reinstitute the 1979 amendments through appropriate legislative channels. The controversy surrounding personal status laws, both supporting and opposing views, dominated the media for several months. Several Islamic organizations and political activists opposed any revision of these laws, which they argued contradicted Islamic legal codes. The Committee for the Defense of the Rights of Women and the Family often defended their policies by reinterpreting Islamic law in ways which, they argued, provided stronger legal rights for women. All parties to the debate presented their positions with reference to the family and all claimed their policies would strengthen, not weaken, familial solidarity. These debates reveal the centrality and relevance of the familial ethos to public discourse and political debate in Egypt. When some women in this group suggested staging a demonstration to call for the reinstatement of the 1979 personal status codes, the government made it quite clear that it would not issue a permit. The government was not very worried about the trouble this committee might cause but was apparently far more fearful of the counterdemonstration that Islamic activists threatened to call if such a demonstration was allowed.

In this study of one particular community in central Cairo, I have argued that the shaᶜb use the familial ethos, informal networks, and informal institutions to further their interests. Situating my research at the level of the household revealed a political universe, with particular interests, which I hope can complement rather than replace or contradict traditional analyses of Egyptian politics, which rely upon elite and interest group analyses. By understanding the range of interests within the Egyptian polity and the various mechanisms men and women have devised to further their ends despite the climate of repression, we may be in a better position to understand the voices which may make themselves heard in the future, once an opportunity presents itself.

NOTES

An earlier version of this chapter appeared in the *Journal of South Asian and Middle Eastern Studies* 13 (Summer 1990).

1. The regressive, traditional, and inegalitarian aspects of the family were emphasized even more in nations which retained explicitly kin-based rule, such as Jordan, Morocco, Kuwait, and Saudi Arabia.

2. Bill and Leiden not only identify the family in the Middle East as patriarchal, but extend this characterization to argue that patrimonial politics dominates the Middle East: "Patterns of leadership in the Middle East have been highly congruent from institution to institution and from community to community. In the family, school, guild, and government, patrimonialism prevails. In patriarchal or patrimonial societies, the patriarch is the main social and political reality. He is the model, the guide, the innovator, the planner, the mediator, the chastiser, and the protector" (Bill and Leiden 1984, 157).

3. For example, Andrea Rugh argues that " . . . the special character of social institutions like the family in Egypt tends to promote an authoritarian rather than a democratic style of leadership, with a policy that acquiesces to rather than challenges that leadership" (Rugh 1984, 45).

4. This situation was even more complex, since the husband was the son of a worker in her mother's bakery. The husband's family, from a lower economic and social position, resided in the basement of his wife's maternal relatives' home and were therefore indebted to them.

5. Suad Joseph discussed the role of the public in arbitrating conflicts in working-class multiethnic communities in Lebanon. For example, Armenians would argue in Armenian but when arguments spilled out into the neighborhood streets they would graciously switch to Arabic so that their neighbors could understand the argument and take sides (Joseph 1983).

6. In 1986 the official exchange rate of the pound, except for tourists and Egyptian expatriots, equaled approximately $1.20. The market value of the pound equalled $1.43 in 1985 (see Economist Intelligence Unit 1988, Appendix).

7. Such tactics are encouraged by the spatial arrangement of these neighborhoods. Densely populated areas minimize privacy among neighbors, creating public space out of stairwells, doorsteps, and, most important, windows. Houses are attached to one another and alleyways are so narrow that windows can be less than five meters away. For a more detailed discussion of the relationship between architectural forms and community, see El-Messiri 1975.

8. These women, it is said, *ta'amil 'amil*. They use prayers or written scraps of Qur'anic verses to protect people from the evil intentions of others and spirits. They are also asked, in different situations, to protect an individual from a specific enemy. Although many people are not entirely convinced of the powers of these people, when crises occur they often ask them to intervene with God, on their behalf.

9. In Lebanon, the reputation of a family is so important that the head of a family association will pay for an advertisement in local papers which disassociates the family from a recently arrested criminal with the same family name and condemns the criminal's behavior (see Khalaf 1986, 169).

10. The primary source of income referred to each person's official position of employment (which was registered with various government agencies), or the occupation or income-generating activity in the informal economy which supported them. Secondary sources of income usually referred to part-time jobs and semiregular employment or income-generating activities. Tertiary sources of income were rarer and included in-kind exchange and skills of the self-employed.

11. In this community, secondary sources of employment were widespread (47 percent of the sample had a secondary source of income and that rate rose to 63 percent among public sector employees) due to the rising cost of living and the declining value of public sector wages.

12. An investigation of the presence of the informal economy in this community (economic activity which is unregulated, untaxed, and unenumerated by the government) revealed that family enterprises were proportionally better represented in the informal economy than the formal one. They accounted for 48 percent of all primary economic activity and 19 percent of all secondary economic activity within the informal economy.

13. Many of the women who were primarily housewives earned additional income through activities such as leading a savings association, sewing, raising poultry, and organizing black market activities (largely in redistributing food that had been acquired or stolen from government food cooperatives). These activities were not occasional activities, since women devoted significant and consistent amounts of time to them.

14. Men in this sample also participated far more extensively in the labor force than national indicators suggest. Eighty-six percent of the men in the economically active population participated in the labor force as a primary economic activity, 61 percent as a secondary activity, and 98 percent as either primary or secondary activity.

15. The definition of work used in the World Fertility Survey was "occupation apart from ordinary household duties, whether paid in cash or in kind or unpaid, whether own-account or family member or for someone else, whether done at home or away from home" (CAPMAS 1983, 10).

16. Unfortunately, the secondary occupation of 93 people in the sample was unknown. Of the known secondary occupations (including those people that had none) the percentage of family-related economic activities increases to 62 percent.

17. Grocery stores have recently begun to advertise themselves as supermarkets. In poorer neighborhoods the distinction means that more processed, expensive goods are available in addition to the inexpensive food staples of the community. Supermarket groceries are also quite unlikely to offer credit to their customers, although this grocer in a more shaᶜbi neighborhood still did.

18. Many of these students attend technical training institutes where it is possible to enter university faculties if one does well. Others attend the faculties at universities which accept applicants with relatively low secondary school examination scores. But some students in the community were admitted to the most prestigious and competitive faculties of engineering and medicine.

19. This is quite similar to the practice of middle-class parents in the United States, who begin saving money for the college education of children as soon as they are born. Parents decide that an education, one of the most promising paths to social and economic mobility in the United States, is worthy of financial sacrifice.

20. Certain policies of the government, however, directly affect the ability of young couples to marry. The government's retreat from guaranteed employment has lengthened engagements as recent graduates of higher education wait three to five years before securing a permanent job. The government's subtle but steady withdrawal of public subsidies from food, housing, transportation, and education has decreased the ability of families to save money for marriage. The prevailing savings strategy in shaᶜbi communities was to minimize daily expenses in order to allow men and women to save a high proportion of their cash income. The shaᶜb's sometimes violent response to the withdrawal of government subsidies must be seen in the context of the effect of these policies on the ability to save for such critical expenses as marriage.

21. For elaboration on the costs and politics of marriage within this community, see Singerman 1995, 75–160.

22. The marriage rate for 1986 was estimated from information from five previous years, available in figures in CAPMAS, "Marriage and Divorce Statistics," 8 (9.2 per thousand). The number of marriage contracts was calculated according to the 1986 population census figures (CAPMAS 1987, 2).

23. While individuals use informal savings associations as a savings vehicle, an economist might argue that they merely finance someone else's consumption, since each lump sum payment is immediately disbursed to a member of the association, who then spends it on consumption. For example, a young man who contributes £E100 per month

to a gamʿiyya may be saving for an apartment, but each month the person who receives the lump sum payment uses it for consumption (i.e., gross savings, as opposed to net savings for the economy). Research is needed to understand whether the final payment of a gamʿiyya is used primarily for consumption or investment.

24. The results were disastrous in one case where the mother of a young girl was very happy to accept the offer of a young engineer who had supposedly returned from his job in the Gulf to find a wife. The family was not very careful in asking about this young man and went ahead with signing a marriage contract (*katb il-kitaab*). After an argument the fiancé visited them at home, tied them up and gagged them, stole their gold and household appliances, took the key to their second apartment, and emptied that out as well. They lost over £E30,000, a husband for their daughter, and the time and expenses for prosecuting the case.

25. While most women prefer *ghuwayaish* (gold bracelets), other women ask for a necklace and bracelet set of precious metals or stones. Women from lower-middle-class origins typically receive jewelry valued at £E500–1000. The value of the gift is public knowledge and the receipts are kept with the mother of the bride in case they need to be returned or sold in times of financial crisis.

26. This almost exclusively female profession has persevered despite rapid social, political, and economic changes in Egypt. In the late nineteenth and early twentieth century, these women sold products to wealthy female clients secluded within large households. Middle- to upper-class women relied on these women for information from other households, since they had little freedom of movement or mobility and less access to markets. Often these women were instrumental in arranging marriages and political alliances among the elite. For a description of the economic role of dallalaat in nineteenth-century Egypt, see Tucker 1985, 82–84, and Messiri 1978, 63–64.

27. According to the most recent population census, 49 percent of the total population over ten years of age is illiterate, 24 percent can read and write, 22 percent have qualifications less than a university degree, and 4 percent have obtained university degrees and above (postgraduate degrees). The discrepancy between the educational qualifications of men and women is largest in figures for Egypt as a whole: 38 percent of men are illiterate in comparison to 62 percent of women (30 percent of men can read and write, 18 percent of women); see CAPMAS 1987, 52–55.

WORKS CITED

Abdalla, Ahmed. 1988. "Child Labor in Egypt: Leather Tanning in Cairo." In *Combating Child Labor*, ed. Assefa Bequele and Jo Boyden, 31–47. Geneva: International Labor Office.

Abdel-Fadil, Mahmoud. 1980. "Informal Sector Employment in Egypt." Series on Employment Opportunities and Equity in Egypt, no. 1. International Labor Office, Geneva.

Abt Associates, Dames and Moore, and the General Organization for Housing, Building, Planning, and Research. 1981. "Informal Housing in Egypt." Report to the U.S. Agency for International Development, Cairo.

Abu Liwaayah, Muhammad. 1986. "Will a Plate of *Kushari* Turn into a Tourist Dish?" *Al-Sha'b*, August 12, 3.

Alderman, Harold, and Joachim Von Braun. 1984. "The Effects of the Egyptian Food Ration and Subsidy System on Income Distribution and Consumption." International Food Policy Research Institute Research Report, no. 45.

ᶜAshmaawy, Ibrahim el-. 1986. "Egyptian Youth: Between Tourist Marriages and Foreign Marriages." *Al-Sha'b*, August 19, 9.

Bill, James A., and Carl Leiden. 1984. *Politics in the Middle East.* 2d ed. Boston: Little, Brown.

CAPMAS (Central Agency for Public Mobilization and Statistics). 1983. *Egyptian Fertility Survey 1980.* Vol. 2, *Fertility and Family Planning.* Cairo: CAPMAS.

———. 1987. *Preliminary Results of the Population, Housing, and Establishment Census of 1986.* Cairo: CAPMAS.

Chazan, Naomi. 1988. "Patterns of State-Society Incorporation and Disengagement in Africa." In *The Precarious Balance: State and Society in Africa,* ed. Naomi Chazan and Donald Rothchild, 121–148. Boulder: Westview Press.

De Soto, Hernando. 1989. *The Other Path: The Invisible Revolution in the Third World.* Trans. June Abbott. New York: Harper.

Economist Intelligence Unit. 1988. "Egypt." Country Profile Reports, no. 4 (Appendix).

Elshtain, Jean Bethke. 1981. *Public Man, Private Woman: Women in Social and Political Thought.* Princeton: Princeton University Press.

Folbre, Nancy. 1986. "Cleaning House." *Journal of Development Economics* 22: 3–40.

Geertz, Clifford. 1973. *The Interpretation of Cultures.* New York: Basic Books.

"Government Price Regulation: What's Wrong with It and So What?" 1986. *Akhbar il-Yoom,* July 27, 5.

Handoussa, Heba. September 1988. "The Burden of Public Service Employment and Remuneration: A Case Study of Egypt." Monograph commissioned by the International Labor Office, Geneva.

———. 1991. "Crisis and Challenge: Prospects for the 1990s." In *Employment and Structural Adjustment: Egypt in the 1990s,* ed. Heba Handoussa and Gillian Potter, 3–24. Cairo: American University in Cairo Press.

Hart, Keith. 1973. "Informal Income Opportunities and Urban Employment in Ghana." *Journal of Modern African Studies* 11: 61–89.

Hinnebusch, Raymond A., Jr. 1985. *Egyptian Politics under Sadat: The Post-Populist Development of an Authoritarian-Modernizing State.* Cambridge: Cambridge University Press.

Joseph, Suad. 1983. "Working-Class Women's Networks in a Sectarian State: A Political Paradox." *American Ethnologist* 10 (February): 1–22.

Khalaf, Samir. 1986. *Lebanon's Predicament.* New York: Columbia University Press.

Khouri-Dagher, Nadia. 1986. "Food and Energy in Cairo: Provisioning the Poor." Report prepared for the Food-Energy Nexus Program, United Nations University, Cairo.

Ikram, Khalid. 1981. "Meeting the Social Contract in Egypt." *Finance and Development* 18 (September): 30–33.

March, Kathryn S., and Rachelle L. Taqqu. 1986. *Women's Informal Associations in Developing Countries: Catalysts for Change?* Boulder: Westview Press.

Messiri, Sawsan el-. 1978. *Ibn al-Balad: A Concept of Egyptian Identity.* London: E. J. Brill.

Muhammed, Ghali. 1986. "*Sha῾bi* Macaroni: Why Has It Disappeared from the Market?" *Al Musawar,* August 18, 52–53.

Murphy, Kim. 1992. "Egypt Rounds Up Islamic Extremists." *Los Angeles Times,* December 14, A12.

Nadim, Nawal al-Messiri. 1975. "The Relationship between the Sexes in a Harah of Cairo." Ph.D. dissertation, Indiana University.

Oldham, Linda, Haguer El Hadidi, and Hussein Tamaa. 1987. *Informal Communities in Cairo: The Basis of a Typology.* Cairo Papers in Social Science, no. 10.

Pateman, Carole. 1980. "The Civic Culture: A Philosophic Critique." In *The Civic Culture Revisited: An Analytic Study,* ed. Gabriel A. Almond and Sidney Verba, 57–102. Boston: Little, Brown.

Portes, Alejandro, Manuel Castells, and Lauren A. Benton, eds. 1989. *The Informal Economy: Studies in Advanced and Less-Developed Countries.* Baltimore: Johns Hopkins University Press.

Rugh, Andrea B. 1984. *Family in Contemporary Egypt.* Syracuse: Syracuse University Press.

Scott, James C. 1990. *Domination and the Arts of Resistance: Hidden Transcripts.* New Haven: Yale University Press.

"The Sha῾b Warns the Government: Stay Away from a Cup of Tea." 1986. *Al-Sha῾b,* August 19, 3.

Shihbun, Hussein. 1986. "The Artificial Rise in Prices: It Has No Connection with Decisions from the Ministry of Food Supply or Its Pricing Policies." *Al-Ahram,* August 15, 7.

Singerman, Diane. 1995. *Avenues of Participation: Family, Politics, and Networks in Urban Quarters of Cairo.* Princeton: Princeton University Press.

Sokkari, Myrette Ahmed el-. 1984. *Basic Needs, Inflation and the Poor of Egypt, 1970–1980.* Cairo Papers in Social Science, no. 7.

Springborg, Robert. 1982. *Family, Power and Politics in Egypt: Sayed Bey Marei—His Clan, Clients, and Cohorts.* Philadelphia: University of Pennsylvania Press.

———— 1989. *Mubarak's Egypt: Fragmentation of the Political Order.* Boulder: Westview Press.

Tucker, Judith E. 1985. *Women in Nineteenth-Century Egypt.* Cambridge: Cambridge University Press.

Verba, Sidney, and Norman Nie. 1972. *Participation in America: Political Democracy and Social Equality.* New York: Harper.

Waterbury, John. 1983. *The Egypt of Nasser and Sadat: The Political Economy of Two Regimes.* Princeton: Princeton University Press.

Wolin, Sheldon S. 1981. "Max Weber: Legitimation, Method, and the Politics of Theory." *Political Theory* 3 (August): 402–403.

World Bank. 1989. *World Tables: From the Data Files of the World Bank, 1988–89.* Baltimore: Johns Hopkins University Press.

Zaytoun, Mohaya A. 1991. "Earnings and the Cost of Living: An Analysis of Recent Developments in the Egyptian Economy." In *Employment and Structural Adjustment: Egypt in the 1990s,* ed. Heba Handoussa and Gillian Potter, 219–257. Cairo: American University in Cairo Press.

Zurayk, Huda, and Frederic Shorter. 1988. "The Social Composition of Households in Arab Cities and Settlements: Cairo, Beirut, Amman." Regional Papers. Population Council, Cairo.

CONTRIBUTORS

Nawal Mahmoud Hassan is the Director and founder of the Center for Egyptian Civilization Studies in Cairo. She obtained an M.A. degree in Sociology from Smith College and has worked in a variety of capacities to help maintain the social fabric, cultural heritage, and historical legacy of the urban inner city. She also founded the Association for the Urban Development of Islamic Cairo, which is a voluntary association situated in the heart of the historic city. She has served as a consultant to Terre des Hommes, OXFAM, the Ford Foundation, and the World Food Program and published several articles on urbanism and population pressures in Cairo. More recently, she has been active in a number of environmental organizations and projects in Egypt.

Homa Hoodfar is Associate Professor in the Department of Sociology and Anthropology at Concordia University in Montreal. She is a British-trained Iranian social anthropologist and has carried out research on the impact of development and social change on the lives of Muslim women in Cairo, Tehran, and Montreal.

K. R. (Kathy) Kamphoefner is Assistant Professor at Manchester College in North Manchester, Indiana. She received a Ph.D. degree from Northwestern University in Communication Studies in 1991. Her areas of study include intercultural communication, communication and development, and Middle Eastern studies. She has conducted extensive fieldwork in Egypt.

Nadia Khouri-Dagher obtained a Ph.D. degree in the Socioeconomics of Development from the Ecole des Hautes Etudes en Sciences Sociales, Paris. She has published extensively on poverty, development, and gender issues in Egypt and the Arab world. She is also a writer and a journalist and author of *Food and Energy in Cairo: Provisioning the Poor* (United Nations University, Paris, 1987) and *Bleu Marine* (Editions La Nef, Tunis/L'Harmattan, Paris, 1992).

Arlene Elowe MacLeod is Associate Professor in the Department of Political Science at Bates College in Maine. She is the author of *Accommodating Protest: Working Women, the New Veiling, and Change in Cairo* (Columbia University Press, 1991). She received a Ph.D. degree from Yale University and has written several articles on gender and power in the Middle East.

Diane Singerman is Assistant Professor in the Department of Government, School of Public Affairs, at The American University (Washington, D.C.). She is the author of *Avenues of Participation: Families, Politics, and Networks in Urban Quarters of Cairo* (Princeton University Press, 1995) and several articles on gender, informal politics, and the informal economy in Egypt. She received a Ph.D. degree from Princeton University and studied at The American University in Cairo.

INDEX

autocolonization, 142

bread, 112, 113–14, 123–24

cash earning activities, 7 (table), 98, 162–63; among migrants' wives, 56, 65. *See also* employment: cost benefit analysis of private, public, and informal sectors

cash economizing measures, 14; shopping and management as, 15, 65, 104; carrying water as, 15; home repairs and improvements as, 16; home production of food as, 16

cash economy: and education, 101; and women, xviii, 100–101

Center for Egyptian Civilization Studies (Cairo), 134. *See also* housing: lobbyists

child-rearing: role of father in, 58, 59

Committee for the Defense of the Rights of Women and the Family, 182

communication: shift from orality to literacy, 98–99

conflict, 154–55; staged in public, 157. *See also* family: and conflict resolution

consumer price index, 117

consumption: and social reproduction, 1–2; and social integration, 18, 20–21; as investment strategy, 9, 16, 20, 22, 55, 64, 166; patterns, 2, 18–19, 31, 76n31

cooperatives. *See* government shops

dallalaat (petty traders). *See* cash earning activities; food: black market

development policies, xvi; and gender, xx

diet, 32. *See also* food

divorce: after wife's illness, 156–57; division of property and alimony, 4, 172–73; rate, 23

domestic work, 12; in low-income neighborhoods of Cairo, 12–14; sexual division of domestic work as strategy, 13, 22. *See also* housework

dower. *See mahr*

education, 29, 32, 60, 179; among Saᶜayda (Upper Egyptians), 91, 93; and employment, 6, 7, 82, 96; and family resources, 96–97; and gender, 6, 7, 60–61, 88, 89, 96–97; and inequality, 103; and social class, 81; costs to family, 86–87; curriculum, 85–86, 105; dropout and nonenrollment, 84–86; government spending on, 85; in trades, 60; private lessons, 87, 130, 179–80; private schools, 81; schools, 82–83; statistics, xiii, xv; teachers, 83–84, 180; under Nasser, 81; under Sadat, 81; women's attitudes towards, 93–95, 96, 103

emergency relief, 139–40

employment: and double workload, 102; and social class, 29, 41; and workplace hierarchy, 33, 104; cost benefit analysis of private, public, and informal sectors, 2, 6–11, 30; dispute over dismissal, 159; influence of economic ideology on, 41; multiple jobs, 8, 38, 161; in public sector, 30–31, 32–33, 39, 66, 163, 164; labor force statistics, 161; state guaranteed jobs, 130; women's, xviii, 2, 10, 28–29; women's attitudes towards, 9, 42, 89, 103–104, 121, 161. *See also* education: and employment; informal networks: and employment; income; wages

engagement, 172; broken, 174

familial ethos, 151, 153–54, 158, 159, 164. *See also* informal savings associations (*gamᶜiyyat*)

family, xvii, 145–46, 152, 155, 168, 176; and conflict resolution, 155–56, 156–57, 157–59; as economic and political institution, 146; as support network, 145; in political theory, 148; size of, 90. *See also* family business; household

family business, 160–65; conflicts within, 158–59; employment in, 65–66

feminist scholarship, xxi

food: attitudes towards cost and availability of, 116–18; availability of, 113, 114–15, 117, 118, 120–21, 176–79; black market, 113, 114–15, 126,